GATHERED AND SCATTERED

Also in this series:

This Is the Day: Readings and meditations from the Iona Community
Neil Paynter

GATHERED AND SCATTERED

Readings & meditations
from the Iona Community

Neil Paynter

WILD GOOSE PUBLICATIONS
www.ionabooks.com

Readings © the individual contributors
Compilation © 2007 Neil Paynter
First published 2007 by
Wild Goose Publications, Fourth Floor, Savoy House,
140 Sauchiehall Street, Glasgow G2 3DH, UK,
the publishing division of the Iona Community. Scottish Charity No. SCO03794.
Limited Company Reg. No. SCO96243.

ISBN 978-1-905010-34-9

Cover design © 2007 Wild Goose Publications
Cover photograph © Neil Paynter

The publishers gratefully acknowledge the support of the Drummond Trust,
3 Pitt Terrace, Stirling FK8 2EY in producing this book.

Overseas distribution
Australia: Willow Connection Pty Ltd, Unit 4A, 3–9 Kenneth Road, Manly Vale, NSW 2093
New Zealand: Pleroma, Higginson Street, Otane 4170, Central Hawkes Bay
Canada: Bayard Distribution, 10 Lower Spadina Ave., Suite 400, Toronto, Ontario M5V 2Z

Printed by Bell & Bain, Thornliebank, Glasgow

CONTENTS

The topics for the days:

A mouse can do little but a nest of mice can work great havoc.

George MacLeod, Founder of the Iona Community

FOREWORD

In work and worship
GOD IS WITH US
Gathered and scattered
GOD IS WITH US
Now and always
GOD IS WITH US.

The closing responses of the daily Act of Prayer of the Iona Community

Powerful yet tender words.

When Neil Paynter asked if I had any suggestions for this book's title, I thought of the phrase 'gathered and scattered'. For me they are empowering words, which have spiritually encouraged and strengthened the many people around the world who hold them in their hearts and say them on a daily basis. Whether gathered or scattered, God's light, hope and healing enfold us.

The words in this book will be scattered in many places, yet their roots are in that shared vision of an engaged and radical Christianity. Although the reflections come from many sources, they are all propelled by the knowledge that God is to be found in everyday living – in the uncertainties, contradictions and laughter of our times.

And whether we are gathered or scattered, may these often prophetic reflections take us all into a renewed commitment to God, to this amazing earth we all walk upon and to our sisters and brothers everywhere.

Peter Millar

Introduction

Each day of the month Iona Community members pray for one another, for the wider work of the Church, and for the community's shared concerns. Like *This Is the Day*, this book explores some of those concerns.

These readings and meditations were gathered over the past few years, during which I have been working as an Editorial Assistant at Wild Goose Publications, the publishing wing of the Iona Community.

Some of these readings are taken from Wild Goose books; some are from *Coracle*: the magazine of the Iona Community; some are from other magazines and from newspapers and radio broadcasts; many are original to this publication.

Also included are short prayers for each day, and a list of scripture readings which readers might like to work through as part of a daily discipline.

The Iona Community believe 'that social and political action leading to justice for all people, and encouraged by prayer and discussion, is a vital work of the Church at all levels' (from the Rule of the Iona Community).

I hope that these readings and meditations will aid in prayer and reflection, and serve to encourage thoughtful, committed action in God's world.

Gathered and Scattered was edited in a flat in Biggar, Scotland. The collection is again dedicated to all who believe in the power of the Word (and of words), and to all those who are working to make their communities more just and peaceful places.

I would like to thank everyone who contributed to this book, especially Ian Fraser, Tom Gordon and Peter Millar. Thank you also to everyone at Wild Goose Publications: Sandra Kramer, Tri Boi Ta, Jane Darroch-Riley, Alex O'Neill and Lorna Rae – you are amazing.

Neil Paynter, Eastertide, 2007

Month 1

NEW WAYS TO TOUCH THE HEARTS OF ALL

The GalGael Trust: The rekindling of community

Thought for the Day on BBC Radio Scotland is supposed to be an up-to-the-moment reflection on current affairs. If you're presenting it, the producers phone about 18 hours before the broadcast is due, to start agreeing the topic and wording that will go out, normally live, just before 7:30 the next morning.

But it's a minefield out there! As the 2-minute *Thought* aims to be thought-provoking but not confrontational, you have to be terribly sensitive. The art is to phrase things in a way that deepens people's thinking, yet minimises the chances of putting a foot in the porridge when set loose from the news studio.

For fifty quid, it's a tough shift. Not only does planning, writing and agreeing the draft take up much of the creative energy of the previous day – you don't sleep well that night either. At least, I don't! I keep waking up with fantasies of the alarm not going off and the imagined ignominy of letting down an awaiting nation – not to mention an awaiting mother on the Isle of Lewis!

It's also advisable to leave enough time to check the internet news before setting off at the crack of dawn. Once I referred to a British soldier's death in Iraq, but rapidly tweaked this on learning that more casualties had been announced overnight. The newsroom would probably have alerted me as I'd gone in, but it's easy for glitches to slip by and for the hard-fought-for airspace that the *Thought* enjoys to appear less than cutting edge.

Recently I received a letter from one of the most senior generals in the British army. He said he always listened to *Thought for the Day* as 'part of my daily fix before I leave for work … so that I know what the nation has been told and may appear in some form in my in-tray half an hour later!' He was London-based and was referring to the Radio 4 version, but still, one can imagine the same influence at a Scottish level.

All in all, to broadcast the morning's 'God-slot' pulls you, for a moment, onto the cutting edge of current affairs. And that is why it was so very strange, on 10th November 2005, for me to have had occasion to present *Thought for the Day* from a studio in Stornoway spoken … posthumously!

Now, if that sounds like a George MacLeod story coming on, you're on the right tracks. For it concerns a man who, with his wife, often worked in Govan at a massive desk that had once been the powerhouse of none other than George MacLeod's secretary.

Sometimes in my role as a board member of the GalGael Trust, I'll lean over that same desk and say, 'You know, there's only one person I could imagine with a greater capacity for getting things done than the Big Man himself, and that was his secretary!'

The GalGael is an award-winning community organisation. Local unemployed people started it, some of whom had met at protests when the M77 motorway took a slice off Pollok Park. Participants are ordinary members of the community, which includes youths who have just left school, retired shipyard workers filled with elders' wisdom, recovering drug addicts, folk recently out of jail, the occasional academic, and the even more occasional clergy person.

Vibrant workshops resound with boat building, silversmithing, stone carving, basketwork and weaving. But more than that, the GalGael's a test bed and repair workshop for the software of human beings – for the rekindling of community.

It's a testimony to all that George MacLeod had in mind that day a wee laddie's stone apocryphally broke the stained-glass inscription on a church window and rendered it, 'GLORY TO GOD IN THE HIGH ST'.

To read Ron Ferguson's magisterial biography of George is like looking back over a blueprint for the GalGael Trust and seeing the dream come to fruition. 'George found that as men cheerfully offered their labour in a worthwhile cause, community began to form quite naturally.' That's GalGael for you, and the key visionaries in the GalGael all see the historical connection. For George, in his pre-Iona incarnation, it was Fingalton Mill that would 'provide a Govan in the country at the lowest possible charges, where folk can get good air fresher than at the coast'.

For today's GalGael, it's Barmaddy Farm, presently being established on lease from the Forestry Commission at Loch Awe and with longer-term plans for a rural resettlement project to connect city and country – because human beings need both.

Phrases like 'Work is worship' run daily through the Fairley Street workshop. We're not a religious organisation and few of the participants would see themselves as potential 'bums on pews' to fill the churches. Equally, few would want to shy from the crucial role that *spirituality* and its articulation in *community* are playing in their lives' journeys.

Addictions run hand in hand with poverty, but behind material poverty there's a much wider spiritual malaise at the heart of the modern world. Those who see this very clearly ARE THOSE whose ego defences are lowered … lowered, because, unlike the 'better placed' in society, they no longer have anything to hide.

Addictions, crime and violence are all forms of emotional anaesthetic. 'Heroin took away my pain,' says Billy, a GalGael metalsmith, '… but it also took away my soul.'

Another GalGael participant with a similarly colourful, hard-pressed background, told me his story in the pub, and I worked it into a poem that ends like this:

… *for the more they come on me*

and more that all's gone
the more that all's left
is mah spiritual song

That's the kind of banter that goes on these days around George MacLeod's secretary's old desk!

You see, the old Celtic shaman was onto something. For all that he might have been a product of his class and his times – 'for a' that and a' that' – George MacLeod was onto something that runs in the spirit of Govan. Although no relation, at least not in the flesh, Colin Macleod, who founded the GalGael, tapped into the source of that same ancient quicksilver.

Colin dropped dead of a heart attack on 2nd November 2005, aged just 39. By the time his funeral started in Govan Old, presided over by the Iona Community's Norman Shanks, there were no pews left on which to park a tardy bum. Police had to halt the traffic past Govan Cross for two hours – and that on a football day.

As well as leaving Gehan, he left their children – Tawny, Iona and Oran – whose names are compass enough to the source of his spirituality. Like the Master Carpenter himself, people were this visionary artist's primary raw material.

And that brings me back round to Radio Scotland, and its unprecedented posthumous *Thought for the Day*.

Very occasionally, exceptional circumstances will cause a *Thought* to be recorded slightly in advance. This happened when Colin was due to deliver it during the unusually busy week of the G8 Gleneagles Summit. However, the piece couldn't be used. On the Friday it was to go out, a live but sombre substitute had to stand in and deliver a thought different to the one planned. It was the day after the 7/7 London bombings. Colin's wonderfully crafted missive from Govan to the G8 was canned.

We buried Colin on 9th November 2005, at his father's home village of Gravir on the Isle of Lewis. But it just so happened that I was scheduled to do *Thought for the Day* the next morning. As George would have said, 'If you think that was a coincidence, I wish you a very boring life.' I managed to procure special dispensation from the BBC's religion team and Colin's family to use Colin's recording. Here are the words; and if you want to hear his own powerful voice reading it, go to www.GalGael.org:

I'm going to tell you a wee story that I sometimes tell my kids. It comes from the Clan Macleod tradition. Many years ago there was a big feast at a clan gathering in Argyll, a kind of Highland G8. Right in the middle was a wooden stake with a poor clansman tied to it.

Word was, his only crime had been to take a deer from the hill to feed his family. Now, as a punishment, he was to be gored to death by a wild bull for the entertainment of all. But nobody said anything. Naebody, that is, until the chief of the Clan Macleod could stomach his dram no longer.

Quietly he stepped forward and faced the host. 'Why don't you let the man go,' he suggested, 'as a gesture of your generosity?'

The host raised his arm. He pointed to the man at the stake. 'You can secure his freedom, but only if you can stop the bull.'

The gate was thrown open. The bull charged. Quicker than thought, Macleod leapt into its path. He grasped it by the horns. With all his power he wrestled it. At that, the crowd erupted: 'Hold fast! Hold fast!' And he held fast.

The captive was set free and there was great feasting and what a party they had that night.

And to this day the motto of Clan Macleod is 'Hold Fast'.

This is how it is with the G8 today. The poor are tied to the stake. Our leaders have a chance to show whether their power is for greed or for service. They must decide whether or not to confront poverty and help end these injustices.

Let the cry of the people be heard: 'Hold fast! Hold fast!'

Month 1 Day 1

Some complain that the Iona Community has deserted Govan. There's maybe truth in that, but equally, it might depend on how we understand the 'Iona Community'.

Adomnán's 7th-century biography of St Columba tells how the saint's deathbed command to the early Iona Community was: 'Love one another unfeignedly. Peace.'

Colin said the same in a slightly different way. He too knew that making community is like making compost. 'What matters is how you shovel it,' he'd say, and, 'Hold fast mucker!'

Alastair McIntosh is a patron of the Iona Community's Growing Hope Appeal, the author of Soil and Soul, and Treasurer of the GalGael Trust in Govan.

Glory to God in the High Street

A boy threw a stone at the stained-glass window of the Incarnation. It nicked out the 'E' in the word HIGHEST in the text GLORY TO GOD IN THE HIGHEST. Thus, till unfortunately it was mended, it read GLORY TO GOD IN THE HIGH ST.

At least the mended E might have been contrived on a swivel so that in a high wind it would have been impossible to see which way it read.

Such is the genius, and the offence, of the Christian revelation.

Holiness, salvation, glory are all come down to earth in Jesus Christ our Lord. Truth is found in the constant interaction of the claim that the apex of the Divine Majesty is declared in Christ's humanity.

The Word of God cannot be dissociated from the Action of God. As the blood courses through the body, so the spiritual is alone kept healthy in its interaction in the High Street.

George MacLeod, Only One Way Left, 1954

Month 1 Day 1

ECONOMIC WITNESS

The spirituality of economics

I am not an economist, I am a practical theologian. But I am a theologian whose practice has involved a lifelong engagement with people living in poverty, and, therefore, of course, with economics. And increasingly I have become interested, some might say obsessed, with the spirituality of economics.

Now these are two words which are not often found together. A friend said to me, 'I see you are giving a lecture on the economics of spirituality' and it may very well be that that is what I am doing. But I think they are actually inseparable if we are truly to understand either of them. Spirituality is a word which is understood in a multiplicity of ways, so, in the interest of precision, I will give you my definition of it, which will form the basis of what I say. You may not agree with this definition, but hopefully you'll know what I'm talking about. It's indebted to the Latin American theologian Jon Sobrino.

Once, Jesus was talking to the Pharisees about spirituality, or was it economics?, and he used the analogy of a cup, saying, 'Did not God, who made the outside, also make the inside?' (Luke 11:40). Our spirituality is our profoundest motivation, those instincts, intuitions, longings and desires that move us, animate us, inspire us – literally, breathe through us. Is the force that moves us from behind or below or before. But it is also our ultimate concern or orientation or goal, that person, object, ideal or value that attracts us, that draws us, towards which we incline … to where we go. If you like, it's the inner life of the cup.

But our spirituality is not just interiority. It is also our choices and actions;

it is where spirit is given flesh, where intention becomes action, where we practise what we preach. Our spirituality shows up just as much in how we spend our money, our time, our abilities, as in how we say our prayers. If you like, it's how we use the cup. And our spirituality is also our relationships: with our environment, with other people, with our own most hidden and unknown selves. If you like, it's whom we share the cup with.

Everyone has a spirituality, just as everyone has a physicality …

Money and time are the two currencies that people use most in our society. These are what we spend, time and money, and we are more and more accustomed to having to translate our spending of time into the currency of money. 'Time is money' we say, and we calculate our earnings by time. If we look at how we spend our money and how we spend our time we can get a real insight into what our core values really are, into what really moves us, rather than what we think, say or hope they are. Above all, our spirituality shows up in what we do. It is where we put our theories into practice … put our money where our mouths are.

If, as a Christian, I believe in a relationship that unconditionally values every person regardless of status, wealth, success or virtue, that conveys intrinsic worth on the worst as well as the best, with no value addition necessary, how am I to regard an economic system, and its underlying spirituality, which determines worth purely by external market forces, which actually relieves people who are poor, disabled, unemployed, single parents, elderly, of their intrinsic worth? We take care of what we value. Ultimately, people know whether and how they are valued by their society, and by its systems and institutions. Who do we give value to?

Speaking recently in South Africa, Archbishop Njongonkulu Ndungane said that: 'it is wrong and unacceptable for some people to have much, much more than they need, and others to suffer the cries of hungry children … economics should be in the service of compassion and civilised values … there is no intrinsic value in the accumulation of money and possessions … these are positively harmful to humanity's spirit if they coexist with poverty.' [1]

Kathy Galloway, from the *Christian Socialist Movement Wheatley Lecture, 2003*

Youth Concern

Sauce bottle

'Sauce bottle' wasn't his real name of course. In fact, it wasn't even his real nickname. His name was Robbie McGinley, and his real nickname was 'SB' – short for sauce bottle, I expect. For as long as anyone could remember, Robbie had a penchant for liberal dollops of tomato ketchup on everything he ate. There were even stories of tomato-sauce-flavoured ice cream. Whatever the truth was, Robbie McGinley and tomato sauce were a legendary combination.

Robbie never took to the nickname 'sauce bottle'. 'He goes nuts if you call him that,' I was told. So SB it was – anything to stop a young man going nuts. In fact, SB was prone to going nuts fairly regularly. That's what got him into trouble. Trouble and SB – like Robbie McGinley and tomato sauce – were pretty well inseparable. He'd 'done time' in List D schools and YOIs (young offender institutions). It seemed it wouldn't be long before SB and the inside of an adult prison would form a lasting acquaintance.

SB found his way to Iona with some other lads from a local outreach project on his estate. He'd not really wanted to go, but his best mate, Dekko, had signed up, and, anyway, SB had nothing particular planned that week. It was in the days of the old youth camps, when youth work on Iona had its own unique style – a bit rough and ready, working at a lot of different levels, and changing lives. And one of those was SB's.

Unbeknown to most of the lads from the estate, the group gathered together in the youth camp that week was as varied as you could get – and on purpose. There were kids like SB and Dekko, already on the slippery slope to major problems; there were lads from a YOI, on a pre-release programme; there were what were known then as 'handicapped' people and their able-bodied carers; there were teenagers with learning difficulties; and there was a smattering of youth and project workers.

'Why you called SB when your name's Robbie?' one of the disabled kids asked after the introductory session.

'If you fucking find out and tell anyone, I'll bloody pan ye, ye crippled doughnut.'

'Hey, it's no fair. SB never takes his turn at the chores.'

'Shut yer face, Thicko, ah'm daein' nae lassie's work.'

It was going to be that sort of week.

A lot could be written about SB as the week unfolded – good and bad – and a lot will never ever be clear – because all of that was going on in SB's head. But what was obvious to everyone was that things were changing. 'Thicko' – aka Bobby – actually learned table tennis from SB, and Bobby and SB reigned supreme in the tournament doubles by the end of the week. 'Crippled doughnut' – aka Sandra – had a squad of lads lifting her wheelchair over rocks, and SB was the foreman organiser and Sandra's minder. And I swear I saw a tear in SB's eye when the week's participants were boarding the ferry for the journey home – or maybe it was just a bit of sea spray that had splashed his face.

I learned later that Bobby and Sandra had arranged for a present to be given to SB at the end of the week. Maybe it's because SB had cleaned the youth camp kitchens out of tomato ketchup by the last day – well, people notice these things, don't they? Or maybe they'd found out something SB didn't really want them to know. But I gather no panning of innocent people took place. And, rumour has it, there's a bottle of tomato sauce on the top shelf in SB's bedroom that's got pride of place, that's never been opened, and, I suspect, never will.

Monday:

Dear God,
my name is Sandra,
and I can't walk any more;
a bad boy called me a crippled doughnut today –

so I really loathe him.
I despise this wheelchair,
I hate being here –
so, there.

Friday:

Dear God,
my friend is SB –
he gets me lifted over rocks
so I can get outside with the others
and not feel useless and left behind.
I like my friend; he likes me.
It's good being here.
Amen

Monday:

Dear God,
my name is Bobby,
and people say I'm slow;
a bad boy called me a thicko today;
I didn't like that and so I hate him,
and I hate being so slow;
an' I hate this place
all the time.

Friday:

Dear God,
my friend is SB,
he plays table tennis with me;

he helps a lot – when I'm rubbish, he isn't.
I like my friend; I think he likes me too –
well, I really, really hope so.
It's good being here.
Amen

Monday:

So, Big Man,
my name's Robbie –
or do you know me as SB too?
Why am I here, surrounded by thickos?
Everyone's a doughnut – except for me.
They're all really rubbish, eh …
So, I hate this place –
right?

Friday:

OK, Big Man,
what's happenin' here?
Table tennis with Thicko – sorry, Bobby – is OK;
and I think I might even fancy wee Sandra, too …
Friends with these people? What's happenin', man?
This is so uncool – but what's to do?
It seems OK up here …
My God!

Monday:

O, God,
my name is gullible …
What possessed me to come up here
to work with people like these, I'll never know.
It's so hard to make sense of what's happening.
Is no one uncomplicated any more?
And will it work out,
O God?

Friday:

Dear God,
my friends are … well …
some pretty remarkable people,
who've done some pretty remarkable things,
forged some pretty remarkable friendships.
Let's hear it for SB and Bobby
and Sandra, and … well …
for me too, if that's OK.
Amen

Tom Gordon

THE WORD

God's authority

In a Latin American country, which shall remain nameless, peasants working the land have banded together in basic Christian communities in which they analyse the oppressive situation they find themselves in and gain resources from their faith to deal with it. The book from which they draw their strength is entitled *Vivir Como Hermanos* (*Live Like Brothers*). It contains the Exodus story, some sections of the New Testament, some exposition. The words of the Bible speak to them very directly. Nothing spoke to them with such power.

In the region in question, vaccine was imported from a neighbouring country to inoculate cattle against diseases. On one occasion instead of doing so it killed the cattle. The peasants – assuming, rightly or wrongly, that this was a deliberate plot on the part of outside interests to take their livelihood in stock-rearing away from them and capture the market – marched on the police station in the main town. The chief of police met them, and ordered them to disband. He was backed up by policemen with guns at the ready. The peasants still came on.

'Stop or we shoot!' said the chief.

'You may as well shoot us,' said the peasants. 'We may as well die that way as through hunger. Our livelihood is gone.'

'Don't you know that I have the authority to preserve law and order in this area?' said the chief. 'As one who has that authority, I order you to disband.'

At that point, a peasant took out of his pocket a copy of *Vivir Como Hermanos* and waved it in the air, saying: 'There is an authority above you and above us, and we must both bow to it.' Then all the peasants took copies from their pockets, waved them in the air and shouted to the police chief that they lived under an authority which stood over every other authority.

The chief was nonplussed. 'What is it you really want?' he asked. 'If you have a real grievance I'm prepared to talk it through with you.'

'Not when guns are pointing at us,' said the peasants.

So the chief sent his men away.

He then took a seat and invited the peasants to squat down around him and talk about it.

'No, no,' they said, 'not you on a seat and us on the ground. All seated, or all on the ground.'

So the police chief sat on the ground and talked it out with them.

The next day a police search was undertaken throughout that whole area. Every piece of the Bible that could be found in the peasants' huts was confiscated as subversive literature.

Ian M. Fraser

Month 1 Day 4

HOSPITALITY AND WELCOME

Energy, new ideas, skills, youthfulness

I was once reduced to weeping over the morning paper when I read the story of a child: a small 12-year-old Kenyan boy, who had set out to be an illegal immigrant into Britain – or maybe into somewhere else, or who knows if he knew where he was bound – by climbing high up under a jet plane and into the tiny space behind the wheel carriage. But when the wheels retracted, they retracted back into his body, and he was crushed to death, suffering terrible injuries. He had no identification, no name, but it was thought that he was probably one of 40,000 street children who live in Nairobi. I read the story, and I found myself weeping uncontrollably for an African child. I don't know why it was his story – it could have been the one about the Albanian children being hosed on a southern Italian beach. Or the one about the Glasgow family removed from their home of five years in a dawn raid and deported back to Pakistan without being given time to contact the 16-year-old son who was away, and who has subsequently disappeared.

I write as a Scot who has relations in Australia, South Africa and right across Canada. Scotland has been an emigrant country, and hundreds of thousands of Scots made similar lengthy, dangerous and squalid journeys to find a new and better life for themselves and their families. A minority went because of political and religious persecution, but the vast majority were economic migrants. I imagine that many readers in North America, Australia and New Zealand have ancestors who arrived in the same way. Our attitude in Britain to those who went this way is interesting. We think of them as brave, resourceful, heroic even. We are compassionate towards the plight that led them to leave: the famines, clearances, poverty and destitution they suffered. We sing songs and write poems about the pain of leaving the glens and the ones they loved behind, and about the hardships they endured in the new world. And when their descendants return to the old country to visit, we rightly welcome them with open arms, and praise their achievements and their prosperity. We believe that they had no alternative but to go, and we are proud of what they did.

How curious, then, that our attitudes to those who are migrants into Britain (and indeed, into the rest of Europe) should be so different. To read the tabloids is to understand that there is no lower form of life than the asylum-seeker or the economic migrant. They are to be vilified in order that they may be condemned, to be described as 'scroungers' or 'work-shy' – though the truth is that they want to work more than anything but are forbidden to, that they receive less than the standard state benefit, and that if their case for asylum fails, they are evicted from their houses and cut off from all financial support – they are, in fact, rendered destitute. Even if they have leave to remain and to work, many of them work in appalling conditions, doing jobs that no one here will do – the fruits of which labour we are, nevertheless, happy to accept. Misunderstanding, racism, relentless hostility are daily experiences; and even when the many who are Christian attend churches here, they do not always receive the welcome that our faith demands of us. The irony is that we need them as much as they need us. Scotland, for instance, has a declining population, along with much of Western Europe. We need the energy, new ideas and skills, labour, youthfulness, that immigrants bring.

Kathy Galloway

Month 1 Day 5

THIS IS THE DAY

Delight

I cannot help it.
This world delights
me. I know
I should dig around
in peat bogs for insight
or ironize the life
out of all and sundry;
cautious, careful, critical,
pacing the poetry
until it is flattened
to prose.

Even in the
bare purple of
a wych elm
in midwinter
mourning
I can
hear the sap
rising again
to meet me
with my name.

The wind can have my caution.

Alison Swinfen

THE IONA EXPERIENCE

Prayers of concern from Iona

God who gathers us in and sends us out,
welcoming and challenging God …
We pray for all who gather in your name today:
In the centres on this island,
where worship is offered in different traditions;
in the Heritage Centre, which will welcome
thousands of visitors in the weeks to come –
may they find inspiration and grace for the task.

We pray for all who travel to new places,
as tourists, as pilgrims, as exiles, as refugees,
as migrants, seeking a better life –
may restless people find their rest in you.

We pray for those who come to this island
weary, and needing refreshment,
and those who come full of hope and with gifts to share –
may all know that they are needed and accepted;
may this continue to be a place of creativity and blessing.

And we pray for those who find life hard here
on this small island, with work and housing hard to find,
who are anxious for those they love,

tired, taxed in strength, troubled in mind –
give them your energy, to begin again, or to carry on.

We pray for all who gather in your name today
in places far away from here: in small rooms
as well as ancient abbeys, in drop-ins
and thrift shops, in hospital wards and works canteens,
in old people's homes, in prison chapels,
round kitchen tables, in the here and now –
may they find companionship,
share bread for the journey,
be encouraged to travel on.

We pray for the peoples of the world,
of which we are a part, a world of suffering and hope;
for places of conflict, and places of encounter;
for those who gather in solidarity, who work for peace and justice,
and those who go out to share, and to live, the Good News –
in Jesus's name

Jan Sutch Pickard

Life in Community

Yes, friends

Yes, friends, you are now among the people I miss.
When the going gets rough and in between.
The best we ever do is
to open ourselves, to share our lives.
And not fail each other.

Yes, friends, you are now among the people I count on.
When my imagination fails me and I wonder how we can make the world
a bit more just and peaceful.
I hold on to the hope that
next time we meet we'll eat together
and pray and get bold together
and know
God is with us,
friend and lover of all.

Reinhild Traitler

In work and worship
GOD IS WITH US
Gathered and scattered
GOD IS WITH US
Now and always
GOD IS WITH US

Responses from the 'Daily Office' of the Iona Community

WOMEN

There is a line of women

Women in Black

The Women in Black movement is an international peace network. At demonstrations, its members (dressed in black) stand in silent protest against war, and in solidarity with victims of violence. See www. womeninblack.net

Women in Black is an international network of women opposed to war, militarism and violence. It is a non-party-political, non-aligned network of women who work for peace and justice by:

– supporting peaceful alternatives to militarism, arms sales, war and violence
– increasing understanding of conflict and non-violent strategies for peace

We stand to bear silent witness against the futility of war and the devastation that comes in its wake.

I used to stand with Women in Black in Jerusalem against the Israeli occupation of Palestinian lands. At the onset of the war in Afghanistan, Women in Black Scotland started in Edinburgh, and we have held a silent vigil in Edinburgh every Saturday since.

What do I do standing in silence for one hour?

As the crowds of shoppers pass I think: *Is it nothing to you, all who pass by?* (Lamentations 1:12). Some pause to read our posters; some (more often than not, visitors from overseas) stop and ask our spokesperson what we are doing, and take our photos and are generally very supportive. Only very occasionally are we harassed. And I pray: for people caught up in conflict; for those imprisoned unjustly; and for the world's leaders.

'There's a song in every silence, seeking word and melody,' says Natalie Allyn Wakeley Sleeth in 'Hymn of Promise' (*Church Hymnary 4*). As I stand there, the song I sing is 'in praise of forgiving love, the love God has for all humanity'. [2]

Runa Mackay

Interwoven with the wire

Interwoven with the wire
dry grass, dying bracken
snaps of children, reeds and flowers.
Interwoven with the stillness
women's voices, singing, crying
songs of justice, sighs of pain,
soft, yet heard.
Interwoven with individuals
an incredible sense of solidarity
holding hands – a shout for freedom.
Interwoven with the darkness
ten thousand flares and candles burning
daylight drifting into evening.
Interwoven with the coldness
the warmth of thirty thousand hearts and lives.
I, one in that thirty thousand,
knelt at the wire
and lit my candle
from another
and left it burning.

Ruth Burgess

Written after 30,000 women, on December 12, 1982, gathered at Greenham Common cruise missile base in Berkshire to protest against nuclear weapons and to celebrate life.

There is a line of women

There is a line of women
extending back to Eve,
whose role in shaping history
God only could conceive.
And though, through endless ages,
their witness was repressed,
God valued and encouraged them
through whom the world was blessed.

So sing a song of Sarah
to laughter she gave birth;
and sing a song of Tamar
who stood for women's worth;
and sing a song of Hannah
who bargained with her Lord;
and sing a song of Mary
who bore and bred God's Word.

There is a line of women
who took on powerful men
defying laws and scruples
to let life live again.
And though, despite their triumph,
their stories stayed untold

God kept their number growing,
creative, strong and bold.

So sing a song of Shiphrah
with Puah close at hand,
engaged to kill male children,
they foiled the king's command.
And sing a song of Rahab
who sheltered spies and lied;
and sing a song of Esther,
preventing genocide.

There is a line of women
who stood at Jesus' side,
who housed him while he ministered
and held him when he died.
And though they claimed he'd risen
their news was deemed suspect
till Jesus stood among them,
his womanly elect.

So sing a song of Anna
who saw Christ's infant face;
and sing a song of Martha
who gave him food and space;
and sing of all the Marys
who heeded his requests,
and now at heaven's banquet
are Jesus' fondest guests.

John L. Bell

PRAYER

Be still, my children

Be still, my children.
My voice is not always
heard in the thunder and earthquakes
of your experience.
I do not only speak when you are
physically and mentally involved in living.
Be still – and in the stillness I will speak.
When you are quiet
when you are resting
when you are aware of me pulsating within
you and around you
when you are waiting and listening,
I will break through
and enrich your silence
releasing my peace and glory
and transforming your experience
until in the stillness
you find yourself longing
to shout for joy.

Ruth Burgess

A way of interceding (A meditation)

In your day make a space to stop, relax and be still.
Listen to some music or
listen to your breathing.

When you are quiet …
recall the things you have enjoyed today:
the sounds, the colours, the tastes,
the people,
and be grateful for their gift …

Now gather together the situations and people concerning you at this time.
It might help to hold your palms open before you
and to imagine holding each person/place/situation/task
in your hands.

Now focus on your breathing …
and as you breathe out
focus on giving these things which you are holding
into the hands of God –
let them go – hand them over – let God hold them.

Trust them to God's touch.

Lynda Wright, Tabor Retreat Centre, Key House, Falkland, Fife

---

Month 1 Day 10

JUSTICE AND PEACE

Let's pretend we're Christians (A letter from India)

In New York there was a conference of Christians. They had met together to discern the meaning of the Gospel in the world. There were priests, pastors, nuns and church leaders from all denominations and backgrounds.

During the meeting an American Indian stood up. He looked out over those assembled and said: 'Regardless of what the New Testament says, most Christians are materialists with no real experience of the Spirit … Regardless of what the New Testament says, most Christians are individualists with no real experience of community.' Then he paused for a moment and said quietly: 'Let's pretend for a moment that we're Christians, just pretend.'

Now this was quite a respectable group of Christian leaders. But he said: 'If we were Christians, really Christians, we would not accumulate, we would share what we have with one another and with the poor. We would actually love one another and we would treat each other as if we were a family.' And then he asked: 'Why don't we do that? Why don't we live in the way of Jesus Christ?'

There was a long silence after he spoke. No one had an answer to his question.

Yet that American Indian's question is a central question in our broken world. His question may not be easily answered: we may dismiss it as too idealistic or as naive; we may not want to hear it. But that central question remains.

To put it another way, our scriptures, our confessions, our creeds are all very public. They're not hidden away. They've not been kept secret. They're not behind locked doors. And our own lives as Christian people, like our scriptures, are also very public. And that's our problem.

For in India, as at home, the enormous gap between our public scriptures and our public lives in the churches has become a principal obstacle to belief in our time. We are so half-hearted in our witness.

That on the one hand. On the other, we are faced with an increasingly broken world. Here in Tamil Nadu the drought has been very bad and thousands of families are suffering.

In other countries – especially in Latin America – more and more people are being imprisoned or killed because they believe that justice, in its deepest sense, belongs to the heart of the Christian Gospel. In Britain there are many new tensions within society.

And over all our heads, the most terrible threat of all – nuclear weapons, 'perfected' in such a way that humans, not buildings, will be destroyed. (Can we really write that – 'humans, not buildings'– and remain sane?)

And in the midst of these afflictions, the American Indian's question becomes more and more central. For the sake of Jesus Christ, why cannot we live out the Gospel more? Whether in India or in Britain or in another country we are faced with this challenge. Do we want to cling to some comfortable Gospel which, in the end, can only bring us false comfort? Or do we want to wrestle against 'principalities and powers' for the sake of our Lord?

As we struggle with our witness to Jesus let us pray to be rid of this 'comfortable faith'. And to rid ourselves of it so that, in the power of the Holy Spirit, we may be able more faithfully to proclaim the incredible riches of Christ in our increasingly broken world.

May we together be people of prayer in these times.

But not only of prayer, but also of committed and costly caring. That kind of concern which comes from one place and one place only: the heart of our living Father.

Peter Millar

Prayer of confession

We confess, O Lord,
that we live with the demonic powers of violence:
that we grow rich by daily oppression of the poor,
that we sleep in the white sheets of racism,
that we say 'Peace, Peace', but do not make peace,
that we prostitute our science and knowledge in the cause of war,
that we have made this planet perilous to our children,
that we have lost the spirit of peace in our restless, disordered lives,
that the times we live in are evil.
And so we are accomplices by our violence,
by our most grievous violence.
We have turned away our face from the face of Christ.
Lord, have mercy on us.

A prayer from the Iona Community

THE INTEGRITY OF CREATION

Moved to action

One of my main reasons for believing in some kind of divine purpose comes from the sheer wonder and beauty of creation. Where we live in the far northwest of Scotland we are privileged to be able to enjoy the darkness, and even occasionally the wonder of the Northern lights. Seeing great curtains of light flickering like searchlights in a great canopy across the sky, or pausing to reflect on the time it has taken for the light of an individual star to reach our tiny planet, makes me so aware of how infinitesimally small we are in the whole cosmos.

Or at the other end of the spectrum, consider the tiny magic of a seed unfurling in the warm earth, or the little interlocking feathers of a wren, or the green brushes of a larch in spring, or the minute perfection of a seashell, and wonder at the beauty of it all. In that sense I cannot but believe in a creator, not so much as initiating an organised act of creation, but as a purpose for good behind the universe. 'And God saw that it was very good.' As the letter attributed to Chief Seattle says, 'To harm the earth is to heap contempt on its Creator.'

I am not a scientist and confess profound ignorance of the finer points of chaos theory and the physics of the universe, but I have a vivid memory of being shown a video at Woodbrooke, the Quaker study centre in Birmingham, which showed computerised images of fractals, explained for the lay person. Seemingly random objects such as forests, clouds or mountain ranges were programmed into the computer in such a way as to show the most amazing patterns and designs. I was profoundly moved and thrilled, as it seemed to me to show a design for life far beyond our understanding, full of sheer beauty.

It is this love of the environment that we live in, and of the infinite variety of

people around me, that inspires in me a deep reverence and gratitude for life, and so moves me to action.

My understanding of God, then, could be described as being in the connectedness of all life. God for me is like the divine spark that links me to another human being, to the animals, to all of creation – a kind of great web of connection, alive, shimmering with energy, creating flashes of inspiration and profound love.

Helen Steven

Prayer from Iona

Dear God,
we thank you for earth,
stars, planets
and moon;
for fields and farm,
for tree and bush –
and for all the other things that you made.

Mary Sharples, age 7

COLUMBAN CHRISTIANITY & THE CELTIC TRADITION

And God saw that it was good

A main characteristic that distinguishes the Celtic tradition from the Mediterranean tradition is the belief that creation is essentially good. Genesis 1 is like a foundational text. At the end of each day in the creation story is the phrase, 'And God saw that it was good.' Then at the end of the sixth day are the words, 'And God saw all that had been made, and behold it was very good.' In the Celtic tradition creation is viewed not merely as something that occurred at one point in the past. Creation is forever being born. It is forever coming forth from the womb of God, from the realm of the invisible into the realm of the visible. And God forever sees what is created as essentially good.

Not only is creation viewed as a blessing, it is regarded in essence as an expression of God. In his commentary on the prologue of St John's Gospel, and in particular the words, 'In the beginning was the Word … and all things have come into being through the Word', John Scotus Eriugena says that all things have been uttered into being by God. If God were to stop speaking, he says, creation would cease to exist. Creation is a theophany, i.e. a showing or revealing of God. At the heart of the Christian mystery is the belief that God is love, that God is Self-giving. All that God does, therefore, is a giving of Self. Creation, the great work of God, is essentially an offering of God's Self. It is a Self-disclosure to us of the mystery of God.

In relation to the question, 'Where do we look for God?', the answer is not, 'Away from creation', but rather 'Deep within all that has been created'. Within ourselves, within our children, within all that has been spoken into being, we can listen for the expression of God.

Eriugena says that God is speaking to us through two books. One is the 'little book', he says, the Book of Scripture. The other is the 'big book', the Book of Creation. This is not to be naive about what has gone wrong in creation. It is not to pretend that creation, like the human soul, has not been infected by sin. It is to affirm, however, that creation is like a sacred text that we can learn to read in our journey of knowing God. It is also to say, as George MacLeod used to say, again and again, that what we do to matter is a spiritual issue, whether that be the matter of our human bodies, the matter of the body of creation, or the matter of the body politic and how we handle the resources of the earth. All these matters are central to spirituality in the Celtic tradition. In the Mediterranean tradition, on the other hand, there has tended to be a separation of spirit and matter. The mystery of God has been distanced from the matter of creation. What we do to creation, therefore, too often has been regarded as not an essential part of our spirituality.

The Celtic tradition was formally rejected by the Synod of Whitby in the year 664. Part of the debate at Whitby reflected the Celtic mission's conviction that it was continuing the way of the beloved disciple who had leaned against Jesus at the Last Supper. The Synod's rejection of the Celtic tradition was a tragedy for Western Christianity. The reality, of course, is that it has lived on in the Celtic fringes of Britain over the centuries. And today it is being recovered. Scottish spirituality has been heavily influenced by many aspects of the Mediterranean tradition. Another part of our Scottish inheritance, however, is the Celtic stream. The reclaiming of it can be an important resource for spirituality in the 21st century. It can help us listen again for the beat of God's presence in this moment and in every moment, in our own lives and in the life of all that has being.

J. Philip Newell

Iona invocation

(Facing north)

Welcome, Spirit of earth,
of mountains, trees, the green earth, vast white sands, ancient rocks and minerals,
bright flowers and rich abundant fruit.
In balance with your rhythms and seasons
we celebrate the joy of our physical bodies
and the holy ground beneath our feet.
Spirit of the earth, hail and welcome.

(Facing east)

Welcome, Spirit of air,
of the eagle, the whispering wind, wide sky and tornado,
of rising sun and flowing air.
We claim the wide open space of your freedom
to soar with your Spirit;
we breathe in time with your breath.
Spirit of the air, hail and welcome.

(Facing south)

Welcome, Spirit of fire,
of volcanoes, of the hearth, of glowing flames, of transformation,
of candlelight and sunlight and heat.
We claim your passion, courage and energy;
kindle in our hearts a flame of love.
We share the light and warmth with all.
Spirit of the fire, hail and welcome.

(Facing west)

Welcome, Spirit of water,
of dolphins, whales and sea creatures,
of oceans, lakes, rivers, rain and tears,
of turquoise Iona waters, crashing waves and calm seas.
We claim your abundance and power.
Flow through us:
we are channels of the water of life.
Spirit of the water, hail and welcome.

(Facing the centre)

Welcome all you saints.
Saints of this island,
all you Celtic saints.
Welcome all you angels.
Welcome all you people.
Blessed be!

Lotte Webb

RACISM

This is your country

'Imagine a country where uniformed men come to your door in the dead of night … Imagine a country where your children are taken away … Imagine a country where you are locked up without trial … You don't have to imagine: This is your country. Welcome to Dungavel.'

This is the voice-over from a short film on so-called 'dawn raids' on asylum-seekers in Glasgow, made by my friend Lucinda Broadbent. Lucinda, from London, has been in Scotland for 22 years. She tells me that she has never felt more ashamed of her adopted land than recently. But she takes heart from the solidarity of ordinary people – neighbours, friends and even schoolmates – who come out in the early winter mornings to stand beside the most vulnerable and, in some cases, hide them in their own homes, risking criminal prosecution.

There is no doubt that a 'first-century asylum and refugee system', driven by the xenophobia of the tabloid press, would have caught up with the fleeing Mary, Joseph and Jesus, and returned them to King Herod. After all they had no 'right' to be in Egypt, they could not provide documentary evidence of previous persecution, there were no visible marks of torture, and the Massacre of the Innocents was simply a storm in a teacup that was unlikely to be repeated. The Egyptian authorities needed to keep in with their neighbours, trade was valuable – and what was a Judean peasant family when measured against that? These Jews were always stirring up trouble.

In the 1980s, the Sanctuary Movement saw churches and synagogues in various parts of the USA hide from the authorities those fleeing the death squads of Central America, whose regimes were being supported by Washington. It was against the law to obstruct the return of illegal immigrants and today similar groups are threatened with prosecution for providing water and medical help to 'undocumented' people crossing the Arizona desert. The congregation of a New York synagogue in the 1980s were discussing whether to offer sanctuary. The rabbi was unable to persuade them, until a middle-aged man rose to his feet. 'Forty years ago,' he said, 'I was a child lying in a ditch in Germany. My parents had been taken away. A farmer and his wife came by and took me into their cart and then to their home. I asked them whether they realised that it would be certain death to be found sheltering a Jew. "Oh yes," they said, "but we are Christians. And our faith compels us to assist anyone in need." '

Mary (not her real name) lives in daily dread of being returned to a country whose political leaders have killed her husband and her father. Emmanuel (not his real name) has a wife and child in another country but cannot visit them for fear of special branch police from his own land, which is on the Home Office 'safe return' list. He was taken from Dungavel in chains on a ten-hour van journey with little food or water – the kind of thing we used to protest about in apartheid South Africa.

Stanley Hope, a member of the Iona Community and for so many years a tireless campaigner on these issues, continually warned us that British immigration policy was becoming more and more racist. Tacitly many of us, myself included, felt that his perception was a wee bit over the top. But Stanley was of course a prophet. The time may come soon when Christians will need to undertake some costly witness not only on behalf of the most vulnerable in our society but on behalf of us all. After all it was Pastor Martin Niemöller in the 1930s who famously wrote:

First they came for the Jews
and I did not speak out –
because I was not a Jew.

Then they came for the communists
and I did not speak out –
because I was not a communist.

Then they came for the trade unionists
and I did not speak out –
because I was not a trade unionist.

Then they came for me –
and there was no one left
to speak out for me.

Iain Whyte

Prayer of confession and commitment

For our treatment of asylum-seekers,
for all who have been ignored,
humiliated, degraded by the system;
for the loss of our humanity,
we express our shame and ask forgiveness.

We commit ourselves to work for a fair and just immigration policy.

Stanley Hope

Prayer of intercession

God who is seen in the fear and faith of the asylum-seeker,
in the passion for people of neighbours and friends,
in the burning desire for justice of campaigners and protesters,
we pray for our leaders who exercise power over the most vulnerable members
    of our society.

Help them to stand in the shoes of those who have been running for too long;
help them to see through the eyes of those whose vision is always clouded
    by anxiety;
help them to make decisions that put people before popular prejudice,
    and so let the net of reception be lowered,
that sanctuary and sanctity may walk hand in hand.
We ask this in the name of the refugee child and man of compassion, Jesus Christ.

Iain Whyte

COMMUNITY

Something almost counter-cultural

This Saturday in Glasgow it will be 'Doors Open Day': a chance for people to visit nearly seventy buildings throughout the city that are of special architectural or historic interest. All over Scotland this month there will be similar opportunities to see places, some of which are not normally open to the public, some others that you usually have to pay to get into. If it's anything like previous years, a surprising number of people will be out and about going the rounds.

There's something almost counter-cultural about keeping your doors open. Perhaps in a few rural areas where everybody knows everybody else people still keep their doors open – even at night. But I doubt if many houses in our towns and cities have their doors open. It's rather a case of burglar alarms proliferating, sophisticated mortise locks and specially reinforced glass. In our church we have padlocks galore, grids over the windows, an alarm system, and steel plates behind the doors where in the past people have used axes to try to break in.

We live in times that are ultra-security-conscious. And, post 9/11, perhaps that's inevitable. But a culture of threat, suspicion and fear diminishes us as human beings. We presume that people are out to get us. Every stranger is a potential mugger or burglar – so bar the windows, pull up the drawbridge and turn on the surveillance cameras.

Fortunately, it's not always like that. In some places, among some people, you can see a culture of trust, built on relationships of mutuality, sharing and caring.

The reality is that we can never be or feel completely safe and secure. Life is a risk. And let's remember, in the words of one of the Iona Community's Wild Goose songs, that 'the love of God comes close where stands an open door'.

Norman Shanks

The love of God comes close

The love of God comes close
where stands an open door
to let the stranger in,
to mingle rich and poor:
the love of God is here to stay,
embracing those who walk his way.

The peace of God comes close
to those caught in the storm,
forgoing lives of ease,
to ease the lives forlorn:
the peace of God is here to stay,
embracing those who walk his way.

The joy of God comes close
where faith encounters fears,
where heights and depths of life
are found through smiles and tears:
the joy of God is here to stay,
embracing those who walk his way.

The grace of God comes close
to those whose grace is spent,
when hearts are tired or sore
and hope is bruised or bent:
the grace of God is here to stay,
embracing those who walk his way.

John L. Bell and Graham Maule

Month 1 Day 15

Pilgrimage

Traidcraft on Iona: Retreat and advance

In April 1996, in the first week after Easter, Traidcraft reps, retailers, helpers and staff journeyed to Iona. 'We said we were on retreat but … renamed it an advance!' Traidcraft is the UK's leading fair trade organisation, which was set up in 1979 to challenge the unfair way in which international trading systems are usually structured.

These prayers were written by Pat Bennett during the Traidcraft week and follow the route of the weekly pilgrimage around Iona:

At St Martin's Cross

Lord of the intertwining –
go with me on this pathway.

So weave my walking with yours,
that the steps of my feet
may become transformed
into a journey of my spirit.

At the Nunnery

Lord of the excluded –
open my ears to those I would prefer not to hear;
open my life to those I would prefer not to know;
open my heart to those I would prefer not to love;

and so open my eyes to see
where I exclude You.

At the Hill of the Angels

Lord of the touch –
here I am.
Consecrate my body – head, heart, hands, feet –
that today, by some word or action,
I may be your angel
to touch someone You love.

At Loch Staonaig

Lord of all resources –
forgive us that we so wantonly waste
what You have given:

The food and water we regard so lightly;
the gifts of your Spirit we spurn so proudly;
the joy of your life we negate so easily.
Forgive us, Lord.

At the Machair

Lord of the land –
it is so easy for us to reach out
and take what we want from the world.
Help us to see
when our bargain
is someone else's impoverishment;

when our pleasure is paid for
with someone else's pain;
and break our hearts
as yours is broken.

During the pilgrimage there is usually a simple, shared lunch at the Machair.

Grace

For sunny sky and calm sea and the wonderfully attracting beaches,
and also for the lovely smell of cheese and the taste of drop scones to share,
thank you, loving and caring God.
Amen

Annie Sharples, age 8

At the Marble Quarry

Lord of creation –
here,
    in the surging of the ocean
    in the beauty of the stone
    in the sweep of the iron
    in the symmetry of the wood
your creativity stands
hand in hand with ours.

In all that You have given us –
both the natural world
and our relationships with one another –

may we always be creators
and not despoilers.

At St Columba's Bay

Lord of sorrow –
my tears are for my sin;
my tears are for my selfishness;
my tears are for my penitence.

Your tears are for my brokenness;
your tears are for my marring;
your tears are for my healing.

May my tears join with yours,
and may that flow
become a healing balm –
for my life
and for the life of your world.

At the Hermit's Cell

Lord of the silences –
speak to me:
in the blowing of the wind;
in the rustling of the grass;
in the sound of the sea;
in the beating of my heart;
in the stirring of my spirit –
speak, Lord.
I am listening.

On Dun I

Lord of the high places –
fill me with your power:
– creating power of the Father;
– life-giving power of the Son;
– liberating power of the Spirit.

May I know such an infilling of You
that my life may be no longer silent,
but become a glorious, joyful affirmation
of your Kingdom.

At the Relig Oran (Journey's end – journey's beginning)

Incoming tide of God – cover my feet
I yield the direction of my life to You.

Incoming tide of God – cover my knees
I yield the rule of my life to You.

Incoming tide of God – cover my hands
I yield the shaping of my life to You.

Incoming tide of God – cover my heart
I yield all my emotions to You.

Incoming tide of God – cover my head
I yield my need for control to You.

Incoming tide of God – overwhelm me
Carry me out into your unimaginable depths!

Paradox

Lord, as we retreat these shores
may we advance with You:
To bring freedom for the captives;
justice for the oppressed;
love for the unwanted;
healing for the broken;
life for the dead.

Thus may the Kingdom of God advance from our retreat.

Pat Bennett

SEXUALITY

All are one in Christ Jesus

The biggest problem I have with people morally gay bashing is that it fuels and 'validates' homophobia. Homophobia isn't just insecure macho blokes punching poofters and raping dykes, which does happen. Homophobia is also about families full of shame and people who learn to feel so awkward in their skin that they hate themselves. Yes, our country is progressive, because, unlike in some other countries, you won't be sentenced to death for being in a same-sex relationship, but we give a very strong message of queer = wrong + shame + sexual perversion. Our culture's judgement, which borders on hatred in many places (schools, building sites, etc), creates internal homophobia within many lesbian, bi and gay people. Internal homophobia, which I can only describe as shame or self-loathing, wrecks lives and families and sometimes results in suicide. Type in the words suicide+gay on Google and you get *'Page 1 of 746,109 results containing gay+suicide'.*

Every Tuesday evening in the Iona Abbey service of prayers for healing, we talk about wholeness and we explain that we believe God intends for us a life of wholeness as expressed in the life and teaching of Jesus. It's much harder to achieve that when you hate yourself and when you don't have the freedom to be open about a very important part of yourself. The church's stance – that homosexuality is perverted and against God's divine path – damages people. It results in mothers wishing they had never had their children, and in gay people repressing their true nature. It also means that many lesbian, gay, bisexual and transgender people (who make up 5-10% of the population) feel unable to go to church and be accepted for who they are.

All are equal in Christ Jesus. This is what the message should be. This is not the same message as 'hate the sin, love the sinner', which is what a lot of queer people hear when they are judged by Christians. I am very accepting of interpretations of Christianity and rarely tell others how they should read the Bible, but I do believe we should never use the Bible to justify judgement. The slave traders justified their riches and profession using the Bible. How can people be free if they are not allowed to be themselves?

Because I am not a biblical scholar, and because there are hundreds of other articles on biblical interpretations of homosexuality, I'm not going to say much about it. However, I'd like to point out that these discussions tend to focus on sex rather than on love, intimacy and companionship. It's interesting that this issue and the issue of the ordination of women are dividing churches. If issues of sin (where no one is harmed by the sin, which may or may not be a sin) is where the cutting edge of Christianity is, it's no wonder there are fewer bums in pew seats! Along with the judgement of women as unworthy of ministry/priesthood, this issue of sexuality reeks of judgement and 'you are less holy than me and my pals'.

Why is marriage exclusive to straight couples? My brother (who is not Christian) tells me that the balance and union of male and female is sacred in a way that is unattainable for two people of the same gender. Yes, men and women produce children, which is possibly the most sacred thing humanity achieves, but we don't stop post-menopausal couples from marrying. And, contrary to popular opinion, homosexuality is natural – it occurs commonly in the animal kingdom. So where is the extra sacredness that my brother sees? All I know is that I have seen just as many straight people having non-loving casual sex as I have queer people, and I don't see a lot of difference between my marriage and that of my two best friends, who are lesbians. My friends own a house, a future and two dogs together; they balance each other's personalities beautifully; they support each other to be more compassionate and better human beings.

This specific issue is the main barrier and reason my non-Christian friends don't want anything to do with Christianity. And for my lesbian, bi and gay friends, the judgement makes churches places that reject rather than welcome them. Jesus didn't teach anything about sexuality, but what he did go on about was tolerance, acceptance of the rejected and loving each other and ourselves. All are one in Christ Jesus and for me that's what it's all about.

Simon de Voil, a member of the Resident group on Iona

HEALING

I want to be healed

I want to be healed.

Do you know what you're asking?
For healing's a journey through doubt and through pain.
And the healing that God brings may take a whole lifetime
with no guarantee that you'll reckon it gain.

I want to be healed.

Then you're asking for changes
that shake the foundations you've built upon sand.
For the healing that God brings doesn't follow our patterns
and shapes us in ways we may not understand.

I want to be healed.

Then drop your defences,
and open your heart, your mind and your soul.
For the healing that God brings probes scars you've forgotten,
cauterising and cleaning and making you whole.

I want to be healed

At least, in the future.
Perhaps I'll just wait till the time feels right.
I'm not sure that God's healing will suit at the moment.
I'll hold on to the things that I'm used to – all right?

Alix Brown, Iona 2004

SOCIAL ACTION

Holding someone in the Light

The simple words 'I'll pray for you' can be hugely encouraging. Some years ago I organised a meeting of military generals, top civil servants and defence experts, coming together with assorted peace campaigners and church leaders for a week on Iona. At the start of the week I was understandably nervous, and a guest at the Abbey who was not a participant in the conference came up to me and said, 'Would you like me to pray for you all during the conference?' I accepted her offer, rather with the attitude of 'Oh well, if she would like to do that it can't do any harm.' From time to time throughout the week we would meet in passing and she would simply give me a little nod of acknowledgement. Gradually I realised that the knowledge of her prayerful support was becoming more and more significant. By the end of a truly amazing week, I realised just how important her prayers had been. It was not just that I personally felt calmed and supported by her thoughts; it was also a tapping into some kind of intangible energy that could be felt at our meetings. I think we were all surprised, and one of the military men summed it up with his parting words as he stepped onto the ferry: 'Only the hand of God could have dumped me into the midst of a bunch of raving peace women!' Then he looked me directly in the eye and said, 'And I mean it.'

This highlights a crucially important form of activism, that of the prayerful supporter. For some years our non-violent action group was supported by a nun in an enclosed Carmelite order. Most of us never met her, but she wanted to know whenever we were doing an action or had an important decision to make, so that she could uphold us in prayer. I believe it strengthened our group in unseen ways, and I also believe strongly that her prayers were as valid a form of activism as our demonstrations and protests, but that one without the complementary activity of the other has an inherent weakness and lack of balance.

Friends [Quakers] speak of holding someone in the Light and I have always found this a particularly helpful way of expressing it. The idea of going beyond words to a different level of being, to enfold another in the Light and Love beyond our physical experience, is a very attractive image.

A powerful example of 'holding someone in the Light' occurred during the trial of the Trident Three at Greenock Sheriff Court. Ellen Moxley, Ulla Roder and Angie Zelter were on trial for dismantling part of the acoustic testing facility for the Trident nuclear submarines by throwing the computers into the loch. The three maintained that their actions were to uphold international law, basing their defence on the ruling of the International Court of Justice in the Hague in July 1996 that nuclear weapons are in contravention of international humanitarian law. Only a few days into the trial Sheriff Margaret Gimblett was faced with a crucial decision whether or not to allow this defence under international law or to treat it as a straightforward case of criminal damage. Everything hinged on her decision. She adjourned the court while she considered the case. Immediately a small group gathered on the pavement outside the court and stood in silence holding Margaret Gimblett in the Light. In many ways similar to upholding the Clerk at Yearly Meeting, this was one of the most powerful experiences of focused prayer that I have ever had. An hour later the Court reconvened, and her decision to allow a defence under international law became legal and campaigning history, as the trial moved on to the acquittal of the Trident Three four-and-a-half weeks later. Sheriff Margaret Gimblett's profoundly moving summing up reflects the moral courage of the decision she took, influenced, I am certain, by the power of prayer.

I have the invidious task of deciding on international law as it relates to nuclear weapons. I am only a very junior sheriff without the wisdom or experience of those above me. I have a knowledge of the repercussions which could be far-reaching. As a sheriff I took an oath to act without fear or favour in interpreting the law … I have to conclude that the three accused, in company with many others, were justified in thinking that Great Britain's use and deployment of Trident … could be construed as a threat … and as such is an infringement of international and customary law. I have heard nothing which would make it seem to me that the accused acted with criminal intent. Therefore I will instruct the jury that they should acquit the three accused.
(Gimblett 1999)

Helen Steven

Life beyond death row

The man had been sentenced and sent to death row. Terrified by the noise, the control inflicted by the institution, and the madness of some of the inmates, he cowered in his cell. His arrival had been noticed, and his name was shouted down the block. That evening an orderly swept a full paper bag into his 'cage'. He sat for hours imagining what horror it contained. At last he opened it, to find soap, toothpaste, chocolate.

The next day he asked the orderly how he could pay the other inmates for these supplies. 'You cannot pay,' he was told, 'except by giving something when someone new arrives.'

Month 1 Day 19

My pen friend, Twin, has spent twenty-one years on death row. The appeals process is drawing to a close. He has become a gentle, thoughtful, spiritual man, with a respect for others. He has found again his childhood faith, Islam, and draws strength from it. He writes, and assists other prisoners. He reads and thinks and prays, and sometimes depression overcomes him. But he is a child of God – made for a life bigger than this one – living out God's laws in circumstances worse than we can imagine. His life is not wasted, but is a source of life to others.

Becoming a pen friend to a stranger is not an easy decision. You don't know who will write back, but you are committed to keep writing, regularly, to the end. You may develop an enriching friendship with someone the world has rejected. It is not about control, or pushing a religious or political viewpoint, but about strangers finding their common humanity.

As a Christian, I am called to believe that everyone on death row is a valuable person, loved into existence by God and designed for eternity.

The charity *Life Lines*, a secular organisation, looks for mature individuals to write to people on death row in the United States. www.lifelines-uk.org

Rosemary Power

While this was going to press, Twin's death sentence was overturned. He was sent for re-sentencing, which may mean prison until death. Even so, the State Prosecutor has appealed. Twin waits to hear.

CHURCH RENEWAL

'I havena gien up on God'

On May 4th, 2006 I took the 10:15am bus from Gargunnock for Glasgow with a change at Balfron. In Kippen, the gears stopped functioning and we could go no further. The driver phoned for a replacement bus and a double-decker was sent (though at that point I was the only passenger). A mechanic came with the replacement bus to attempt a repair. The drivers had a word with one another, and then said to me: 'When does your meeting in Glasgow start?' I said: '12:30.' 'Is it important to get there in time? – because if it is we should get a car laid on to take you straight in.' I told them that my being late would not matter. So a double-decker bus/taxi took me the seven miles to Balfron.

There the driver did not leave me at the bus stop, where I would get a connection in 20 minutes, but took me to the small bus station and into the drivers' howff; there he gave me a chair and a hot drink, and we had time to talk.

I asked one of the drivers if he liked his job or if it was the only one he could get. He said he quite liked it, and told me about the training he got to make sure he could handle single and double-decker buses responsibly. I said that the work he did was important in keeping the whole world going. He said: 'Eh?' seemingly incredulous to hear his work so highly valued. I said that in the book of Ecclesiasticus the people who sustained the created world were declared not to be the 'high-ups' or intellectuals but to be labourers, ploughmen, blacksmiths – the equivalent in that time to drivers and mechanics. 'Is that right?' he said. 'In the Bible? Are you a minister?' I said I was but that I had started ministry working in labouring gangs because I believed that the church had been too distant from working folk, and that there I acted as a kind of chaplain.

'I was once in the church,' he said, 'but I gied up on it. I havena gien up on God! But I gied up on the church.'

So I said what a waste it was that people's gifts weren't used; that they were dumbed down in the pews.

'That's it!' he said. 'You're treated as if you are only meant to be spoken to.'

So I told him I was going into Glasgow to check on a book which advocated that kind of change.

'Gosh!' he said. 'I'd fairly like tae read a case made oot for that!'

When *The Way Ahead* was printed, a copy was sent to the Drivers' Howff, Bus Station, Balfron, with a word of thanks.

'The Way Ahead: Grown-up Christians' by Ian M. Fraser was published by Wild Goose in 2006.

Prayer (Behind the scenes)

God the Lord, you sustain us invisibly by the air we breathe, the energy granted for daily tasks and conversation, the capacity to relate to you and to one another. This is the Lord's doing and it is wonderful in our eyes. The day itself is a gift of grace, not guaranteed, for we might not have wakened to it. We give thanks.

We give thanks for those who are servants of your sustaining grace, not only those we see but those who are invisible – bakers, butchers, candlestick makers, who supply our needs.

We switch on the light and the cooker, scarcely giving a thought to those who bring electricity to our homes – except in times of storm when the lines are down and we crouch in the cold. Now we take time to thank you for them.

We remember with gratitude those who drive vans, buses, trains, trucks, allowing networks of contact to be maintained and goods and people to be moved to where they can meet and work and be of use to you. We give thanks for those who maintain our highways, those who resurface roads …

We bless you for those who make and sell clothes; for volunteer workers in charity shops; and for all kinds of service in shops that supply our daily needs and wants.

We pray for those who, invisible to us, seek to heal divisions in and between nations – in Northern Ireland, in Palestine/Israel, all those working to make peace sustainable and just.

God, who sustains us, we give thanks for all those working behind the scenes. Amen

Ian M. Fraser

Month 1 Day 20

WORSHIP

A new heaven and a new earth

… I remember last year, the Jubilee year, my colleagues and I were responsible for producing a liturgy, an act of worship to celebrate the biblical requirement that debts be cancelled and people burdened with debt be restored to their full dignity. I remember something which happened on Iona and in York Minster and in a Lutheran cathedral in Karlskrona, Sweden, and in a Catholic church in New Orleans.

The liturgy allowed people, if they wished, to make signs of their commitment to God's future of justice and responsible living. Towards the end of the service, people could engage in any of four symbolic actions. One of these required worshippers to come up to the altar on which there was a basket with small pieces of string, each tightly knotted. They were invited to take a piece of string and remember someone who was indebted to them morally or financially, someone they had not forgiven, someone who was the victim of their unwillingness to let the past be put behind them. Then, in front of the cross of Jesus, they could untie the knot and lay the string on the altar and declare before God their decision to cancel the debt, to forgive.

And I watched grown men cry and teenagers cry and proud people come away changed, because in that action they glimpsed a new heaven and a new earth where reconciliation might win the day rather than hatred.

This must be what the church and liturgy are about …

John L. Bell

CALLED TO BE ONE

Holy risks: The ecu-comical movement

It is our conviction that, as a matter of policy at all levels and in all places, our churches must now move from cooperation to clear commitment to each other, in search of the unity for which Christ prayed, and in common evangelism and service of the world.

From the British Churches' Swanwick Declaration, 4th September, 1987

We confess anew with shame, however, that Christians too are divided in various ways. A Church called to God's work of reconciliation in the world will only be credible if it is a body that demonstrates within its own life the reconciling power of Jesus Christ. We cannot do this effectively unless we begin to overcome within the Church not only ecclesiastical and doctrinal, but also social, racial and economic divisions, as well as disunity between the churches. Our task as the Body of Christ is to go out in love with the whole gospel for the whole world. We are called to trust one another and to take 'holy risks' for the sake of common mission. On every agenda the first question should be: 'Is this a priority?' and the second: 'How can we do this together?'

From the British Churches' Swanwick Report, 1987

Whilst much has been achieved in the twenty years since these statements were made it can hardly be said that many 'holy risks' have been taken. As summed up by an atheist university lecturer some years ago, the 'ecumenical movement' still looks to many outside the churches to be more like the 'ecu-comical movement'. Seventy years or so ago when Stanley Jones preached the gospel to Mahatma Gandhi and asked him if he would become a Christian, the Mahatma replied: 'Yes, I will become a Christian tomorrow.' At which point Jones's heart missed a beat, till Gandhi continued: 'If you will tell me to which church you would like me to belong.' End of conversation!

Or as Brooks Atkinson once said: 'I have no objection to churches so long as they do not interfere with God's work.' Or as Jesus once said: 'Every kingdom divided against itself is laid waste, and no city or house divided against itself will stand.'

God's work is not about Presbyterianism, Catholicism, Methodism, Calvinism, Evangelicalism, Ecumenism, Anglicanism, Congregational-ism or any of the other 'isms' to which so many of us seem to be so attached. It is about unity and reconciliation and peace so that the world may believe.

Murdoch MacKenzie

Month 1 Day 22

MISSION

On our doorsteps

What else is there to do if Christianity has proved to be simply part of an oppressive system?

An Amerindian has written in anger: 'To us, Hitler killing 6 million was not the world-shaking event it was to Europe – from our vantage point of having over 20 million killed by Europeans, of having whole nations of Indians completely destroyed.' He goes on: 'Who is oppressing Indians in general? Only the US, Canada, Brazil, Mexico, Peru and the other 'governments' of those two continents? Who is oppressing, then, the natives of Australia and of Africa? Who benefits from the rubber, chocolate, petroleum, minerals and lumber of North and South America? Western civilisation as a whole – Europeans (who may enjoy calling themselves Americans, Australians or whatever). And I almost insist that there is no Christianity except that which exists. That spoken of and thought of by theologians cannot really concern us who must fight the effects of what exists in the real world.' And again: 'Can you look at the world and say that Western civilisation is good? Can you look at the world and say that Christianity, as it is, is good?'

Following are some extracts from an Institute for Cultural Action (IDAC) document on the experience of the Aymara Indians in Peru:

> Destruction of the Aymara socioeconomic life was accompanied by the imposition, at the hands of the Catholic clergy, of an authoritarian and oppressive deity completely foreign to Aymara cosmology, (page 3)
>
> To fit in and be productive in a capitalist society, the Aymara had to change their whole value system and world vision, (page 5)
>
> Resignation and acceptance of suffering – so fervently preached by the

priests – had become prevailing attitudes, (page 17) … (from Document 4, Political Education – An Experience in Peru, IDAC)

In Ilesha, Nigeria, a group from the local community met to contribute to the World Council of Churches 'Participation in Change' programme. One of the questions used to focus discussion was 'What should be prominently on the agenda of the Fifth World Assembly of the World Council of Churches?'. The chairman summed up contributions from the floor and made his own emphasis in the following words: 'Christianity came through the West to us. But Westerners are not acting at all like Christians towards us. The inhumanity, exploitation and oppression which we suffer, coming from those from whom Christianity originally came, hurts us and shames the Church. I went to an Anglican church when I was in Geneva a short time ago, and it was so obvious that people were unwilling to sit beside me – the Church of the West is full of racism. The churches of the West have the money and the power – but they need to learn from the rest of the world what real humanity means.

'Evangelism to the West is badly needed. A rebirth of genuine Christianity needs to be produced. The gospel is being brought into disrepute by the people who had originally been its bearers and representatives. The big question for the Fifth Assembly is how can the World Council of Churches begin a mission to the West to evangelise people there in all their dealings with other countries? There is nothing more important than this to face.'

A dominating flow of history based on wealth and technology has been as much a mark of missions from the West as the theology of the West. People have been crushed and silenced by the gospel which should set people free. They turn from it, sick in the stomach, to search for true life elsewhere. If they care at all about the faith, they have no doubt about where the main field of mission lies – on our doorsteps.

Ian M. Fraser

Month 1 Day 23

Time to rest and recuperate

For six years you shall sow your land and gather in its yield; but the seventh year you shall let it rest and lie fallow, so that the poor of your people may eat; and what they leave, the wild animals may eat. You shall do the same with your vineyard, and with your olive orchard.

Exodus 23:10–11 (NRSV)

When you reap the harvest of your land, you shall not reap to the very edges of your field, or gather the gleanings of your harvest. You shall not strip your vineyard bare, or gather the fallen grapes of your vineyard; you shall leave them for the poor and the alien: I am the Lord your God.

Leviticus 19:9–10 (NRSV)

As I read these passages from the books of the Law I think of the experience of the Aymara Indians in the highlands of Bolivia. In that tribe, individual families own areas of land, but it is the community that determines what will be grown for the benefit of all. Each landowner is told what crop to grow, and is regularly instructed to leave an area fallow. This communal organisation of agriculture ensures that an adequate diversity of crops, such as potatoes, quinoa and oca, are grown to meet community requirements. It also gives the land time to rest and recuperate. If a family's land is to be fallow for a year, the produce of other members of the tribe will take care of all needs. As a result the Aymara agricultural system has functioned for hundreds of years without destroying the soil.

Ghillean Prance, Science Director of the Eden Project (Cornwall), and former Director of Royal Botanic Gardens, Kew

---

Month 1 Day 23

WORK

To see it is to make you cry

When we realise
that all our scientific discoveries
are sacramental unveilings of the Body of our Lord:
when we realise
that we cannot lift a stone to build a fortification
but the presence of God moves in to occupy the hole that we have made:
when we grasp
that the houses men live in
(and not just the men who live in them)
are offerings for His glory:
that the food men eat
(and not just they that eat the food)
are aspects of His presence:
when the angels reveal to us
(as science, that modern trumpet of the angels, reveals)
that 'the fullness of the whole earth is His glory':
when we realise all that
and grasp what we *do* with
stones and iron and food and houses,
there is no other cry that can escape our lips than
'Woe is me' …

Woe is the people among whom I live, yes:
but, firstly – 'woe is me:
for I am a man of unclean lips
and mine eyes have seen the King, the Lord of hosts.'

George MacLeod, from a sermon, 1944

THE POOR AND DISADVANTAGED

True or false?

How would you answer this question?: God has a bias towards the poor. True or false?

I had to work on that question while I was at college, training for the ministry. And before I started I had to admit my own bias. I'd been very influenced by the then-Bishop of Liverpool, David Sheppard, who believed so strongly that Jesus *did* have a bias to the poor that he even wrote a book by that title (*Bias to the Poor*, Hodder & Stoughton, 1983).

Jesus certainly had plenty of time for wealthier people. Many of his friends were among the better-off folk of his community – he ate at their homes, they supported his work. He wasn't prejudiced against them.

But Jesus made it plain that there is a special place in God's heart for the 'poor'. He spent a great deal of time with those people.

He had a lot to say about wealth and poverty, far more than about any other issue. (I once saw a speaker hold up a bible he'd cut up with scissors – he'd cut out every reference to money, wealth and poverty: the Bible literally fell apart in his hands.)

Jesus condemned those who build their wealth up while exploiting their workers, and those who lift up their hands in prayer while neglecting needy people around them.

He challenged the religious people about their values, their friendships, their use of time and money. He asked them to do things with their money which would go beyond even charity and generosity – made them wonder if they'd got their place booked in heaven after all.

And he did a lot of this while he was eating. Once Jesus said: 'The next time you put on a dinner, don't just invite your friends and family and rich neighbours, the kind of people who will return the favour. Invite some people who never get invited out, the misfits from the wrong side of the tracks. You'll be – and experience – a blessing. They won't be able to return the favour, but the favour will be returned – oh, how it will be returned! – by God' (Luke 14:12–14, *The Message*).

So many of the stories about Jesus take place around a table where the guests are a real mix of people – the well-off hosts and the people Jesus has dragged in off the streets. There are all sorts of odd conversations as lawyers talk to fishermen, as prostitutes chat with businessmen's wives, as burglars pour wine for bishops and as society's celebrities pass the salt to folk they'd normally pass by lying on the street.

For the poor people, sharing in those meals would have felt like heaven. For the rich people it could have felt very uncomfortable. Or it could have opened their eyes and helped them see life in new ways. Imagine a meal like that at your house, how strange and wonderful it could be.

There *is* a bias to the poor in all of this, but also a blessing for the rest of us if we open our eyes and hearts.

John Davies

Jesus said

Leader: Jesus said: Blessed are the comfortable,
for God has shown them his favour.
RHS: OH NO HE DIDN'T!
LHS: OH YES HE DID!

Leader: Jesus said: Blessed are those who have good pension funds,
for God has shown them his favour.

RHS:	OH NO HE DIDN'T!
LHS:	OH YES HE DID!

Leader:	Jesus said: The strong and powerful will inherit the earth.
RHS:	OH NO HE DIDN'T!
LHS:	OH YES HE DID!

Leader:	Jesus said: Blessed are the winners, for they will inherit everything.
RHS:	OH NO HE DIDN'T!
LHS:	OH YES HE DID!

Leader:	Jesus said: Don't do anything to undermine the existing order – to do so is to go against God.
RHS:	OH NO HE DIDN'T!
LHS:	OH YES HE DID!

Leader:	Jesus said: Look after yourself, then if you have something left over, give a coin to the poor.
RHS:	OH NO HE DIDN'T!
LHS:	OH YES HE DID!

Leader:	Jesus said: God is a nice old man, who doesn't want anyone to rock the boat.
RHS:	OH NO HE DIDN'T!
LHS:	OH YES HE DID!

Ron Ferguson

Basic Christian Communities

The concrete cross

May I dare to revert to how the Iona Community got started?

I had been minister of a West End congregation in Edinburgh. St Cuthbert's at the West End of Princes Street. We had 3,000 members; 1,000 in the Sunday school! Four clergy. It was before television, so the 6:30pm service rarely had fewer than 1,500.

This was true of many churches. In short, Scotland was 'religious'.

Yet, paradoxically, Social Security was at a minimum. A man with his wife and one child got, in total for all three, 28 shillings (today a similar family receive £37) …

In the thirties we had gone 'religious', and forgotten the true nature of the Gospel. I found myself then the minister of a real unemployed parish – Govan, with its 3,000 members, and 1,000 in the Sunday school. Poverty was rife.

But what a revelation it was to see how Christian were the unemployed, though comparatively few came to church.

Was there a widow starving in the top flat? … In no time the poor rallied round and fed her! … Were children without clothes on the next stair? At once the poor around brought in clothes. Were people in trouble, sometimes criminal? … Well, then the unemployed rallied round to comfort them.

'I was an hungered and ye gave me meat, naked and ye clothed me, in prison and you came to me.' The three great signs of Christian obedience!

There were four of us on the staff, all bachelors living together in the top flat of our church hall. We thought these 'unchurched saints' had a great message for our young clerics in the divinity hall. So we bought the ruined Fingleton mill for a song.

We bought a second-hand bus. We asked these unemployed masons and carpenters to come out with us, bringing their senior sons with them – most of them unemployed – and we got our young clerics to come and camp with these crafts-men, and learn 'true religion' from them to outpass the stodgy theology of the divinity hall.

We built a swimming pool and made [the mill] a wonderful holiday house at minimum cost to the craftsmen of Govan and their kids.

In summertime, we clerics also escaped to Iona and learnt more of St Columba. We knew he was a congenial saint for our purpose. He was no recluse monk.

Through St Ninian he had learnt of the great Martin of Tours who (equally amazed at the down-to-earth saintliness of the civilians and the farmers in France) deserted his monk's cell and set up 'family groups' of clerics and citizens to meet the real Christ who loved the poor.

Martin built no churches. His churches were real people living in fellowship, the clerics tilling their fields and going out to the fishing, and not expecting the citizens and peas-ants to feed them.

This seemed to be the Word for the Church of our time.

On one of our Iona walks we plotted – to our own amaze-ment – the possibility of 'doing a Fingleton Mill' with the ruined Iona Abbey! To our amazement the trustees (who held the ruins for the Church of Scotland) gave us permission to do it! So we got started in Iona.

To our amazement money came (and a lot of criticism!). We were accused of 'imitating monks' when we were doing the very opposite.

That first year we discussed one day (the six young ministers and the six young unemployed carpenters and masons who had found the common faith at Fingleton) what our uniform should be. It was not difficult. The main occupation of the permanent residents on the island was fishing (and tilling the soil). So we all bought fishermen's blue suits, to wear on weekdays and on Sundays!

It was 1938, and divinity students, who had finished their university course, came and joined us.

We only built in summertime. In winter, the divinity students went and served in industrial parishes, while the craftsmen went back to Govan. The spiritual had got merged with the material; as Christ had so often pleaded.

The ruined buildings in summer inspired us. The whole history of the Church was there. St Martin's time, already described. Then the fatal retiral of the Church into theoretical theology. The widening gulf between the clerics and the citizens.

To be sure, they built wonderful cloisters, but these were for clerical contemplation rather than revealing conversation with the peasants.

That was the 11th century … Came the 15th century and the rupture was complete. Nought but a Reformation was adequate: and so the walls of the monastery fell down. The 10th-century St John's Cross lay splintered on the ground.

But our craftsmen had what seemed a good idea. Painstakingly, they cemented its carved stones into a modern cross for our century: outside, beside the west door.

It was a sermon in stone: 'our age'-cement had taken over the next age of faith on the original site. But came the '60s, and it was blown down!

Annoyed at first, I came to see that God had blown it down! – to remind us that the Cross does not speak to us through the centuries at ever greater intervals! God's Cross confronts *each age* in contemporary terms.

So there was constructed a new concrete cross, embodying the past, to be sure, but contemporaneous with the differing needs of the present time. And it is this concrete cross which challenges our generation now, standing outside the west door.

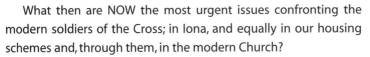

What then are NOW the most urgent issues confronting the modern soldiers of the Cross; in Iona, and equally in our housing schemes and, through them, in the modern Church?

Feeding the hungry has a different connotation in the 1980s to what Govan faced in the thirties. In the eighties, with all our modern consciousness of a united world, it is starvation in the Third World countries!

Every 15 seconds, someone dies of starvation – brothers and sisters as they are of our opulent West! We can hardly pass that by, when the 'least of our brethren' are in fact the embodiment of Christ!

By the same token, clothing the naked has new meaning. Too many firms in the West do not want the Third World to prosper! They want to keep the Third World poor, that they may continue to buy from us!

… And the international banks seem unaware that what confronts them, the Third World, is the Body of Christ!

By the same token 'visiting the people in prison' has a similar challenge, now that we know the material is shot through with the spiritual. That is, now that we know salvation is about bodies.

Feeding the hungry, clothing the naked, visiting the imprisoned is politics, politics, politics! Bodies, bodies, bodies! … They are all about what we do with the Body of Christ!

Such are the vast challenges of the Cross for our day …

George MacLeod, an extract from a sermon preached in Easterhouse in the 1980s

NON-VIOLENCE AND PEACEKEEPING

God in the other

Personally, I derive much … comfort and inspiration in the idea of a God who is 'closer than breathing', the very ground of our being. This shifts the entire focus of the divine away from distant inaccessibility, to an immediate immanent presence within every one of us, constantly present and constantly loving. Thus, not only is God the very essence and core of my own being, there is also 'that of God' in every person I meet. The Nepalese greeting *Namaste,* usually coupled with a folding of the hands and a bow, means 'The God within me greets the God within you'.

There is a direct connection between a belief in this kind of God and the respect that forms the whole basis of non-violence. If every one of us embodies an aspect of the truth of God, the divine, the very essence of humanity, then this must immediately affect how we treat that person. This was at the heart of Gandhi's teaching. If we kill or use violence against another human being, then we are doing violence to the truth of God within them.

Even enemies, those with whom we profoundly disagree, have this element of the divine, and it becomes our task to seek that out in order to be able to move forward in mutual respect. Non-violent action is based on the assumption that by one's own actions, by confronting people openly and lovingly in a new and creative way, one can reach this deep inner core of the divine, appeal to the very highest nature within a person and so effect change. And of course the change may need to happen within oneself. This is why part of non-violence training teaches one to look one's opponent in the eye, thus encountering the window on the soul, meeting as human to human and saying, 'You cannot ignore my humanity, just as I respect yours.' And of course this is also one of the reasons why secret police wear visors and dark glasses, precisely to avoid such a deeply challenging contact.

At the start of the Options for Defence week on Iona, during which military generals, military experts and peace campaigners gathered for a conference, we all assembled in the Chapter House of the Abbey. It was a distinctly stiff beginning, suspicion in the air and each side eyeing the other with proverbial hackles raised. To begin the introductions and attempt to ease the atmosphere, I said that we all sincerely believed that we were working for peace, but simply differed over the methods. The relief was almost palpable as shoulders came down, people relaxed into their seats and began to look each other in the eye.

I remember an occasion at the peace camp at Greenham Common. We had been blockading a gate for several hours, when a decision was made to open the gates forcibly from the inside by driving at them with a large truck. The gates were being forced open slowly and women were being crushed under the gate as it swung. Those of us lined up on the outside, hemmed in by a solid row of police, felt totally helpless and at a loss as to what to do. Eventually we decided to stand up and speak to the police officer directly in front of each one of us. I was opposite a very young man, and, as I was angry and distressed, I said, rather unkindly, 'Do you like doing this kind of thing?' To my consternation his eyes filled with tears and he said, 'I am hating every minute of it and I wish I was anywhere else.'

Of course there are times when it seems impossible to discern that of God in the other; times when all appeals fail and attempts to make peace can lead to suffering and even death. Yet unbelievably, in some of the most extreme situations, there are amazing stories of how the deep humanity of another has been touched and a seemingly horrific situation transformed.

Helen Steven

Month 1 Day 27

INTERFAITH

A story from England and a story from Sri Lanka

From the mouths of children

Guests from all faiths gathered in the Muslim Resource Centre by special invitation, one evening near the end of Ramadan. We joined the Muslim congregation in the *Iftari* prayer for breaking the fast.

The imam led prayers, and speaker after speaker appealed for support for the victims in the remote mountain villages of Pakistan, wounded and cut off by the terrible earthquake.

The Lord Mayor of Coventry, a Hindu, working side by side with the Deputy Lord Mayor, a Muslim, spoke movingly of the work of the Islamic Relief Fund. Four Sikh elders from the gurdwara nearby arrived with £500. So many families of the local Asian community had friends and relatives directly affected.

Then, at the very end, at sunset, before the meal began, the Muslim children: Sabrina, a teenaged member of the National Youth Parliament, spoke simply, clearly and from the heart. Then her younger friends, three girls and a little boy, said they wanted to sing a song they had learnt at school:

'When I needed a neighbour, were you there, were you there?
When I needed a neighbour, were you there?
And the creed and the colour and the name won't matter,
were you there?

I was hungry and thirsty … when I needed a shelter … were you there?'

Jesus's challenging words of love in Sydney Carter's song, shyly sung; and then, picking up confidence, the last verse:

'Wherever you travel I'll be there, I'll be there,
wherever you travel, I'll be there.
And the creed and the colour and the name won't matter,
I'll be there.'[3]

The whole hall fell silent for a long moment.

God was recognised by each one there – alongside us all and with our suffering brothers and sisters overseas.

We hadn't needed all the adult speeches – the children said it all.

David Hawkey, an Associate member of the Iona Community

Putting the window back together again

Although I'm a Kiwi living in Glasgow, I have not travelled much apart from the long-haul flights between New Zealand and Scotland. Recently an opportunity came up for me to visit friends in Sri Lanka; they are working in the Anglican church in Kandy, right in the middle of this beautiful, teardrop-shaped little country.

My first impressions of Sri Lanka included the Third World poverty, which I found very sobering; the all-pervading mix of religions; the influence of Buddhism; the open friendliness and generosity of the Sri Lankans; the stunningly beautiful beaches and mountains – and the fast and furious driving!

Month 1 Day 28

There is one story which has lingered with me and which I want to tell. In Kandy, all the major religions sit beside each other, cheek by jowl – St Paul's Anglican Church; the Temple of the Tooth, the world-famous Buddhist temple; the Muslim mosque; and the Hindu temple. The Anglican church was built over 100 years ago and in a style typical of the Victorian period – red brick with a large clock tower at the street front and a large stained-glass window at the rear of the church. About nine years ago a bomb was set off in the grounds of the adjoining Buddhist temple and this blew the church's stained-glass window into over 20,000 pieces and part of the roof was destroyed.

As soon as this happened, a group of Buddhist volunteers kindly came to the church and, over two years, painstakingly put the stained-glass window back together again. When I was told this story I was in the church looking at the beauty of the window – and I could not believe that it had been damaged in this way. However, on closer inspection I could see the hairline joins in the glass pieces – amazing! At the same time as the Buddhists, a local Muslim businessman came to the church and offered to immediately hire a construction firm to repair the church roof; this kind offer was accepted by the Anglicans. I understand that both the Buddhist and Muslim faith communities met the restoration costs as a kind gesture to the Christian church.

Today the voice of religious difference is very shrill and it frightens all members of the human family across all cultures – where will it all end? In this context I found this story heartwarming and faith-affirming – it needs to be told as a counterpoint to the seemingly relentless media stories of religious conflict and intolerance.

Brett Nicholls, an Associate member of the Iona Community

COMMITMENT

Unafraid to be

The God of Heaven, the God of earth,
of stars, of sky, of sea:
the One who spoke into the void,
created us to be.

Created us to be His voice,
to be His hands, His feet:
to be His image constantly,
to everyone we meet.

He made us, every one, unique
in our humanity
and daily challenges each one
to be what we can be.

Why, then, are we still so afraid
to listen to His Son,
whose life has shown us how to be
and what we can become?

When others judge and can't respect
my vulnerability,

then echoes of a thousand hurts
leave me afraid to be.

And often I, in arrogance
and insecurity,
will play my part in making you
become afraid to be.

When justice fails and no one heeds
the cries of agony,
He speaks to us: 'Be not afraid,
be not afraid to be.'

He's asking us to walk with Him
the path to Calvary
and take the risk of showing that
we're not afraid to be.

So Christ within and Christ without,
Christ in whom all are one,
teach us not only how to be
but also to become.

Alix Brown

THE REDISCOVERY OF SPIRITUALITY

Political meetings, law courts, pubs

As I walked down the street after a political meeting, a young woman caught up with me: 'Can I have a word with you?' she asked. She came to the point straight away: 'Tonight's meeting did it. You never try to hide the belief that motivates you to struggle against injustice. Now, I'm in the same struggles. But I don't have a basis to draw on. More and more I feel the want of that. It grows on me that the source you have is what I am looking for. I'm not a church person. But I'd like you to talk about the Christian faith with me. Could you come up some evening?' I did so and we talked for some hours. The woman and her husband became clear that the Christian basis for living was what they could affirm.

◆

It was a fight against the Poll Tax which brought Mrs McMenemin and me together in Stirling. She had been rallying opposition through her secretaryship of the Raploch Tenants' Association. I had been fighting the tax through the courts. I went to her house for an update on her activities. At the end of a long spiel on the effects on poor people, I said to her, 'You've put your finger on the theological basis for resisting the Poll Tax.' 'Have I? What did I say?' 'You said, "God's no' for injustice. God's for fowk".' 'Did I? Well, I was right. That is the theological basis for fighting it!'

◆

By the time the government abandoned attempts to enforce the Poll Tax, my case was before the European Court. At the previous stage, when being judged by three Law Lords in the Court of Session, some frequenters of Gargunnock Inn asked me to tell them about my arguments against the tax. I started to do so: the legal argument based on the Act of Union, the theological argument based on requirements of natural justice, the moral argument against partners and neighbours keeping tabs on one another and telling tales. Then I had a better idea: 'I'll tell you what. I'll put a copy of my case against the Poll Tax on the pub counter and you can read it and judge for yourselves.' It was in the local inn that the case, with its theological core, was debated.

There is no end of places appropriate for doing theology – political meetings, law courts, pubs!

Ian M. Fraser

THE THIRTY-FIRST DAY

On the thirty-first day of each month, Iona Community members pray for members who have died and for their families.

A prayer and a blessing

In God alone my soul finds rest
After Psalm 62

Along the road
I've travelled far,
I've been lost and found,
I've fallen and been raised,
by God!

My weary soul found rest
in some beautiful places,
in some wonderful people.
Thank God!

My soul wearies more easily now.
The 'closed' signs are going up,
and the road ahead is hard.

God, help me!

In God alone I find rest now,
in the beauty behind all beauty,
in the wonder behind the wonderful people.
O Christ!

My soul
finds rest
in God alone.
My God!

Ian Cowie

Death

'Death is the last great festival on the road to freedom.'*

Go gently on your voyage, beloved.
Slip away with the ebb tide,
rejoice in a new sunrise.

May the moon make a path across the sea for you,
the Son provide a welcome.
May the earth receive you and the fire cleanse you
as you go from our love
into the presence of Love's completeness.

Kate McIlhagga

*Dietrich Bonhoeffer

Month 2

New Ways to Touch the Hearts of All

In the whole of my life

Jimmy Cunningham was broken-hearted when his wife, Margaret, died. Forty-eight years of marriage, the sharing of good and bad times, and his dependency on his wife for the stability of the family home, all combined to make bereavement a devastating experience. We invited him to the hospice bereavement support service. He said he intended to come. We were relieved.

On the afternoon of the first evening meeting that Jimmy was due to attend, his son phoned our hospice. He explained that his dad hadn't been doing too well, and that, in fact, he had been hitting the bottle really hard. He'd been on a drinking session over the weekend, and was in no fit state to go out anywhere, far less attend a meeting for bereavement support. Maybe it would be better if someone visited him at home, he suggested.

That's why, later in the week, I found myself calling at Jimmy's home with one of our specialist nurses. She had known him during his wife's illness and intended to introduce me and leave me and Jimmy together. It didn't work out that way. The man who opened the door was in a pretty sorry state. He was unshaven and dishevelled. He smelt of stale beer. His hands shook and his shirt was stained. It was clear that he was in no condition to talk about anything, least of all how he was coping with his loss. So I suggested that I call another day when he felt more up to it, and we arranged to meet the following Tuesday at 2:30.

When I got back to the hospice, I was concerned that Jimmy wouldn't remember our arrangement. So I wrote him a letter – handwritten on hospice-headed

notepaper – reminding him of the day and time I would call, saying he was a good man and we would give him all the help we could, and suggesting that if he wanted to be in touch at any time he could phone the hospice. The following Tuesday I stood apprehensively at Jimmy's door as 2:30 arrived. I rang the doorbell. I didn't know what I would find. I was more than pleasantly surprised. The man who greeted me was in an altogether better state – no shaky hands, a clean shirt and tie, clean-shaven and hair combed, black polished shoes.

'C'mon through to the kitchen while I finish making the coffee,' he suggested. I noticed as I passed through that the living room was in pretty good shape. Jimmy had obviously made a big effort. Straight sixes for presentation, I reckoned. The kitchen was the same. But the thing that caught my eye, attached by a fridge magnet to the upper section of the big fridge/freezer in the corner, was my letter. And underlined in red was 'Tuesday at 2:30'. Sensible man, I thought. But that wasn't all that was underlined, for lower down the letter was a bold red line under the words 'You're a good man.'

Jimmy caught me staring at the letter. 'Puzzled by the underlining?' he asked, obviously reading the quizzical look on my face.

'Not by the top bit,' I replied. 'That's sensible. But why have you underlined these words down there?'

'Oh, "You're a good man"?' Jimmy replied. 'It's simple really … 'Cause no one's ever said that to me in the whole of my life.' And Jimmy Cunningham was seventy-two years old.

Month 2 Day 1

I always seem to fall short –
not quite good enough,
always second best,
never pleasing the people who matter.

I always seem to come off worst –
failing to make the grade,
missing perfection,
down the ranks from where I should be.

I always seem to be left behind –
last one to be picked,
far from special,
never chosen to be up front.

Then someone says I'm a good man –
someone believes in me,
when I don't believe in myself,
and offers a different voice.

And I ask, 'Can this be true?
Am I a good man after all?
Whose voice is this
that calls me good for the first time?'

Self-belief from such a small beginning?
Maybe not, and maybe not yet …
But a small voice against a lifetime of put-downs
has to be a good place to start …

Tom Gordon

Month 2 Day 1

ECONOMIC WITNESS

We must call them to account

The way that the resources of the Earth are divided between the people of the planet is the stuff of economics. The economic system decides who earns what for doing what. This is not an automatic or technical matter. It is the result of decisions made by political policy-makers. The system is man(kind) made, and it can be changed by mankind. There is nothing inevitable about it.

The way the resources of the Earth are divided between people is also the stuff of the gospels, and of the scriptures of all world religions. Jesus of Nazareth, the Buddha, the Prophet Mohammed, and the Jewish prophets representing Yahweh all speak unequivocally of the need for sharing as a function of God's abundance. They have clear ideas about how the resources of the Earth should be used and shared so that we may reach our fullest potential as co-creators with God.

It is not only a matter of God's morality: it is about our fundamental belief about the character of mankind itself. The economic system profoundly affects the character of a society and the people living there. Economics is about power relationships in society. Power relations affect the way people think and behave towards each other, their aspirations and their values. The morality of a society – the human and spiritual relationships between people – cannot be separated from the way the economy works.

For example, market domination based on global competition has a number of effects on the human psyche. Worldwide it has vastly widened the income gap. Alongside huge wealth live excluded people who have failed to compete successfully, and literally lack food and shelter. Their material poverty becomes accepted by the rich as natural; and it destroys the sense of human solidarity.

Other kinds of poverty follow. People living with failure, poverty and insecurity do not often make happy families in which children are cherished and supported. Parents worried about survival are inclined to quarrel; families break up. Children who grow up with anxiety, violent adults and physical deprivation are stunted in their emotional and physical growth. Mental illness is highest in the US, the home of the worship of competitiveness. Suicide is rife in all 'advanced' countries.

Not only very poor families experience financial insecurity. Worldwide, few middle and professional class people feel in control of their livelihoods. You can have a good job today and tomorrow something happens at the other end of the world that shatters your prospects. Employers guard against unexpected blows by putting everyone on short-term contracts. It is called 'flexible' labour; and it has profound effects on family life and security.

Gross income inequality creates a profound sense of injustice. That is the cause of the urban terrorism that threatens everywhere. If people do not have access to justice, they think they have nothing left to lose. Street violence arises where vulnerable people are ravaged by impersonal economic forces. Mad snipers, serial killers and random shooters, apparently 'motiveless', are the understandable outcome of an abused childhood and a sense of societal injustice – all outcomes of an economic system.

Where material consumption is the sign of success, personal greed becomes the driving force. Life at the top is a jungle where personal integrity has no chance against the requirement to obey, flatter, cheat, destroy colleagues and toady for advancement. The stakes are high: galactic incomes or the sack at a moment's notice. How do such people remain sane as they go home to families where love, trust and mutuality of care are expected – and to church on Sundays where personal morality is preached?

The commercialisation of public life, another aspect of market domination, eats into public life. Commercial sponsorship of political party congresses is common. Democratically elected governments hold exclusive functions to which rich people – lobbying for their own interests – can buy access.

So people are affected profoundly by the economic system: Kibbutzniks have a different worldview from New Yorkers; welfare-state nurtured Swedes do not see life like Singaporeans. Tibetans' traditional philosophy has little in common with Britons'. It is not about genes, but about their economy. The current dominance of international competitiveness is producing a uniform tooth-and-claw callousness and a destruction of community values. The economic system is changing the expression of human nature.

So economists are more powerful than they think. They must begin to take responsibility for the implications of the policies they advocate. Like the physicists who invented the nuclear bomb, they tend to wash their hands of the consequences of their discipline. We must call them to account.

Prayer

Dear God, you are the source of everything we have.
Yours is the vision of abundance,
and the light of our vision:

Bless our longing for your Kingdom,
our hunger for shared bread, wine and joy;
and our striving for their incarnation.
Amen

Margaret Legum

YOUTH CONCERN

Spending time with children

'Who is the greatest in the Kingdom of heaven?' Jesus called a child, whom he put among them, and said, 'Truly I tell you, unless you change and become like children, you will never enter the Kingdom of heaven.'

Familiar words from the Gospel of Matthew. What do you imagine the child was doing just before Jesus drew her into the circle? Having a little skirmish with her little brother? Making faces to see if she could get Jesus to laugh? Earning frowns from those trying to listen to Jesus? We might imagine many poses, many expressions. One thing we likely do not imagine, however, is that this child had just been shopping.

Yet at the recent 13th International Conference on Children's Spirituality in Lincoln, England that is an image of children we were challenged to consider. In one of the keynote addresses, sociologist Zygmunt Bauman looked at the way Western economies target children as consumers. He reported that in 2002, children aged 4-12 influenced $300 billion of purchases in the United States; they purchased $30 billion worth of goods and services themselves. By stimulating their desire for new products, advertising generates in children a state of continual dissatisfaction with what is old and used in favour of 'the flavour of the month'. Children under the age of 5 now recognise brands and know what they want to eat, to wear, to play with, to watch, as parents well know. So it seems most parents now consult shopping-wise children not only on what the children prefer for themselves but on what they recommend for the home. While making collective

decisions about family purchases in and of itself is not a bad thing, Bauman worries that the soul of the child is under siege as childhood becomes a preparation for the 'lifelong task of selling the self' by acquiring symbols of desire affirmed in the marketplace.

Even here on Iona I know the truth of his quip, 'All roads lead through the shops.' Many children who visit the MacLeod Centre express their identity through brand loyalty – in clothing, in football, and in pot noodles! 'Where do you shop, Nancy?' they press again and again. 'The SPAR' is not an answer they can comprehend! They just cannot understand how we can survive out here without the choices offered in urban shopping malls …

The second address at the conference was given by theologian Mary Grey, no stranger to Iona, who moved the conversation in ways that knit social analysis together with a theological vision for childhood. She began by offering insight into 'childhood's disenchantment'. Not only are children targeted as consumers in developed economies; at least 250 million children are victimised around the world as sources of cheap labour and as prostitutes. They are forced onto the street and into militias. Their humanity is manipulated and degraded. Grey's concern for 'the once and future child' included a plea for adults to return to our senses and face up to our own addictions and desires that we play out in the lives of children around us. She advocated a liberation theology for children that can celebrate the Holy Spirit as the energy in curiosity, play, joy, friendship and a child's special relation with nature, core dimensions of a child's spirituality.

The complex roles that children play in the global market remind me not to create too innocent a picture of the child Jesus drew into his circle. Surely, if so many children in privileged countries are economic players and so many children in poor countries are exploited workers, we adults have to engage children seriously to awaken their awareness of both power and manipulation. In this we are helped by a child's innate sense of fairness. Every brother or sister can spot favouritism on the part of a parent. They rankle when things are not shared in equal proportion. Children can call us all to fairer trade if we adults help them learn the true costs of what they consume. In Canada a few years ago, there was a panel of children that travelled the country raising awareness on the exploitation of child labour around the world. Such children call us to act for fairness and justice in our everyday purchases and practices.

As I reflect on my time on Iona, I see ways in which the themes of the conference come together. This year, we were deeply moved by evaluations turned in by members of a school party who spent a week with us. The young people spoke in gratitude for the confidence they'd discovered and for the value they'd recognised in their own lives – some for the first time. These same students had taken on fair trade issues in a workshop, and spent an evening giving voice to their heartfelt concerns for complete strangers as they wrote letters for Amnesty International. Confidence in themselves led to confident action for others. Such are the memories I shall treasure and the stories I'll tell as I move back to the theological classroom in Canada. The smile on a child's face when I can pull the right name out of my memory bag; the transition from troublemaker to troubleshooter among those who return year after year; the pride and satisfaction evident when plans for a commitment service come together in a wonderful way – small details that demonstrate the value of bringing children into the centre of the circle.

Creating opportunities for children and young people to explore their own potential and examine questions about the world and their place in it is soul-affirming work – for child and adult alike …

Nancy Cocks, from a sermon in Iona Abbey

Prayer from Iona

Loving God, we turn to you to help people who are homeless, hungry and thirsty.

Eve Sharples, age 6

THE WORD

Bread and stories

Treasure chest

Imagine, if you can, the Bible as a chest, full of old treasures that are the ancient stories of human experience and God's wisdom. Largely consigned to gather dust, abandoned in the attic of the house of our modern living, unneeded, discarded.

What instinct or longing lies within us that makes us want to pull out and examine the dated photos and cards and books and garments and myriad of yesterday's remnants? A seeking for the 'security' of times past perhaps? What then do we do when we find, as we constantly do, that these stories – though expressed in the imagery of another age – are far from being tame relics of yesteryear? What do we do when we find they contain essential truths that we lose sight of at our peril?

In the quick rummaging through of the treasure chest, we constantly find items that attract and delight the modern mind. Like stories that tell of a creation that is 'good'; or like the story that tells of a man created from the dust of the earth and given life by the very breath of God, which reminds us of the God-given and inalienable dignity of all women and men, and of our relationship with the Earth we inhabit.

These are stories that tell of a God-ordained rhythm to life: that we should not be working every hour that God sends, nor be excluded from work; stories that tell of God's purpose of social cohesion: that there should be mechanisms to stop the rich getting out-of-sight rich and the poor being trapped in unending poverty. Critically, there is a story of the unveiling of the nature and purpose of God in the mundane detail of the single human life of the carpenter of Nazareth, who in the mystery of faith turns out to be the Son of God.

Erik Cramb

Lectio divina* – The Word as the Bread of Life

In this method of prayer we do more than hear or read the Word of God. Through reflection it becomes like food to be savoured, chewed and enjoyed until all the nutrients it contains energise us to live its truth.

There are several different stages to this prayer:

– Read a short passage of scripture very slowly.

Read the passage again and again if necessary, listening for a word or short phrase which takes your attention.

– After you have been attracted to a word or phrase, concentrate on it. Repeating it over and over again, perhaps in time with your breathing, let it become part of you. Let it sink into your consciousness; let it dwell within you.

– Now ask yourself: 'How does this word/phrase connect with my reality today?'

How is it relevant to where you are at this time?
What is God saying to you through it?

– In the light of the word/s speaking to you, allow a conversation to develop with God.

What do you want to say in response?
It is important that you are honest – express your thanks and praise, but also your doubts and anger, tearfulness; your need for help and guidance.

Listen, God may have another word for you.

– Now try to enter the deeper silence and stillness, holding the word or phrase in your heart, waiting on God, contemplating the mystery.

– As you go out into the world carry the word/phrase with you – it is your bread to sustain you on this day's journey. Return to savour it often.

(Passages from the psalms, the poetry of the prophets, and the epistles are particularly suited to this way of praying.)

Lynda Wright, Tabor Retreat Centre, Key House, Falkland, Fife

*Lectio divina means 'divine reading'.

Prayer

The Maker's blessing be yours
on your road
on your journey
guiding you, cherishing you.

The Son's blessing be yours
wine and water
bread and stories
feeding you, challenging you.

The Spirit's blessing be yours
wind and fire
joy and wisdom
comforting you, disturbing you.

Ruth Burgess

Month 2 Day 4

HOSPITALITY AND WELCOME

Make yourself at home

There is a ring at your doorbell one evening. On answering, you meet the Risen Lord himself, standing in your doorway. Somehow you recognise, without any shadow of doubt, that it is the Lord. In imagination, what do you do now? Tell him to come back on Sunday? Presumably you welcome him in and invite as many of your friends as you can find. In the course of the evening you may find yourself making utterly fatuous statements to the Lord of all creation such as, 'Do make yourself at home.' Jesus gladly accepts your kind invitation.

Now take a two-week leap in your imagination. Jesus is still in your house. How are things at home now? You remember some of Jesus's sayings:

Do you suppose that I am here to bring peace on earth? No, I tell you, but rather division. For from now on a household of five will be divided: three against two and two against three; the father divided against the son, son against father, mother against daughter, daughter against mother, mother-in-law against daughter-in-law, daughter-in-law against mother-in-law.
Luke 12:51–53

You might also remember what the letter to the Hebrews says about Jesus: 'Jesus Christ, yesterday, today, the same forever.' So how have things been over family meals during the last two weeks? What has Jesus said, or done, which has caused tantrums among some members of the family, and who has been leaving the table and slamming the door behind them?

You have invited Jesus to make himself at home, so he is now inviting his friends to your house. Who were his friends in the gospels and what did other people say about them? 'The tax collectors and the sinners, meanwhile, were all seeking his company to hear what he had to say, and the Pharisees and the scribes complained. "This man," they said, "welcomes sinners and eats with them".' (Luke 15:1–2). What kind of people are arriving at your house, what are the neighbours saying about them, and what is happening to local property values?

Having trouble at home and with the neighbours, you might decide to share Jesus's company with your local church, so you arrange for him to give a little talk. You remember the little talk he once gave to the chief priests, the scribes and the Pharisees, assuring them all that the tax-gatherers and the prostitutes would enter the Kingdom of God before they did. He gives substantially the same sermon to the faithful of St Jude's Parish Church and there is uproar; the parish loses its principal benefactors.

You return home with Jesus. The problem of your life now is what to do with Jesus, for he is causing trouble at home, with the neighbours and with your local church. As he is Lord of all creation, you cannot throw him out of the house, so what are you to do? Perhaps look around the house with care, find a suitable cupboard, clear it out, clean and decorate it, have good strong locks put on the door, push Jesus inside, lock the door and place a lamp and flowers outside. Each time you pass, you can give a profound and reverential bow. In this way you have Jesus with you always, but he does not interfere any more in ordinary life.

Gerard Hughes, a friend of the Iona Community

THIS IS THE DAY

Light catching

Let us go light catching.
There are places where
there are great
shafts of it.
And nets lie idle
waiting for the
Catchers
to come.

Let us go light catching.
Let us cease our angry wrestling
with angels and demons
for a while,
and watch it
play in these places,
low and long.

Let us go light catching,
cabbage white,
meadow blue.
And let us be bright, as
the light flutters by.

For the time for
light harvest
is come and
good work needs
tortoiseshell
and painted ladies.

Alison Swinfen

Month 2 Day 6

THE IONA EXPERIENCE

Following are three pieces from former Iona Community guests, volunteers and residents. They give a flavour and feeling of life on Iona for members of the community there.

Over a pot of boiling soup

What was a young, inexperienced cook like me doing in an institutional kitchen on a remote Scottish island?

Less than 18 hours after being welcomed to the staff of the Iona Community, I found myself preparing lunch for 60 people with other volunteers from as far away as Japan and Australia. The Iona Community is a liberal, ecumenical Christian group that operates two centres on the Isle of Iona, offering hospitality and a vision of community to guests from around the world.

I had travelled to Iona with thirteen other college students. We came to explore how we could use our knowledge and schooling to find rewarding and meaningful life paths. Our best conversations occurred not during scheduled discussion times, but as we climbed to the top of Dun I under a full moon, celebrated my 21st birthday at the island's pub and sailed the Atlantic in *Freya*, a tiny blue fishing boat with red sails. Nurtured by beautiful scenery and good company, we tackled the big questions: How can we affect the world in a practical and positive way? How can we use our knowledge and talents?

After our week together on the island, I waved goodbye to my friends as they returned home and I stayed for six more weeks to put my thoughts into action. I discussed international politics over tea and scones, carried my dirty laundry through the sanctuary of the 800-year-old Iona Abbey and sang in four-part harmony while washing dishes. I found insights where I least anticipated them. In the future, I'll seek new experiences in a setting where I can be challenged – not just in the classroom but over a pot of boiling soup.

Sarah Turner

Iona collage (A rainbow time)

The island and the people entwined like some complex Celtic knot –
the weather always an accompanying strand

Changing colours of the Sound
Conversations on the road in passing

Walks in windy silence with new friends –
yellow marsh iris and a shy bird's song

Sharing a house with an ebb and flow of colourful, curious world travellers,
ages and surnames never known and just not important

Learning a new job side by side with thinkers and dreamers:
a gathering of adventurous spirits not knowing what the future holds,
but daring to take the risk –
like Columba and his friends as they set out across wild, dangerous seas

Clashes of culture and misunderstandings of humour
requiring a spirit of openness and wonder at how different we all are
and how similar

Demonstrating the use of a vacuum cleaner
  to a volunteer from a village in Uganda
Finally the last job finished –
then turning to welcome new arrivals
as the rhythm of a new week begins

Noticing how folk can both work well together
and avoid each other,
how the ageless challenge of being yourself
  with others gives you real opportunities:

to face your fears,
to try to resolve conflict,
to learn to love when it's hard to

Singing and playing
  in an 800-year-old abbey
where words and music mingle and fly,
as workers and pilgrims worship
  in their own way

Recycling and reshaping faiths

Food for thought,
food for sharing round a table

Words of wisdom and advice softly spoken
from people who have lived and
learnt from life

Hot drinks outside –

Month 2 Day 7

sitting on a bench with blankets watching the vibrant night sky
shoot stars over your head

Village hall disco DJing and dancing in your walking boots and jumper,
not giving a toss how you look –
just as long as you're movin' to Marvin's soul

Ambling over to do a bleary-eyed breakfast shift,
with the early-morning sun awakening over your shoulder

Beaches and birthdays
with cakes made by a Hungarian confectioner;
handmade cards and thoughtful, crafted presents

Juggling lettuces down the nave in a children's service:
'Lettuce pray!'

'Bring your thing' Coffee house nights, with creativity and laughter
and time to talk and meet the new faces

Sitting in the office
talking to an insomniac Tasmanian Franciscan nun on the phone:
about what's sold in the shop;
describing the day to the other side of the world

Staffa boat trips to see the painted puffins' clumsy clown arrivals

Scraping ferry-gate-goodbyes:
struggling to give the meaning of a friendship a final worthy word
or gesture

Month 2 Day 7

A rainbow time:

A group of folk from far and wide suddenly together –
just for a brief time and then they're gone,
touched by the rain and the sun and each other.
Maybe changed and challenged;
and wondering what's next
and whether
that spirit of togetherness
can be found in another place.

Kath O'Neil

Nothing more

In times when life is hard,
inner voices speak alluringly,
of easier loads and simpler lives.

Yet, to stay amidst the raw emotion,
to feel its waves thrashing
against the coastlines of our humanity,

to live there,
is to be,
and nothing more;
to live, to learn, to grow, to love.

Scott Blythe

Life in Community

Mother's letter

This story from a young mother made me think:

My sister and I live in the same part of the town, and yet, for one reason or another, we didn't see each other that often. Well, there were the kids, and work, and the church, and all the rest. There never seemed to be enough time. My mother lives a long way away, and when she writes, she always asks the same thing in her letters: *When was the last time you saw your sister?* Once, when I wrote back: *Three months ago, I think …* our mother obviously decided that enough was enough. It was time to act.

So, shortly afterwards, I had a strange kind of letter in the post. It was from mother – another of her regular epistles, I thought as I opened the envelope. But when I examined the contents, that's when I knew it was strange. For what I drew out from the envelope was a letter that clearly wasn't finished, for all I had were pages 1 and 3. When I looked at it more carefully, I saw that the greeting at the top of the letter was to me *and* my sister.

I was puzzled. Was my mother losing the plot? I was worried. What was she on about? I just didn't get it. Had dementia set in, or was I missing something? I phoned my sister to express my concern, and told her about my letter and my worries about our mother's state of mind. She laughed – not the reaction I expected at all.

'You'll never guess what I got in the post today,' she said. 'I got a letter from mother, addressed to both of us, and, like yours, it only has two pages – but my pages are numbers 2 and 4.'

We laughed together. The penny had dropped! Mother wasn't going senile after all. She knew exactly what she was doing. To understand the whole letter, and to have the complete epistle of our mother's news, we had to get together. We had no choice. Pages 1 and 3 had to go together with pages 2 and 4.

Since then – and that's a fair while ago now – we each get half a letter every month, and so we enjoy spending an evening putting the letter together and catching up on news from mother – and from each other too. Finding time for that doesn't seem to be a problem any more. It's time for us to be together, and we're the better for it. And you can bet that mother is delighted.

'When did you last see your sister?' she asked me on the phone recently.

'A couple of days ago,' I was pleased to report.

And I could *feel* my mother smiling down the phone.

Tom Gordon

Month 2 Day 8

WOMEN

The wound of the daughter of my people

From 1988 to 1998, the World Council of Churches sponsored an Ecumenical Decade of Churches in Solidarity with Women. Its team visits to women in churches around the world identified four key concerns that showed remarkable consistency, whether the women were coming from poor Southern countries or rich Northern ones. They were:

– **the invisibility of women** – their low level of access to and participation in structures of both society and church, in leadership, in decision-making, in availability of resources, education and information;

– **racism and xenophobia**, which are emerging in new forms across the world, in ethnic cleansing, in the increased numbers of refugees and asylum-seekers, in internal ethnic and racial conflicts, as well as in their wearily familiar guises;

– **economic injustice** – the adverse impact of globalised economic systems affects women and children disproportionately;

– and last, but by no means least, **violence** against women.

Of course, these four are not the only concerns of Christian women, whose interests are as diverse as their situations; and they are not concerns only of women. But they are overwhelmingly the most important ones, confirmed by dozens of local, national and international women's organisations, raised again and again from Canada to Cameroon. Furthermore, they unite women of different faiths and none. They are also, broadly speaking, the agenda which emerged from the UN Decade for Women and its global consultation in Beijing.

Nor do they affect only women – it would be ludicrous to suggest that. But they affect women more often, more acutely and with more profound consequences than they do men. Women make up half of the world's population, do 66% of the world's productive work, and own 10% of the world's wealth and 1% of the world's land (UN figures). Women are still massively disempowered and the more powerless you are, the easier it is for power to be wielded against you. Added to the onerous responsibility of being the harder-working sex, women suffer more because of their role as primary carers of children, of the very old, and of the dependent ill and infirm. And their low profile in decision-making means that the kind of policies that would be family-friendly for women and their dependants often take second place to other interests, whether these be the interests of corporate shareholders, of the military industrial complex or of powerful local elites.

Local/global

All of these things affect women everywhere. In a globalised world, the violence of poverty may affect 95% of women in one country and only 20% in another. In one country poverty may mean extreme destitution, even starvation, and death at 30. In another, it may mean eking out an existence of social exclusion on the margins of an affluent society and having a life expectancy of 10 years less than the woman in the leafy suburb next door. But the causes of their poverty will be the same. They are redundant to the requirements of a globalised free-market economy. Poor women in Britain don't have very much visibility and are afforded little respect, failing as they do to conform to the media- and consumer-driven image of the 'have-it-all, do-it-all' successful woman. Their only crime is to be poor, but in our culture that is treated as a moral failing.

Invisibility affects women in rich countries in other ways too. It is only very recently that the relentless onslaught of violence against women has even begun to be acknowledged in this country. This is a global pandemic recognised as a major health hazard to women by the British Medical Association. It takes many forms: domestic violence, incest and child sexual abuse, sexual harassment, rape and sexual violence, unrealistic and degrading representations in the media, trafficking, institutional gender violence, and violence in war. This is by no means an exhaustive list.

And for women already invisible, economically oppressed and at risk of violence, racism and xenophobia compound all of these. Women from ethnic minorities, refugees, asylum-seekers, gypsies, all those perceived to be outsiders have less access to resources and fewer resources to access. They are more likely to be victimised and stereotyped, are less likely to be asked what their needs are or even to be communicated with in their own language, and some women who experience violence may be caught between community pressures to stay silent and racism if they break the silence.

It is sometimes suggested that feminist theology is a preoccupation of privileged white Western women, and is of no interest or relevance to Third World women. But there are feminist and women-centred theologies in every part of the globe, engaging with just these issues, and talking to each other; as the Hispanic *mujerista* theologian Ada Maria Isasi-Diaz comments ruefully, 'If we are women theologians in the First World, we are told we are out of touch with the women in the pews. If we are Third World theologians, we are told "these women" from the First World are unduly influencing us – as if we were not capable of thinking for ourselves.'

A woman living in Drumchapel in Glasgow may have more in common with her sister in Bangkok or Lusaka than her sister next door in Bearsden. Ask me about gender and I'll reply, as a thousand women from all over the world did at the hearings on violence against women in Zimbabwe in 1998, 'Your story is our story.' The wound of the daughter of my people wounds me too.

Ask me about the Church and gender. How long have you got? – for there's a story. I do not forget that every manifestation of violence against women can be found in the Bible, held up as Holy Writ. I do not forget the thousands of women burned as witches by the Christian Church. Nor do I forget the women refused any pain relief in childbirth because it was their destiny to bear children with suffering. I do not forget that, as Monica Furlong rather acerbically said: 'If we had to wait for the Churches to promote tertiary education for women, the Married Woman's Property Act, the franchise, entry to the professions, equal pay for equal work, the Sex Discrimination Act, and many other measures vital to women's well-being, we should still be waiting. Indeed, the Churches frequently opposed such reforms.'

Shall I speak of the suffering of women at the hands of the Church?

No. I would rather speak of the pathology of worshipping a God who could be assumed to place male honour over female life. I would rather speak of a theology which has not only laid on woman the duty to endure violence in marriage but also made her responsible for her abuser's salvation through her own example of 'patient endurance', and which has placed a higher value on the maintenance of the institution than on justice and female health.

I would rather speak of a Church which turns women away from the sacrament and is embarrassed by them in the community when they leave abusive marriages; which has consistently colluded in and been complicit with male violence, has covered up for perpetrators to maintain the fiction that this is just a question of 'a few bad apples'; of a Church which has preferred silence to truth.

I would rather speak of an understanding of gender relationships which has sanctified the domination and control of one gender by another. Domestic violence and sexual violence are rooted in the belief that one partner has the right to control the other, and that, to quote the reaffirmation of Southern Baptists of America last year, the proper role of the woman is one of 'gracious submission'. I was interested to read that former US President Jimmy Carter, a lifelong Baptist, and his wife, Rosalynn Carter, have left their church in protest.

I would rather speak of an idolatry of the Bible which has legitimised the beating and abusing of children on the basis of 'sparing the rod and spoiling the child', and which has made the possession of a penis the definitive factor in authority and decision-making.

I love the story of the feeding of the multitude by the lake, not least for the bit that says, 'everyone ate, and had enough'. It is one of the most beautiful lines in the Bible, this picture of sufficiency, of sharing. But the story also demonstrates simply and rather appallingly two thousand years of a particular blindness of Christian history: 'the number who ate was about five thousand men, not counting the women and children.' Or, as the Jerusalem Bible has it, 'to say nothing of the women and children' (Matthew 14: 21). What a history of exclusion that sums up! A history of the people who are not counted, who have been and continue to be invisible in so many ways – in their poverty, in their unvalued labour, in their wasted potential.

People often ask why abused women don't just leave their abusive partners. Perhaps the difficulty of doing that has some light thrown on it when we ask: why don't abused women just leave their abusive churches? Many do, of course, and continue to do business with God elsewhere. But it's not so simple. For the church that offers hurt also offers healing. I do not want to suggest that all, or even many, men in the Churches are abusers, or that all women are invisible, suffer violence, racism or economic injustice in the church. But being part of the body involves the recognition that if one part suffers, all the other parts suffer with it. The wound of the daughter of my people wounds me too.

If we are beginning, slowly and painfully, to recognise that our Churches are institutionally racist, institutionally sexist, the journey to recognise our institution-alised gender violence seems an even slower one.

Part of that journey has been the struggle for women to distinguish between the God who in Jesus Christ loves, affirms and believes in women, and the Church which doesn't. Women stay because they love Jesus. They know that *'during his life here on earth, Jesus visited the towns and villages and saw with his own eyes the problems facing the people. He saw poverty, the inequality, the religious and economic oppression, the unemployment, the depression, the physically ill and the socially unclean. His heart was filled with pity. He pronounced what his mission was all about: he came to preach the good news to the poor and to release those who are captives and give health to those who are ill.'* (Musimbi Kanyoro)

In him they see the possibility of a new kind of community, a true community of women and men.

In searching for hints of that true community women all over the world have been reading the Bible and the history of the Church from another angle, rediscovering the hidden histories, the silenced voices, the notes on the margins. They are seeking the God of Jesus Christ, the motherly God who comes close in the Word made flesh. They are seeking the women and men whose spirituality is one of hope, of courage, of compassion, of inclusion, of persistence and resistance.

And with eyes fixed on Jesus we also begin to see the outlines of another Church, a Church of those on the margins, those disempowered, those of no account in the eyes of the world or indeed of parts of the Church, a Church in which Jesus is embodied.

As the Church struggles painfully to decolonise, spiritually and materially, that process has to include the decolonisation of women. There are many facets to this, but if we are truly to be part of a world Church, then these four primary concerns for women everywhere must be ours too. For 'the wound of the daughter of my people wounds me too'.

Kathy Galloway

PRAYER

An act of solidarity

Yesterday was the International Day of Peace – designated by the United Nations as a day of global ceasefire and non-violence, an opportunity for education and raising public awareness.

Churches all over the world were encouraged to observe yesterday as an International Day of Prayer for Peace.

What difference do our prayers make? This isn't a question just for people who go to church. Prayer is not the preserve of any one group. There is something naturally human about praying, especially in times of difficulty and need – out of our concern for others and for ourselves. What are we expecting to happen when we pray? Is it that whoever or whatever we are praying to will bring about some miraculous laser beam intervention?

Prayer is essentially an act of solidarity – an expression of our own need, a yearning for a better world, a commitment to belonging together. We pray not only with our lips but with our lives. And every little act of justice, caring and generosity counts.

As part of the International Day of Peace several well-known church leaders from all over the world recorded video messages affirming the power and promise of peace, providing inspiration and hope for those engaged in the quest for reconciliation today. Archbishop Desmond Tutu of South Africa summed it up like this: 'God weeps over God's world, aching because of conflict in Darfur, in Beslan, in Harare, in Colombia, in Jerusalem, in Belfast. God has no one but you to help make this world hospitable to peace and justice.'

Norman Shanks

Prayer

God, lead us, that we may stand firm in faith for justice.
Teach us love. Teach us compassion.
Above all, out of love and compassion,
teach us to act.
Amen

From 'A Service of Prayer for Justice and Peace', *Iona Abbey Worship Book*

JUSTICE AND PEACE

Saving its own skin

They say familiarity breeds contempt and some expressions are so familiar that they lose their impact. Maybe 'justice and peace' is one of them.

Many of us pray for justice and peace in the hope that the world will somehow become a better place, but do we realise the implications of what we are saying? And what we might be getting involved in?

For a start, justice is not an optional extra; it is absolutely intrinsic to our understanding of God.

In as much as we can speak of such things, the nature of God is to do with love. We speak of the grace of God and the love of God. We hold that we are created by the free, outflowing love of God. And we in turn are called to respond in love to God – and to our neighbour.

Love means that we actively seek the well-being of the other. We seek that person's fulfilment; we treat that person with respect – even with reverence. We actively seek their shalom, their peace.

But how can we love our neighbour if we treat that person unjustly; or allow that person to be treated unjustly? Injustice is a denial of love and runs counter to the nature and will of God. The prophets knew it, and Jesus knew it.

Think for a moment about the words of Micah: What is asked of us? 'To do justice, love kindness and walk humbly with God.' How odd the three commands are in that order. Justice comes first. Walking humbly with God comes last. Maybe we walk with God when we seek justice.

Then there is the argument Jesus had with the religious leaders who had concentrated on things that didn't matter and missed the vital issues. What is it that Jesus puts at the top of his list? 'You have neglected the justice and the love of God,' he tells them.

Justice is at the centre of our relationship with God because love, and the justice which is its consequence, is at the centre of what we believe God to be.

The trouble is that justice and the peace which is dependent on it comes at a price. And it is a price the Church has been reluctant to pay.

Why was Jesus was crucified? For healing people? For being good? For teaching his disciples the Lord's Prayer? Or was he executed by the rich and powerful because he challenged their oppressive and unjust systems? Because he threatened their vested interests: their status and their privilege?

One reason there is injustice is that it suits the powerful and rich. It serves their interests. It does not happen by accident: it is part of the dynamic which ensures that the rich stay rich and the poor stay poor.

Jesus made a fatal mistake early on in his brief career: he committed himself to bring good news to the poor. Good news for the poor means an end to injustice and its replacement by well-being and the fulfilling love of God.

Heal a leper? Fine: go ahead. Heal ten if you want. But touch a leper? Share the defilement of a leper? Treat a leper as a human being? Stand in solidarity with a leper whom disease has condemned to utter poverty? Show the leper s/he is loved by God? Challenge and destroy a system of exclusion and injustice? Not if you value your life.

No wonder the rich and powerful hated him: no wonder he had to be silenced.

The Church however has not made the same mistake. And in saving its own skin, it has failed the very people to whom Jesus proclaimed life: the poor and the marginalised. A couple of examples of how this happens:

First, it feels as though the Church has effectively silenced Jesus. No sooner has the Resurrection happened than he is exalted to the right hand of God on high. Out of the way. Out of this world – and certainly out of the gutter where he chose to spend so much of his time. This exalted Jesus now has no one to speak for him but the Church. It is as though his death and resurrection are of such magnitude that they render his life on earth irrelevant. As though his words and highly controversial ministry to the poor and oppressed can be airbrushed out.

In the Creed we affirm that he was born of the Virgin Mary and suffered under Pontius Pilate. Did nothing significant happen between those two events?

In the Anglican liturgy we proclaim the 'mystery' of faith: Christ has died, Christ is risen, Christ will come again. Does the mystery of faith not include why he appeared on earth at all? His challenging words and actions somehow get lost in translation.

Secondly, the Church has killed the poor with kindness. On the occasions when it has expressed a concern for the poor, it has been a pastoral concern for the relief of suffering and comfort for the individual. Ambulance work rather than seriously questioning the underlying cause of the disease. The Church has seldom demanded to know why things are as they are or asked who might stand to benefit from such an unjust state of affairs.

And for this it has earned itself the gratitude of society. Gratitude for relieving us of our guilt at the plight of the oppressed; gratitude for allowing us to kid ourselves that the problems of poverty are being addressed; gratitude that the real issue of justice has been avoided.

Those poor who are selected to receive such caring end up being the passive and patronised recipients of the charitable handouts of the rich: disempowered, unheard and, when the soup kitchen has rolled on, still hungry. Meanwhile, the rich remain secure in their wealth, status and power.

But then along come people like Helder Camara and give the game away. 'When I give bread to the hungry they call me a saint; when I ask why the hungry have no bread they call me a communist,' he said. He earned the disapproval of the rich and powerful by his stand for justice.

Meanwhile, Oscar Romero, who discovered the meaning of God's love from the poor, paid the price of the struggle for justice with his life. Like Jesus, he had made powerful enemies.

Maybe prayers for justice and peace should come with a health warning.

David Rhodes

Send us out

Leader: Jesus said:
ALL: I HAVE COME TO BRING GOOD NEWS TO THE POOR
Leader: Jesus said:
ALL: I HAVE COME TO PROCLAIM LIBERTY TO THE CAPTIVES
Leader: Jesus said:
ALL: I HAVE COME TO GIVE RECOVERY OF SIGHT TO THE BLIND

Leader: And so they took this Jesus –
the one who wanted to overthrow the order of the world –
and brought him to a cliff to throw *him* over
ALL: BUT JESUS WALKED THROUGH THE CROWD AND WENT ON HIS WAY

Leader: And so the powers arrested and beat and bound him,
and spit in his face and stripped him bare,
and nailed him to a cross and left him for dead …
ALL: AND AFTER THREE DAYS
HE ROSE FROM THE GRAVE …

Month 2 Day 11

Leader: Jesus Christ, we are your body on earth,
help us to do your work:

ALL: TO HELP BRING JUSTICE TO THE POOR AND DISPOSSESSED;
TO FREE THE SLAVES OF CAPITALISM AND 'THIRD WORLD' DEBT;
TO OPEN THE EYES OF THE COMFORTABLE AND APATHETIC –
TO TURN THE WORLD UPSIDE DOWN.

Leader: And when things get tough,
in our home towns
or far away in the great cities of the world,
help us to stand firm,
and not be moved by intimidation and threats of violence.

ALL: KEEP US SAFE, LORD CHRIST.

Leader: And if following you should someday lead us to a place
where we are persecuted or arrested,
or where our lives are in danger because of our affiliation with you,
give us the strength not to deny you,
and the peace to know that,
whatever happens,
we have lived our lives for you.

ALL: LORD JESUS, SEND US OUT IN CONFIDENCE, HOPE AND JOY
TO DO GOD'S WORK. AMEN

Neil Paynter

THE INTEGRITY OF CREATION

After the party

The winding path
on the nearby hills –
a place of beauty
as a spring day dawns;
and on it I walk
lost in wonder,
moved
by the song of creation,
touched
by its ever-changing mystery.

But all is not mystery here,
for suddenly
on this gentle path
there are
empty beer cans,
plastic bottles,

cigarette packets,
and other debris
scattered in confusion,
randomly abandoned
as the party ended.

Precise markers of
our affluence,
and perhaps of our
poverty of vision.

And in clearing
the mess
on this spring morning,
my heart is sad –
for how can it be
that a soul
can
bypass
such
beauty?

Peter Millar

Month 2 Day 12

COLUMBAN CHRISTIANITY & THE CELTIC TRADITION

Through which the Spirit speaks to us

The 'Celtic' has become an accepted part of modern Christian spirituality in these islands. Its assumed roots in ancient practice or poetry, or in the popular tradition of more recent times, is at best tenuous, yet many of its themes tell us a great deal about the spirituality of our own times. The Celtic is often a metaphor for modern desires; a tool for pause in a time of rapid change; and a response to living in a society that appears harsh, and destructive of itself and of the individual.

Themes that recur in the books and liturgies that abound on Celtic themes include delight in the natural world in all its vastness and intricacy, and a desire to live lightly upon our planet. Another is the recognition of the Divine as immanent as well as transcendent, and the need to honour this by reverencing creation. The Trinity as the ultimate Christian expression of community and creativity figures highly at a time when community is under threat from mobile lifestyles and increased opportunity not to know our neighbours, and where human creativity frequently appears to be exploited for financial gain. Another theme that resonates with our concerns today is the sense of place, and of places, loved and prayed in over time that now provide a sense of peace and healing for those who visit today. The lives of early saints in all their quirkiness are attractive for their freshness, strangeness and seeming spontaneity, as they aid the reader in looking again at human nature and the joy of place.

The 'Celtic' is seen to reflect the traditions not only of the smaller nations of these islands, but also of the English. Their language, culture and poetic expression were very different, but the joy in the lives of the saints is the same, especially where their legends have come down to us in the Latin of Bede; while the English language produced devotional poems like the Dream of the Rood which touch people as much today as they did more than a thousand years ago.

Ancient poetry and the oral traditions that describe spiritual concerns in unfamiliar ways are intensely appealing, even when known through translation or adaptation to modern concerns. In reality, much of the current belief and practice has been created quite recently. We know nothing from Anglo-Saxon England about dance and little about liturgy, and we know that women were far from equal and that powerful abbesses like Hilda of Whitby were the royal exceptions. We do however have great works of religious art, including the Lindisfarne Gospels, that speak to our common humanity.

Above all, the movement provides a sense of liminality, of being of the edge, of crying out in the wilderness, of warning against impending doom, as we destroy the planet that gave us birth, and as unjust international structures breed anger and despair.

Something is moving in our understanding of church. Some very old material has been rediscovered, and rejoiced in. Some has been much misunderstood, adapted, or diminished in an attempt to select those pieces that seem best to relate and express modern concerns. Much has been discarded or is not known.

But the new expressions that have grown out of all this may well have the light touch of the Spirit as, at their best and as they become filtered through prayer, they guide us to a new understanding of what it is to work out our salvation in the world we have been given. By using the ancient nature poetry of these islands together with the psalms that Jesus sang, through living with the modern tension between our desire for spontaneous self-expression and our acceptance of the discipline of being on the journey with others, we may move into serving our neighbour more deeply. We learn to pray so that we may preserve our earth for future generations to walk on lightly and lovingly, that the joy we have found in travelling through life with our Creator may also be theirs.

Celtic spirituality may be an extended metaphor, but it can be one through which the Spirit speaks to us. Unless we change our ways radically, we will destroy our species, and the poor of the world will suffer first. Following ancient saints, reciting ancient prayers, and trying loving our neighbour through the Trinity, can provide one way among others for people of our own time to make the ancient prayer of praise, penitence and renewal. This is not only for ourselves but for a world that needs to be constantly, radically restored, that all may have life, and life in all its fullness.

Rosemary Power

Prayer

Grant me, sweet Christ, the grace to find –
Son of the living God! –
A small hut in a lonesome spot
To make it my abode.

A little pool but very clear
To stand beside the place,
Where all men's sins are washed away
By sanctifying grace.

A pleasant woodland all about,
To shield it from the wind,
And make a home for singing birds
Before it and behind.

A southern aspect for the heat,
A stream along its foot,
A smooth green lawn with rich topsoil
Propitious to all fruit …

A lovely church, fit home for God,
Bedecked with linen fine,
Where over the white Gospel page
The Gospel candles shine.

A little house where all may dwell
And body's care be sought;
Where none shows lust or arrogance,
None thinks an evil thought.

And all I ask of housekeeping
I get and pay no fees;
Leeks from the garden, poultry, game,
Salmon and trout and bees.

My share of clothing and of food,
From the King of fairest face,
And I to sit at times alone
And pray in every place.

From a ninth-century Irish prayer

Racism

Engaging in conversation

… How much have we learned from our history about the perspective of those who suffer discrimination because of race or colour and are marginalised in society? Have our traditions of freedom and democracy prevented us from behaving with indifference, even brutality, towards non-white people? How can we reach out in meaningful dialogue and friendship to the 'stranger' in our midst? How do we begin to change our own thinking in such a way that we can value and cherish different cultural traditions?

These are enormously difficult questions, and they are also profoundly spiritual ones. We are all products of our culture and carry a range of hidden assumptions. Yet conversion is possible. With God's help, we can begin to look at our society through a different lens. To awaken to the miracle which is the rich diversity in cultures; to walk as a friend with a person whose skin colour is different from our own; to recognise that we have much to learn from our black and Asian neighbours.

In the Gospel of John, we read of a meeting between Jesus, a Jew, and a Samaritan woman at Jacob's Well. There had been centuries of feuding between the Jews and the Samaritans, and the woman was astonished when Jesus spoke to her and asked if she could draw some water from the well for him. Not only was she a Samaritan, she was also a woman, and for a rabbi to be seen speaking to a woman in public was the end of his reputation. By engaging in conversation with her, Jesus, at a stroke, broke down these various barriers of nationality and orthodox Jewish custom. He cut through entrenched attitudes and in doing so revealed a totally new way of understanding 'the other'. A way which the nations thirst for in our time.

Peter Millar

Prayer

Across the barriers that divide race from race;
across the barriers that divide the rich from the poor;
across the barriers that divide people of different faiths;
reconcile us, O Christ, by your cross.

From the World Council of Churches

Litany of celebration

For

Steve Biko
Nelson Mandela
Archbishop Desmond Tutu
For Martin Luther King's 'I Have A Dream' speech

For

Nusrat Fateh Ali Khan singing Qawwali
Amarjit Sandhu singing Bhangra
Louis Armstrong singing What A Wonderful World
Bob Marley singing Redemption Song,

Get Up Stand Up,
No Woman No Cry

For

Ben Okri
Wole Soyinka
Ken Saro-Wiwa

Arundhati Roy
Vikram Seth
Hanif Kureishi
Salman Rushdie

For

John Coltrane
Dizzy Gillespie
Duke Ellington

For

The blues of Billy Holiday
For the strong, deep voice of Bessie Smith

For

Jimi Hendrix
Prince
Sly and The Family Stone
The Jackson Five
The London Community Gospel Choir

Month 2 Day 14

For

The Supremes singing Baby Love
Motown Records
Spike Lee films

For Sister Rosa Parks not giving up
her seat on the bus

For

Talkin' 'Bout A Revolution by Tracy Chapman
Joan Armatrading

For

Lynford Christie
For Mary Seacole –
a black nurse in the Crimean War
who set up a hostel for wounded soldiers

For

Langston Hughes
Gwendolyn Brooks
Bell Hooks
Maya Angelou
James Baldwin

For

TV presenter Trevor McDonald
Cricket star Imran Khan
Diane Abbott – the first black woman MP

Month 2 Day 14

MP Mohammad Sarwar
Comedian Lenny Henry

For

Kofi Annan

For

the Indian family who lived next door to me who used to invite me in for curry
For the couple's three children whom I taught to juggle

For the newsagent who always said Hello

For

'Vannakkam'
'Namaste'
'Shanti'

For

'I and I'

For the amazing people I taught English as a second language to
at the YMCA in Canada
For going out for coffee with them after
and listening to their stories
For learning
how they survived death squads and civil war
how they survived in boats for days
how they walked over mountains with no shoes
how they're glad to be alive

Month 2 Day 14

For

the Caribbean diner where I used to hang out sometimes
and eat all-day Sunday breakfast –
£1.99 with the works and no bother

For

my friend Peter's dreadlocks –
like long thick cables connected
to the energy of the Godhead

For his smile
For the books he was always reading

For

the vegetable samosas the Indian grocer's wife makes
For shopping there instead of Tesco

For a different attitude to time

For

standing at the window and watching
old Chinese women doing Tai Chi in the park,
for the elegance and wisdom of movement

For

the dancing Shiva
the sound of a jembe
For the sound of a steel band playing
a sitar

For

hot jasmine tea in a china teapot in Chinatown
Chai
The Ethiopian cross

For

warm naan bread
For scooping up rice and curry
that turns your fingertips saffron yellow

For the smell of coconut oil

For

a pile of plantains in a market stall
in Tooting

For

Brixton
Nottinghill

For

men dressed in long flowing agbadas
women wearing head ties –
for dignity and directness

For

Edinburgh Mela
WOMAD
For Real World Records

Month 2 Day 14

For

taking your shoes off to enter a mosque
Covering your head to enter a gurdwara
For The Pakistanis of Stornoway
For Chinese kites in Hyde Park

For rich, colourful textiles and handicrafts

For walking down Great Western Road past shop windows full
of the most beautiful fabrics, carpets, jewellery boxes …

For the colours of saris
Bengal silk
For Kanchipuram silk with gold thread

For huge groups of people talking together

For

Portobello Road
For a world of colours and smells

For all of this and more!
Thank You, God of infinite diversity and love.
Amen

Part of a litany of celebration written for a service in Iona Abbey.

Jane Bentley, Helen Lambie, Dorothy Millar, Kath O'Neil,
Neil Paynter, Jan Sutch Pickard

Month 2 Day 14

Month 2 Day 15

COMMUNITY

Valuing the communal joys

A few weeks ago, I was speaking at the National Estate Churches Network Conference in Rotherham, on the theme of 'Singing the Lord's Song in a Strange Land'. As I have done several times this summer, I mentioned that my colleague John Bell is well-known for saying that everyone can sing. With this conviction, he has winkled out people from the back row of the hall (a place they have been standing ever since they were thirteen when an unimaginative music teacher told them to go to the back row of the choir and mime), persuaded them to open their mouths, and told them they have the voice of an apprentice angel. I don't want to put words in John's mouth, but I understand him as saying that everyone has the potential to enjoy singing, because to lift your heart and your voice and express something in song is an enjoyable thing to do. The activity of singing has intrinsic value regardless of one's degree of competence in it.

... I happen to think that the enjoyment of the expressive arts is a God-given gift, and a human right, and to tell someone they can't sing, or paint, or write poetry, or whatever, is a seriously hurtful thing to do, and I said so. What happened next confirmed that. At the lunch break, a man came up to me and said that he had something urgent to tell me. He believed that God had led him there that day to hear what I was saying. He was not a registered participant at the event – he had simply come to give a relative a lift, and was invited to stay and listen. He had arrived at the event very upset. The previous day, he had been attending a prayer meeting at his own church, and, at one point, he had been moved by the Spirit to pray in song. As he was leaving the prayer meeting, his pastor said to him in passing,

'Great song! Pity about the singing!' The man was devastated. He felt humiliated and rejected. Now, however, he felt that God had given him a message through me – a message of affirmation and acceptance, and he felt once more empowered to sing the Lord's song.

I was glad that the man had his capacity to enjoy singing restored to him. I was saddened that still (and it happens all the time) people are discouraged from singing, and from many other creative pursuits, because an authoritative person has mocked or embarrassed them; made flippant or careless remarks that have a long-lasting effect. Encouragement, says Paul, is one of God's gifts for the building up of the body. It's one we ignore at our cost.

Singing is one of the great communal joys, and we live in a time when the communal joys badly need to be revalued. Fewer and fewer people have the experience of sharing as being about enjoyment in common with others. We have less experience of having to rely on others, of having a pleasure enhanced by doing it with others, of seeing ourselves as a part of others, dependent on them, and they on us – and all our politics and all our economics are exacerbating this trend. Such is the competitive nature of the market now that it becomes ever harder to engage in a demanding common task in which cooperation is both a necessity and a joy. Skills, knowledge, information are increasingly commodities to be competitively traded and jealously guarded.

And because we have lost confidence in our capacity to make and sustain relationships, it is easier not to risk the attempt. There are many substitutes now available to protect us behind our boundaries, to ensure that we need have less and less connection with actual people. So we have fewer and fewer opportunities to experience common enjoyment. Breaking open one's isolation, that life may be shared and enjoyed, is a risky thing to do with so little trust in the possibility of common joy – and perhaps I mean common not just in the sense of being with others, but in the sense of joy in the small, the ordinary, the everyday.

For Christians, our Lord, our scriptures, our faith, all teach us that blessing is first and foremost communal blessing. That communal blessing was experienced in a profound way by all, staff and guests, who shared the Iona week for asylum-seekers and refugees. For some who came, this was the first holiday for years, the first time of feeling truly welcomed, accepted, 'at home', since they had arrived in Britain. Recently, a survey said that 41% of Glasgow's population were afraid of asylum-seekers, and would not like to have them living next door. The vast majority will never have to. In fact, it is asylum-seekers who are far more likely to be harassed, assaulted, even murdered (two already have been). And these are people who have fled brutal regimes, experienced threat, torture, rape, fear beyond anything we can imagine.

When did we become such cowards? When did we stop thinking it was both desirable and possible to befriend our neighbours? Was it when we stopped valuing the communal joys? The racism at the root of so much anti-asylum-seeker rhetoric needs to be challenged and confronted. But the possibilities of friendship, of communal joys, of the sharing of experience, faith, ideas, cultures which asylum-seekers offer also need to be affirmed, celebrated and made available much more widely than they are at present.

Valuing the communal joys figures largely on Iona and at Camas. They are there in singing, not just in worship but in ceilidhs and Big and Wee Sings. But people also discover the communal joy of working all afternoon in the craft room, chopping vegetables together in the kitchen, walking on the pilgrimage, learning to kayak or abseil, dancing Strip the Willow in the village hall, breaking bread together in the church but also in the refectory, or in the MacLeod Centre or Camas dining rooms. And in sharing these communal joys, as

so many discover on Iona and at Camas, we find the confidence to
share our stories, our hopes, ourselves.

Kathy Galloway

I will sing a song of love

Chorus:
I will sing a song of love
to the One who first loved me,
and I'll sing it as a child of God,
who is named and known and free.
For the love of God is good,
it is broad and deep and long;
and above all else that matters,
God is worthy of my song

And I will not sing alone
but with earth and sky and sea,
for creation raised its voice
well in advance of me.

Chorus

And I'll sing with every soul,
every language, every race,
which proclaims this world is good
for God has blessed this place.

Chorus

And I'll sing for what is right
and against all that is wrong,
because God is never neutral
who inspires my song.

Chorus

As I bring to God my joy,
so I'll bring to God my pain
for there is no hurt which God
requires me to retain.

Chorus

While my life on earth still runs,
may my song to God be given,
till through grace I join the harmony
of all in heaven.

Chorus

John L. Bell

PILGRIMAGE

Iona pilgrimage: Through thick and thin
(A sermon from Iona Abbey)

How lovely are your dwelling places, Yahweh-Elohim;
my whole being yearns and longs to be in your house.
My heart and my flesh sing for joy to the living God.
Even the sparrows find a home in the Cloisters
and the swallow a nest to settle her young
in St Oran's Chapel, my liberator and my God.
Happy are those who live in your house,
always singing praise to you.
Joyful are those whose strength comes from you,
whose hearts are set on pilgrim roads.
As they pass through the dry valley of Baca,
they find spring water to drink.
Also from pools, you provide water
and cover the valley with blessings
for those who lose their way.
They go from strength to strength:
They will see the God who is Yahweh-Elohim.
O God, hear our prayer.
Give ear, O God of Jacob and Leah and Rachel!
Redeemer, our shield, look and see the face of your anointed.
For a day in your Abbey

is better than a thousand anywhere else;
I would rather be a doorkeeper in the house of my God
or a housekeeper in the Abbey.
I would rather mop the floor in the homeless shelter
than live in the mansions of the Money Boys.
Our God is a sun and a protector who gives grace and honour,
who withholds no good thing from those who do what is right.
Yahweh-Elohim, how happy are those who trust in you!

(Psalm 84, adapted for worship on Iona)

More than a year ago, Eduard Loring and I were invited to come to Iona to share a week with you in considering 'The Spirituality of Solidarity'. We gladly accepted the opportunity to teach with our dear friend Norman Shanks. But an unexpected battle with cancer through this past year has meant that our plans to come have been off-again, on-again. I give thanks today for the healing prayers of the Iona Community, joining those of friends and family at home, and for the rigorous and wonderful medical care that I have received. I am a living and grateful testimony that our God is a healer, and I am more thankful than I can express for the blessing and privilege of being with you in this beautiful abbey on this wondrous island.

When it became clear in late May that we would be able to come, I began right away to think of Psalm 84, which I have grown to love. This is the Psalm of a traveller going up to the Temple in Jerusalem for Sukkot – the Festival of Tabernacles or Festival of Shelters. In the longing to arrive, the Psalmist sings with heart and flesh for joy, for the house of God is a place that makes space for all who come. Even the smallest, the least important birds!

This is the song of a pilgrim whose heart is rooted in the house of God and whose strength comes from God. Or we might say, pilgrims whose hearts find a home in the Body of Christ in the world and whose strength comes from the Spirit of Christ for the costly journey of discipleship through the dry valley of Baca, the valley of the dry bones, indeed even through the valley of the shadow of death.

We go from strength to strength because the Spirit of God is with us and we are given to each other in the Body of Christ – in community for the journey.

Pilgrimage is such a good Iona word! I couldn't count the number of times we've heard the word in the past week. So many come here 'making a pilgrimage', and of course there is a guided pilgrimage around the island each week to visit the important places and buildings – the holy sites. There are groups on Celtic pilgrimages, individuals and families on faith pilgrimage, people seeking meaning in the history of Scotland, folk looking for roots in family history and identity. People leave with great sacks filled up with stones as if to tote off the holiness with them (and I have to admit I've got a few stones in my pockets!). We are *hungry* for the holy: for the bread that satisfies. And the faith journey is such a deep part of what it means to be human – seeking vocation and integrity in solidarity with the human family and all of creation.

But if we worship the one who is God of heaven and earth – if we seek discipleship with Jesus the Liberator – we cannot satisfy ourselves with having visited holy places. A pilgrimage is nothing if it leaves us unchanged. It is so significant that the Psalmist says, 'Happy are those whose strength comes from you, whose *hearts* are set on pilgrim roads.' To come to Iona we have set our *feet* on pilgrim roads. But to receive the holiness of God's presence we must leave with our *hearts* set on pilgrim roads.

George MacLeod, the late founder of the Iona Community, is often quoted as saying that Iona is a THIN place – with small boundaries between material and spiritual. Only the thickness of a tissue between heaven and earth. I love this and I experience it here. This seems to me to be a place 'shot through with the Glory of God'. It's so important to have this experience precisely because it helps us, it nurtures us, when we're in the THICK places – the God-forsaken places, the ugly places – the places of death and oppression where Jesus's presence can hardly be felt or experienced with any spontaneity.

These are the places where Christ comes to us in the guise of a stranger – in the hookers, crooks and thieves just like the crowd Jesus made his best friends and in whom he promises to hide himself.

Is not our spiritual pilgrimage a daily journey of taking up the cross to see the presence of God – to see the executed and Risen Christ in the most unlovely places so that we can be led to resist and struggle and advocate and agitate and present our bodies as living sacrifices against all that hurts and maims and insults and kills God's children? This is not an easy pilgrimage because it inevitably brings conflict with the powerful and the 'money boys' (as George MacLeod loved to call them). Struggling for the poor and exploited means pushing with all our strength against the powerful tides of global capitalism and its manic, frenetic demands to buy more, consume more, trample our neighbours, and ignore the common good in our desperate pursuit of our own personal comfort, titillation, pleasure and convenience. And this struggle is never welcomed by the powers.

Our hearts are set on pilgrim roads not to satisfy ourselves with finding one holy place, not to romanticise this thin place, but to take this experience of the presence of the holy back into the thick of things. When our hearts are set on pilgrim roads, we can come to know God's Spirit who permeates 'every blessed thing' and every blessed body; when our hearts are set on pilgrim roads we struggle to find the HOLY where we are – in the ordinary cities and towns where we live, in this world where, as the Peruvian poet César Vallejo says, 'suffering and death increase sixty minutes in every second'. The life of discipleship brings us to see and know the face of Jesus in his most distressing guise: in the poor, the hungry, the stranger, the abused, the addict, the desperate and deranged, the elderly and the demented, the refugees and war victims, the sick and the demanding, the panhandlers and the prostitutes, the criminal and the condemned. Because these are the friends of Jesus: the poor and the poor in spirit, the vulnerable, those who know their need for healing and cannot hide their vulnerability and desperation. When our eyes can see with pilgrim hearts through the thick grime and human wreckage we know with clarity and certainty that these – the least of our sisters and brothers – are those in whom Jesus Christ hides himself and invites us to recognise him and reach out in solidarity and love.

This is indeed a journey through the dry valley of Baca – the valley of the shadow of death – the valley of the dry bones, the valley of the shadow of death on the cross, the valley of torture and abandonment, of execution and homelessness. For this is where Jesus leads us if our hearts are set on pilgrim roads.

At the Open Door Community, our home in Atlanta, Georgia, our life and work for the past 25 years has been among the homeless poor and the men, women and children of Georgia's death row. December 1983 was a major turning point for us. After six years of ministry on death row, we came to the time that Georgia would execute its first prisoner in nearly twenty years. John Eldon Smith was the first. I had visited Smitty for five years. He had been found guilty of an awful murder. In those early years of my ministry, I had gradually learned that none of us can be summed up by our one worst act. And I came to know Smitty as a friend capable of great caring and compassion – a warm and funny man.

His execution was scheduled in August and September, and both times he came within hours of his death before the courts intervened to stop it. Two weeks before Christmas, the courts did not intervene and he was electrocuted until dead. We gathered with his family to bury him ourselves in a second-hand suit and a donated casket at the edge of a beautiful pasture at the Jubilee Community.

Two weeks later, during Christmas week, the temperatures in our city plunged to sub-zero and stayed there for a week or more. None of the church shelters could be persuaded to stay open extra hours because the volunteers were enjoying holidays with their families. We worked around the clock to keep our dining room open for shelter and to take hot soup and coffee out onto the streets. But before the week was out, more than 23 people had frozen to death on the streets of Atlanta. In the days and weeks that followed, I was heartsick and bone weary. I was disillusioned and angry. I didn't want to hear any more about solidarity or the call to be 'faithful rather than effective'.

I had been taught all my life that if I applied myself to a problem, I could solve it! We were well-educated people. We could *change* things. But what we were finding was that the longer we worked among the homeless, the more there were and the faster they were dying. The longer and harder we worked to abolish the death penalty, the more the American people clamoured for executions and the deeper was this wrenching, dehumanising pain and suffering caused by violence in our personal interactions and by our dehumanising systems of so-called justice. I was indeed passing through the dry valley of Baca. I was becoming a heap of dry bones in the valley of dry bones – I was losing my hold on hope as the pain and bitterness of loss threatened to engulf me. Every time I went to the prison at Jackson (it's called the Georgia Diagnostic and Classification Center), I missed Smitty and I had to look at and speak with the very people who had given the orders and pulled the switches to run 2,300 volts of electricity once, twice, three times through the body of my friend.

I was sick of it and so angry that I began to feel my own capacity for violence. I was angry at everybody, including God. I hurt all over and I wanted some comfort and relief.

Several months down the road, our community, along with the Jubilee and Koinonia communities, had a weekend retreat with Dan Berrigan, the Catholic priest and radical resister who has been a mentor for many of us in the States. As he taught, Dan mentioned, as an aside really, that the Latin root of the word comfort – *comfortare* – means 'to strengthen'. God's Spirit is the Comforter: the one who strengthens us. When the road is hard and the cross is heavy and the valley is dry, the comfort that God promises us is the strength and presence to help us go on: the sustenance of spring water in the desert of our despair.

Nothing changed for me really. The executions have continued and the homeless poor suffer desperately. But gradually the bitterness drained away in face of the simple conviction that God is good and never gives us a work to do without also giving us the strength to do it. To live in solidarity with the poor, the broken and the prisoner is to live with death and suffering, truly to journey through the dry valley of Baca. But pools of water spring up in the most unlikely places. And we find companionship and laughter and singing along the way. And reflected in the pools in the midst of the dry bones we see the brightness of Resurrection.

The book doesn't say, 'Yea, though I walk through the valley of the shadow of death, I will fear no evil, for you take away the death and suffering and make me comfortable and at ease in the Empire.' It says, 'Yea, though I walk through the valley of the shadow of death, I will fear no evil *for thou art with me. Thy rod and thy staff they comfort (strengthen) me.'*

When our hearts are set on pilgrim roads, the Body of Christ is our home in the world. And in the centre of this home is a table, prepared for us in the presence of our enemies. A table spread with ordinary bread and wine, a table that nourishes us to go from strength to strength. A table to which people will come from north and south and east and west to sit together in the Beloved Community.

The Table of God is the remembrance of the hideous, torturous death of a Radical Resister. But it is

Month 2 Day 16

a Resurrection Feast, because the resistance to established religion and the Empire was and is rooted in a Radical Love that calls us into a community of resistance and becomes for us blessings of fresh spring water in the dry valley of Baca.

Even for those who will never come to Iona, the table is a thin place to which we are all invited. A place where our eyes are strengthened to see the presence of God among us, a place where our hearts are strengthened with the courage to live the life in thick places. We receive strength to walk the walk and take the heat for Jesus – the Vagrant, the Executed One – the Risen One who is with us always. May God be praised.

Murphy Davis

Murphy Davis is a Founding Partner of the Open Door Community in Atlanta, Georgia.

'The Open Door Community is a residential community in the Catholic Worker tradition (we're sometimes called a Protestant Catholic Worker House!). We seek to dismantle racism, sexism and heterosexism, abolish the death penalty, and create the Beloved Community on Earth through a loving relationship with some of the most neglected and outcast of God's children: the homeless and our sisters and brothers who are in prison.

We serve breakfasts and soup-kitchen lunches, provide showers and changes of clothes, staff a free medical clinic, conduct worship services and meetings for the clarification of thought, and provide a prison ministry, including monthly trips for families to visit loved ones at the Hardwick prisons in central Georgia. We also advocate on behalf of the oppressed, homeless and prisoners through non-violent protests, civil disobedience, grassroots organisation and the publication of our monthly newspaper.'

From the Open Door Community website
www.opendoorcommunity.org

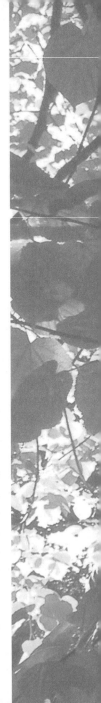

SEXUALITY

A group Bible study

Cursing, yet graced in our sexuality

One of the great issues of the day is who is included and who is, quite deliberately, left out. There is a studied determination in some quarters of the Church to ensure that gay and lesbian people are not only left out, but kept out.

The Iona Community has a Working Group concerned with sexuality which believes that same-sex relationships can be firmly grounded theologically in scripture. This is the first of three studies on this theme.

Bill's story

Bill Clayton came out to his parents as bisexual when he was 14. He was naturally nervous about doing so. But after reading a book which his parents gave him which contained some 'coming out' stories, he plucked up the courage and told them. They helped him to find a support group, continued to love him and were happy when after three meetings Bill told them that the support group was great but not something that he needed.

The Activist Club at Bill's school invited Colonel Margarethe Cammermeyer, a campaigner against the 'gays in the military' ban, to speak at the school. Homophobic parents and community members objected mainly on 'religious grounds'. Bill was one of those putting up flyers to come to the meeting. The meeting was held but homophobic feeling ran high and the local press was receiving hate mail.

A month later Bill and two friends were walking near their school when a group of four teenage lads followed them in a car shouting obscenities. They stopped the car and approached Bill's group. They brutally assaulted Bill, kicking and beating him into unconsciousness. Bill was taken to hospital and the police were called.

A lot of people responded to the crime and a rally against hate-crime was called. With staggering courage Bill spoke at that rally, '… More than ever we, the gay community, need to come out and band together and fight for our right to be safe in our homes and in our streets.' Col. Cammermeyer returned and spoke at the rally to support the young people involved.

A month after the rally on May 8th, 1995 Bill took an overdose. He was rushed to hospital but it was too late. On the way there he told his mother that he was just tired of coping. He could not face the prospect of being attacked again, or his friends being attacked. All he could see of the future was hate and violence and going from one attack to another. He was 17.

From *Lesbian and Gay Christians*, Issue 57, March 2000

Jeremiah's story

The prophet Jeremiah had an experience comparable to Bill's. He knew himself to be as he was: a man burnt up inside with a message which he felt an irresistible urge to share, but which brought him ridicule, persecution and seemingly endless mental and physical anguish – personal suffering which he could hardly endure. He found himself under compulsion to take a path in life which he would never have willingly chosen.

O Lord, you deceived me, and I was deceived;
you overpowered me and prevailed.
I am ridiculed all day long;

everyone mocks me.
Whenever I speak, I cry out
proclaiming violence and destruction.
So the word of the Lord has brought me
insult and reproach all day long.
But if I say, "I will not mention him
or speak any more in his name,"
his word is in my heart like a fire,
a fire shut up in my bones.
I am weary of holding it in;
indeed, I cannot …

Cursed be the day I was born!
May the day my mother bore me not be blessed!
Cursed be the man who brought my father the news,
who made him very glad, saying,
"A child is born to you – a son!"
May that man be like the towns
the Lord overthrew without pity.
May he hear wailing in the morning,
a battle cry at noon.
For he did not kill me in the womb,
with my mother as my grave,
her womb enlarged for ever.
Why did I ever come out of the womb
to see trouble and sorrow
and to end my days in shame?

Jeremiah 20:7–9;14–18 (NIV)

Month 2 Day 17

Paul's story

There is a variety of gifts (graces), but always the same Spirit. And there is a variety of ways of serving, but the same Lord. Working in all sorts of different ways in different people, it is the same God who is working in all of them. The particular way in which the Spirit is given to each person is for a good purpose.

1 Corinthians 12:4ff

Now for the questions about which you wrote (on marriage and virginity). I should like everyone to be like me, but everybody has their particular graces from God, one of this kind, one of that.

1 Corinthians 7:1a,7

St Paul gladly acknowledges that each person is graced by God with varied gifts and that all are given to be used in the service of others for His good purposes. What has not been so readily acknowledged within the Church is that each member is graced in varied ways in his/her sexuality, even although St Paul makes quite explicit reference to this in his letter to the Church at Corinth.

Discussion

1. Share together in the group your personal responses to Bill's story and Jeremiah's story.

2. There are many lesbian, gay, bisexual and transgendered people who are driven close to despair by the attitudes of others who cannot accept what they know to be true of themselves, namely that they are created by God in the way that they are. Some members of the group may wish to share their own experiences of such attitudes.

3. There may be members of the group who would like to declare with clarity and simplicity who they are and what they would want to say to those who deny God's many-splendoured creativity and drive others to despair.

4. Discuss together in the group how those who are graced in differing ways in their sexuality may use their gifts for God's good purposes in the service of others. See Paul's story.

Graeme Brown

HEALING

Cocoa the Wonder Dog

In July 2003, Cocoa the Wonder Dog came into our lives. This was a big step for us (some in the family would say a crazy step), since, being confirmed cat people, we had not really had a relationship with a dog. And, like decisions in many families, this was not a unanimous one.

But it has proven to be a wise choice. For during those long, difficult months of surgery, chemotherapy and hospital stays, which followed our son's diagnosis of Stage 4 cancer, we always had someone at home waiting for us, filled with unconditional love, and never-ending hope. I always thought it was true with cats, but Cocoa reminded us that pets are visible signs of that invisible grace God fills us with in each and every moment of our lives.

And Cocoa got us out of the house, especially on those mornings when bed seemed so safe and warm, and on those evenings when all we wanted to do was 'veg out' in front of the TV. Cats are perfectly content to take care of their business, in their way and time, but dogs – especially a dog like Cocoa – demand to be walked! And so we did – through puddles; in August heat; shuffling through snow, and trying not to slip on the ice underneath – we walked, and walked, and walked …

And along the way – on starry nights and cloudy days, in times of uncertainty as well as faithfulness, with tears marring our vision and joy bubbling on our lips – God was at work in our lives with the gentle presence of the Holy Spirit, and the healing grace of Jesus Christ.

We have grown accustomed to the belief that healing comes through medication, medical teams, hospitals, wonder treatments. And it does happen that way, for many of us. But healing also comes in quiet moments: in the gentle hand on a shoulder, in eating a meal prepared by a neighbour, in the prayers of a community of faith, in the silent moments of the night. All too often, however, we are not alert enough to these moments and ways in which the healing power of God is poured upon us.

God does healing work in many remarkable ways, and often through rather 'unremarkable' people, and sometimes, even through a 'dumb animal' like Cocoa.

Note: We had been looking for a dog off and on for months, when we discovered Cocoa. She was the first dog, in all that searching, who came and approached us, rather than our approaching her first. Not long ago, there was a story on the news about a study which showed that some dogs have a special 'sense' by which they are able to 'smell' cancer in a person. We adopted Cocoa about two months before our son was diagnosed with cancer, and probably at the time when it was 'growing' within him. Gives one pause.

Prayer

Heal this reluctant child of yours,
Holy One:

I despise the truth
that pain is my
faithful companion,
    but am loath
    to place it in
    your scarred hands.

I gnaw on the
bitterness
in my heart,
its tart taste
tingling my tongue,
    so I cannot
    savour the sweet
    Bread of Life.

The millstones piled on my shoulder
by the world
break my flesh,
    but
    I fear
    the peace
    you offer me
    may shatter my arrogant spirit.

Heal me, Holy One,
heal me.

Amen

Thom M. Shuman

SOCIAL ACTION

Damascus Gate

The T-shirt said it for me. I had 'got stoned in Jerusalem'. My barman son tentatively checked out that his minister father wasn't being naive. I *did* know the double entendre? Yes, I did. Some of my more PC friends questioned whether it was right to be flippant about what, for some people, is a life-threatening situation, and, of course, in the Bible, stoning was a sentence for the blasphemer. So let me explain:

It was the third week of my time in Jerusalem. It was good that morning to return to the southern wall of the Temple platform. There I was alone. I walked, took photographs. It was the place where Jesus had walked into the historical crisis of his time. An occupied city. A city of divided loyalties. Sadducee versus Pharisee. Roman versus Jew. City versus country. Jesus had made for the Temple. What then happened has been remembered. What he said about the future of the Temple was so uncomfortable. Disaster was approaching. New life would rise from its destruction. But that new life would come from him. His life in the lives of others. But first there had to be a dying.

I crossed the Old City and out into East Jerusalem through the Damascus Gate. I could hear shouting. Not unusual in that crowded exit, but this time it was more harsh and directed. I could see people looking in one direction. I followed their gaze and walked with the crowd. Boys were throwing stones. I stayed behind them. The noise was incessant. Sirens. Horns. The explosive concussions of gunfire. I had walked into a disturbance. I followed the crowd. I stopped by a lamppost.

The stone came. Blood poured over me. I turned, confused, embarrassed. Hands held me, offers of 'hospital'. I walked. I felt I was running. Stones spun off the pavement around me. The cut was small but the bleeding profuse. Faces. Concerned. Frightened. Little children wide-eyed. 'Why you, a foreigner?' 'Who are you?' There was help in their expressions. It would be repeated again and again in the Palestinians I would meet in the next few days. 'We are sorry. This is not your conflict. It was a blind stone. It was not aimed at you deliberately. When we get angry we throw stones.' There was a reconciliation in their words.

Later I met a Palestinian mother. She had three sons. Each had been involved in the *intifada*. I asked her what I might tell my own family on returning to the UK. She explained that stone-throwing is a sign of despair and frustration. Each time her lads went out she expected one of them to be maimed. 'We pick up stones because there is nothing else to do. The anger is all-consuming. You must live here to understand.'

What I later realised was that I had unwittingly stood near an Israeli police van caught in a traffic jam. The stone-throwers had turned their aim on its plight. It was then I became one of the statistics for that day – a day when some people had lost their lives and many hundreds had been wounded. As Israel celebrated its fiftieth anniversary, for the Palestinians it was a day of grieving. For me it was a chastening experience.

I had been compelled by the crowd, the noise, the sight. It had felt right to do that. That was my historical setting at that time. I'd tried to be a spectator. But the conflict draws you in. Stones flung in anger, despair, frustration, found a target. Stones flung inviting a response hit someone who thought he could just watch. It was a time to learn that, if you want to experience reconciliation, you can't stay on the sidelines and watch the conflict.

John Rackley

Church Renewal

Less concerned about itself

Renewal for the Church has always meant the Church being less concerned about itself and more concerned about the world it exists to serve. Whatever our theories, there can be no doubt that our main conscious aim and intention today is to build up and maintain our own religious institutions – the Church is something to support. We give little time or planning to our real job: the offering of ourselves to God for His use. Reformation for the Church has always meant *service and action*. 'Men and brethren, what shall we do?' was the early Church's response, as we read in Acts, to the preaching of the Gospel. The House Church tries to make us more truly a Church – a body of people who, having professed their faith, mean business about it, who get together to ask, 'Right! What does it mean for us?' Some such set-up seems necessary if this is to be done. If special action is called for, which the Church as a body should undertake, in this kind of way all can be in on the planning and so are much more likely to play their part.

Much more important, however, we must realise that the Church at work does not mean (as we normally take it to mean) a religious institution acting in institutional

ways; it means *Christian people living their lives*. In the same way our personal Christian action is not something which we add on to our ordinary lives, or undertake with that part of our leisure time which we can spare for Church work. It means: living our ordinary lives responsibly, in obedience to Christ. This is how God, through His Church, can get to grips with His world; this is the way of leaven and salt and light; this is the truth, which the Reformation recovered, that the Church is the laity, the whole people of God. The vitality of the Church (this instrument through which God's will is done in His world) depends, in the end, not on decisions taken in Kirk Sessions or in General Assemblies but on the particular decisions and choices we each take each day, often without our thinking about it, as parents and workers and citizens, in the particular circumstances of our particular lives in our particular world. The institutional Church exists, and must exist, to provide the means of grace – the means whereby we can be helped and equipped to make these decisions and choices in accordance with the will of God …

David Orr, an early member of the Iona Community, 1962

A favourable time

In every age we are faced with the determination of God to transform all created life in justice, truth and peace.

In every age we are faced with the deliberate self-limitation of God through the choice of human beings to be partners in that work of transformation.

When the time was ripe Jesus Christ came, in a fully human life. He came among us as *arabon*: 'the colour of God's money staked in a gambler's throw for a new world'. He announced and represented God's Kingdom: the whole fabric of created life working God's way. He called people to join him in this work. From those who responded, church was formed.

The Kingdom must be prayed for and worked for – and also, in the end, be received as a gift: 'Fear not, little flock – it is your Father's good pleasure to give you the Kingdom.'

The church, on the other hand, must be built up, each limb and organ contributing to the life of the body whose Head is Jesus Christ. To be effective in ministering with him to the world God loves, it must 'grow up into him', becoming equipped for the job, all its gifts being exercised with ever greater maturity.

The Church in the West is experiencing what Isaiah called 'a time of God's favour'. What look to be drawbacks hold promise:

- The Church is no longer the power in the land that it once was. It can no longer set itself up as the authorised dispenser of God's judgements on people and events. It is no longer listened to just because it is Church. So it is in a better position to give heed to the words of Jesus about power. Faced with a bid by the mother of James and John to give them a privileged position, Jesus warned: 'You know that, with the Gentiles, rulers lord it over their subjects and the great make their authority felt. That must not be your way! With you whoever wants to be great must serve, and whoever wants to be first must be the slave of all: as the Son of Man came not to be served but to serve and to give his life a ransom for many.' In his letters to the Corinthians Paul insists that it is the weak things which overthrow the mighty; and that, in his own case, it is when he is weak that he is strong. Jesus Christ, treated as a nothing, crucified, risen, testified to the effectiveness of a different power from that wielded by those with clout in the land. Dietrich Bonhoeffer put the matter succinctly and brilliantly. Christians are called to 'participation in the powerlessness of God in the world'. [4]

- The Church in the West is being pruned back. What seems negative has positive implications. Jesus warned disciples that they had to be prepared for times of pruning. He identified himself as the Vine and his Father as the Vinedresser. He told them that they, as branches, would be subjected to the cutting away of dead wood and of spurs which were no longer productive. This was needed to achieve greater fruitfulness, a more abundant harvest.

Month 2 Day 20

- The Church in our time is more alert to the danger of becoming what Swiss basic Christian communities called a *Kuschelgruppe* – a 'cuddling group', absorbed in itself. Yet the media so often measure the church's health as if it existed by and for itself. As football support is measured by numbers going through the turnstiles, so the yardstick for church commitment has been taken to be numbers turning up at a building. How can that be the means of assessing the vitality of a community which is to be like leaven changing solid dough to produce bread, like salt giving life savour, like light active to chase away darkness? As well attempt, by eye measurement, to distinguish the water from the whisky in a dram! The service of the church is to get lost in creative self-giving, that the world be transformed in justice, truth and peace.

Some years ago I visited Fuller Theological Seminary in California. Students approached me with words emblazoned on T-shirts: 'Don't Go To Church'. When I looked after them I read on the back: 'Be The Church'.

I was in London when Bob Geldof and others summed up the efforts to release poor countries from crippling debt. There Gordon Brown paid tribute to the Church and other religious bodies for providing dynamic at the heart of the movement.

When a quarter of a million people marched against the Iraq war where was the Church? In the thick of things, not separately labelled. Faslane protests, G8 summit pressures, the Make Poverty History campaign had Christians at their heart. Veteran Labour politician Roy Hattersley has confessed, as an atheist, that the evidence is compelling that caring friendship for the old, the weak, the vulnerable in our society would be substantially missing were Christians not bedded into local situations, acting there with enlightened compassion.

Ian M. Fraser, 2006

Month 2 Day 20

WORSHIP

The whole

Worship the Lord with all your heart and with all your mind and with all your strength.

I almost used these words recently as a scriptural quote, but realised in time that it was only what I'd *like* to be a biblical quote! The text which inspired me was Mark 12:28–34, where Jesus quotes the Old Testament and says the greatest commandment is to love the Lord your God with all your heart and soul and mind and strength (the original in Deuteronomy says, 'heart, soul and strength').

I wouldn't think much of a card from my partner saying, 'Happy birthday, darling, I love you with all of my mind.' Human love is usually expressed as coming from the heart. But these words remind us that love is bigger than an emotion – God wants every part of us engaged, loving, committed: heart, head, soul and body.

So if we are to love God with our whole being, shouldn't we worship God that way too? To worship God in this way means the whole person – not just the intellect or emotions or just one part of who we are. I believe that if we are to be the people who love God with heart and mind, body and soul, then we cannot help but let that overflow into our worship.

I was schooled well in 'head' worship, growing up in the Scottish Presbyterian Church. There was nothing much to do but sing, listen, listen and listen. The only movement was stand, sit – and certainly sit still! Not a rich sensory experience.

I suddenly noticed a line from a familiar hymn in a new light recently: 'lost in wonder, love and praise' ('Love Divine All Loves Excelling'). Definitely not what we, as Scottish Presbyterians, were supposed to be doing! I suppose I have spent my adult years rejecting, respecting and recovering from that formative experience. I've discovered that, because I am not a 'head' person, it didn't work very well for me.

How do I get lost in wonder, love and praise? Why would I want to? Didn't I spend years being suspicious of folk who look as if they are? Well, praise the Lord – African song has redeemed me and helped me overcome my awkwardness with body and movement stuff in worship. It has helped me to 'be in the moment' and discover that sometimes it's not what I am saying that counts, but how I'm expressing it. It's helped me to worship more wholly.

It's been happening gradually for a long time now – since those early days of singing South African songs of faith and freedom on the streets of Glasgow with the Wild Goose Resource Group. After years of preaching why singing these songs is important, I have had a new awakening of why, as a white Scot, this music matters to me personally.

So, eh … *amandla* and *slainte* and would you like a wee dod of shortie with your cassava?

Alison Adam

Sensual Bible readings (from Iona)

Voice 1:   Touch!

Voice 2:   Then suddenly a woman who had been suffering from haemorrhages for twelve years came up behind him and touched the fringe of his cloak, for she said to herself, 'If I only touch his cloak, I will be made well.'

Voice 3:   All who had diseases pressed upon him to touch him.

Voice 4:   People were bringing little children to him in order that he might touch them.

Voice 1: And a woman in the city … brought an alabaster jar of ointment. She stood behind him at his feet, weeping, and began to bathe his feet with her tears and to dry them with her hair. Then she continued kissing his feet and anointing them with the ointment.

Voice 2: Look at my hands and my feet; see that it is I myself. Touch me and see.

Voice 3: Taste!

Voice 4: The house of Israel called it manna; it was like coriander seed, white; and the taste of it was like wafers made with honey.

Voice 1: My child, eat honey, for it is good, and the drippings of the honeycomb are sweet to your taste.

Voice 2: As an apple tree among the trees of the wood, so is my beloved among young men. With great delight I sat in his shadow, and his fruit was sweet to my taste.

Voice 3: He brought me to the banqueting house, and his intention toward me was love. Sustain me with raisins, refresh me with apples; for I am faint with love.

Voice 4: Smell!

Voice 1: So he came near and kissed him; and he smelled the smell of his garments, and blessed

Month 2 Day 21

him, and said, 'Ah, the smell of my son is like the smell of a field that God has blessed.'

Voice 2: Like cassia and camel's thorn I gave forth perfume, and like choice myrrh I spread my fragrance … like the odour of incense in the tent.

Voice 3: While the king was on his couch, my nard gave forth its fragrance. My beloved is to me a bag of myrrh that lies between my breasts.

Voice 4: Awake, O north wind, and come, O south wind! Blow upon my garden that its fragrance may be wafted abroad. Let my beloved come to his garden, and eat its choicest fruits.

Voice 1: Mary took a pound of costly perfume made of pure nard, anointed Jesus' feet, and wiped them with her hair. The house was filled with the fragrance of the perfume.

Voice 2: Hear!

Voice 3: They heard the sound of the Lord God walking in the garden at the time of the evening breeze.

Voice 4: And after the earthquake a fire, but the Lord was not in the fire; and after the fire a sound of sheer silence.

Voice 1: Raise a song, sound the tambourine, the sweet lyre with the harp. Blow the trumpet at the new moon, at the full moon, on our festal day.

Voice 2: Let the sea roar, and all that fills it; the world and those who live in it. Let the floods clap their hands; let the hills sing together for joy.

Voice 3: Whether there came a whistling wind, or a melodious sound of birds in wide-spreading branches, or the rhythm of violently rushing water, or the harsh crash of rocks hurled down, or the unseen running of leaping animals, or the sound of the most savage roaring beasts, or an echo thrown back from a hollow of the mountains … the whole world was illumined with brilliant light.

Voice 4:   Let anyone with ears listen!

Voice 1:   See!

Voice 2:   Let me see your face, let me hear your voice; for your voice is sweet, and your face is lovely.

Voice 3:   For with you is the fountain of life; in your light we see light.

Voice 4:   Now David was ruddy, and had beautiful eyes, and was handsome.

Voice 1:   A great portent appeared in heaven: a woman clothed with the sun, with the moon under her feet, and on her head a crown of twelve stars.

Voice 2:   Then Jesus said to him, 'What do you want me to do for you?' The blind man said to him, 'My teacher, let me see again.'

Voice 3:   The eye is the lamp of the body. So, if your eye is simple, your whole body will be full of light.

Voice 4:   For now we see in a mirror, dimly, but then we will see face to face. Now I know only in part; then I will know fully, even as I have been fully known.

Lotte Webb

CALLED TO BE ONE

Stumbling blocks

Karl Barth, whose *Church Dogmatics* occupy a fair amount of space on study shelves, was once asked to sum up the faith in one sentence. By way of reply he quoted the opening lines of the hymn by Anna Bartlett Warner:

Jesus loves me! This I know,
for the Bible tells me so.

The theological niceties with which some people seem so strangely fascinated often mean very little to those at the grassroots of our churches. Rather they present stumbling blocks to local Christians who would simply like to love one another with the love with which God in Christ loves them. It was this same Christ who warned against the hypocrisy of the scribes and Pharisees, who were so little conversant with what we now call the hierarchy of truths that they strained out a gnat whilst swallowing a camel (Matthew 23:24).

Just as Fritz Schumacher in his *Small Is Beautiful* urged us to study economics as if people mattered, we have to learn to do our theology as if people matter and to rediscover with Ian Fraser and with John Drane that theology is 'the people's work'. As someone once said, the problem with Jesus as the Word made flesh is that we have turned him into words again. He never wrote a book and the only reference we have to his writing anything was when he wrote in the sand (John 8:6). Yet Christians have spent centuries endlessly filling theological libraries with books and papers, constitutions, canon law, *summa theologicae* and annual reports.

While theologians and doctrinal committees fiddle, local people in local ecumenical partnerships, who simply want to love one another and to share bread and wine together, become frustrated and exasperated. They despair of soporific phrases about 'having patience'; and of being told that 'the mills of God grind slowly' and that unity will happen 'when Christ wills'. There ought to be no doubt in any of our minds that Christ wills it now – that, after all, is what he died for on the Cross, and it is our job to get on with it. Otherwise what do we mean when we piously say, Sunday after Sunday in all of our churches all over the world: 'We who are many are one body because we all break the one bread'? Either that is true or it is blasphemy. If it is true then why don't we do it? Why don't we realise something of the urgency in the face of an increasingly secular and disbelieving world?

It is argued that doctrinal matters must first be settled before sharing bread and wine, and Matthew 5:23–24 is quoted where Jesus said: 'So if you are offering your gift at the altar, and there remember that your brother has something against you, leave your gift there before the altar and go; first be reconciled to your brother, and then come and offer your gift.' Well, if that is so, and if we took it seriously, we would have no more eucharists, and would declare a moratorium on Communion and the Mass, until such time as we were sure that we had so spoken the truth in love that we were at peace with one another. Then, and only then, would we dare to offer the gifts of bread and wine and utter the words stating that we who are many are one body because we all share the one bread.

Murdoch MacKenzie

Affirmation

Christ is like a single body, which has many parts.
We affirm that to his body we belong:
YES, LORD, SO SAYS MY HEART!

If one part of the body suffers
then we will share its pain.
YES, LORD, SO SAYS MY HEART!

If one part of the body is praised,
then we will share its happiness
YES, LORD, SO SAYS MY HEART!

In the one Spirit we are baptised into one body;
in her nourishing power we will travel together.
YES, LORD, SO SAYS MY HEART!

Alison Adam and Iona Abbey guests

MISSION

Here, now

John Harvey, in his address to the community, said … 'George came increasingly to believe, not so much that the mission was to bring the Gospel to every creature as that the mission was to bring all mortals to the awareness of the love and purpose of God already present in all creation, already breaking through.'

This conviction of real presence was lived by George. His life was poured into what Zen Buddhism describes as 'being here'. Again and again from George: 'You can only find God in the Now': God is right now, or not at all! Life is right now, or not at all! Our maturing, our loving, our becoming, is an endless process of being here, now. Here, now, being really present to people, to the real presence in them, so that they might become really present to themselves. Here, now, being really present in confronting the outrages and injustices that divide people from their real presence, that damage their true selves, that prevent them from being all that they can be: the damp house, the racial slur, the material impoverishment, the obscenity of war. Here, now, being really present to the letters on your desk, the knock at the door, the voice in your ear. Being here, now, is discipline married to passion, love wedded to will …

Kathy Galloway, from an editorial in *Coracle*, written shortly after the death of George MacLeod in 1991

Get back to the old Gospel

If therefore we are to be open for revival it is the here and now that must preoccupy us not the there and future. It is *now* that we must build, if we would meet Him then. It is the body of things that must concern us, if we would know the truth of things. Folk say, 'Get back to the old Gospel.' Well, the thought has not escaped us! But it is somewhere here that is the old Gospel. Was it not always the recovery of this that marked the great revivals? Martin, whose cross stands sentinel over this very church, going out with his Celtic mission after the first declension insisting that, of every twelve monks, only two to be the Sunday preachers the rest to be carpenters, fishermen, workers in wrought iron, body healers; there is the authentic note. So that when his missionaries came to the highland glens, and later to the Yorkshire dales, men knew Christ to be the Lord of all good life; that is the arena of the old Gospel.

Again, Francis of Assisi tearing up the imitation flowers and smothering the altar with bluebells and with primroses; Francis, founding a religious order and insisting that their only dress be the habit of farm workers of his day; Francis determined to be involved, identified with man's material needs; that is the authentic note of the old Gospel.

Again, our reformers reasserting the priesthood of all believers with the head of every family as officiating priest; insisting that each man, doctor, lawyer, farmer, had his vocation and ministry till the kitchen table of the farm becomes the table of the Lord; there is the authentic note.

All these, Martin, Francis, our reformers, recovered the marriage of the spiritual and the material that the incarnate Lord might revive their time. They recovered the plan – triumphant in the person of Jesus Christ.

Here, then, is the obligation of the social gospel, that with which we must become inseparably concerned. It is not a derivative of our faith, it is not somewhere on the circumference of our faith, least of all is it a temporary expedient to meet the material passions of modern man … It is the authentic arena of our faith, it is the condition of revival.

George MacLeod, from a sermon in Iona Abbey, 1946

Month 2 Day 23

WORK

The arrogant accountant

Geoffrey was a young accountant who was trying to make his mark on the world. He was going to be famous, the best ever, top of his profession – such was his high opinion of himself. He wanted to get off to a good start. So he rented a magnificent office in a prestigious new building in the centre of town. He furnished it with the most impressive things – studded leather chairs, gold-framed paintings and a wonderful antique desk. He filled it with state-of-the-art communication equipment – fax machines, desktop computers and the like. And his pride and joy was the fanciest of tele-phones, which sat on his desk waiting to be connected.

On his first day in his sumptuous office, a client was announced, the very first of what Geoffrey believed would be a long list of distinguished clients who would come to rely on his consider-able expertise. So, to indicate his busyness and the preciousness of his time, the young account-ant deliberately made the new client wait in the outer office, and left him there for a quarter of an hour. To create an ever bigger impression on the client, when he was eventually ushered in, he picked up the receiver of the fancy telephone and pretended to have a conversation. 'But Director General, my dear sir,' he said, 'we are both wasting our time. Yes … if you absolutely insist that I should take the job – but not for under £20,000. That's the bottom line, for I have many demands on my valuable time … All right then … that's settled. You have made a wise choice. I'll be in touch. Goodbye.'

He replaced the receiver and noticed, to his considerable pleasure, that the client who stood before him was suitably impressed. Indeed, he appeared to be somewhat taken aback by Geoffrey's performance, almost overwhelmed, and certainly confused. So, glowing with pride, the young accountant looked haughtily at the incredulous client, and asked boldly, 'Well, my man, what can I do for you?' And the man paused for a while, as if not quite knowing where to begin. Then, quietly, nervously, he replied to Geoffrey's question, 'Well, excuse me, sir, but, you see, I'm from BT and I've just come to connect your phone.'

'Where your treasure is,
there your heart will be as well,'
Jesus said.

So I place my treasure
in the safe deposit box
of my possessiveness
and selfishness,
a bank strongroom
that is the world's understanding
of worth
and value
and prestige.

And I feel good
and look good
and sound good.

But my heart is hidden away
with my treasure,
in a safe deposit box,
in a bank strongroom,
out of sight,
safe and secure,
never to be seen.

Come into my world, living God,
like an honest client,
and challenge my perceptions
of work,
of value
and of myself.

Break open my treasure store,
and place it in the vault
of your Kingdom.
Let it grow in your hands.
Let it be used by your will.
Let it be shared with your people.

Open my heart;
expose it to your Love.
Call me to take the risk
of believing in the ways of your Kingdom
and not the ways of the world.

And let my treasure be known
for what it always was –
a gift to be shared
and not mine to keep,
and dwell upon,
and hoard in my miser's hands.
And let my heart be given
in love for your Kingdom
and for the good of your people.

Tom Gordon

THE POOR AND DISADVANTAGED

Poverty is neither inevitable nor acceptable

Those of you who live in Glasgow may have often stepped over it or around it, while passing through George Square – the commemorative stone set into the ground on the south side of the Square, facing down Miller Street. It reads:

Paris, October 17, 1987

On this day defenders of human rights from every continent gathered.
They paid homage to the victims of hunger, ignorance and violence.
They affirmed their conviction that poverty is not inevitable.
They proclaimed their solidarity with people throughout the world who fight to eradicate extreme poverty.

'Wherever men and women are condemned to live in poverty, human rights are violated. To come together to ensure that these rights be respected is our solemn duty.'

Joseph Wresinski

Glasgow, October 17, 1999:

People from all walks of life gathered here, united in their commitment to these principles and in the fight to eradicate poverty. Each year on October 17th (United Nations Day for the Eradication of Poverty) people in many countries gather together to bear witness to the continuing struggle against poverty.

Glasgow Braendam Link campaigned for several years to have this stone set in George Square.

Glasgow Braendam Link is a partnership of families, staff, volunteers and friends who work together to support and encourage people living in poverty, and to campaign to make their voices heard. It has its roots in the work of the Gorbals Group, an experimental project from the 1950s to the 1970s which, among other things, sought to put the issue of poverty high on the political agenda. Lilias Graham, a member of the Gorbals Group, established Braendam Family House, near Stirling, where families facing multiple problems could go for rest, renewal and reflection. People have often said that Braendam was the first place where they felt valued as individuals – they were much more used to being written off as failures.

It was recognised that once the families returned to the city they often felt isolated. In 1980, Glasgow Braendam Link was established to continue the support when families came home to face the ongoing stresses of living in areas of deprivation throughout the city.

The Glasgow stone is supported by Glasgow City Council, and serves as a public statement, right in the centre of the city, that poverty is neither inevitable nor acceptable.

Molly Harvey

See
www.gblink.org.uk *and*
www.atd-fourthworld.org

Month 2 Day 25

Remember me

Do you remember me?
Though I am nameless to you
and have no statue or square in my honour,
you will look down and I will be there,
under your feet,
close to the earth where I lived and died.
I could not rise where you might look up to me on a plinth or plate;
too many burdens pinned me down.
Narrow sunless streets and overcrowded closes hemmed me in;
I breathed damp and foetid air from running walls
and cholera, typhoid, tuberculosis, asthma laid me low.
Polio, rickets and poor food shortened my stature and my days,
and heroin and AIDS cut me down.

Remember me, do you?
I turned the wheels that made the engine-room roar.
I dug your roads and built your ships,
I carted your coal and drove your trains,
I forged your iron and unloaded your docks,
I stoked your boilers and fed your production lines,
I cleaned your offices and swept your streets,
I sewed your clothes and emptied your bins,
I made your weapons and fought your wars,
I fried your food and guarded your factories,
until you had no more use for me
and I became an economic liability.
I came from many places to do it:
from the highland glens and island shores,

---

from the slave-mines of Ayrshire and the valleys of Lanark,
from Ireland, Poland, Russia, Italy,
from India, Pakistan, Uganda, China,
from Chile, Vietnam, Iraq and Kosovo;
well that you remember me on the ground beneath your feet.
The city was built on my labour.

You remember me?
Remember the miracles I worked, on low pay, or no pay,
on strike pay or benefit.
Remember the washing I did,
walls, stairs, clothes, weans;
remember the lullabies I sang them when they couldn't sleep,
and the nights I sat up with a sick neighbour.
Remember the wakes when they died.
Remember the allotments I dug
and the jerseys I knitted
and the houses I painted;
remember the matches, the beautiful game.
Remember the singing, remember the dances;
remember the patter, and the drinking, and the laughter,
remember the courting and the weddings and the babies.
Remember the young ones who made it to college,
and the others who didn't, remember them too.
Remember the unions and the co-ops and the tenants' groups,
remember the marches to the Green and the Square.
Remember the suffragettes and the rent strikes, and the poll tax –
remember we tried and we fought and we cared.
Remember that I kept on getting up every morning,
remember my prayers and remember my tears.

Month 2 Day 25

Remember that I lived and my life had a value,
remember that I loved and hungered for more:
for the chance to reach out and look up and see further,
for a life free of want and exhaustion and fear;
for the right to be treated with justice and dignity,
for the right to be human,
for the right to a name.
It's not much to ask, but it's harder to come by,
and it's hardest of all to be seen when you're poor.
So when you walk by, just stop for a moment
and see me, and wonder, and maybe ask 'why?'
And *you* remember me.

Kathy Galloway

Written for the laying of the commemorative stone in
George Square, Glasgow.

BASIC CHRISTIAN COMMUNITIES

God in the thick of things and beyond
(A house church at worship, Panama)

They gathered frequently to pray as a group, together with the women and with Mary the mother of Jesus and with his brothers.
Acts 1:14 (GNB)

One night, when a planned engagement fell through, I wandered among the homes of the community. There I met a man, Bill, whom I had previously talked to as he was washing a car. Nine months ago he had been a hopeless drunk. Now he lived by doing odd jobs.

I asked if there was anything happening which I could attend. He said he was a lay minister and was just going to conduct a liturgy of the Word. I would be welcome to come along. He was still in the same creased shirt and trousers in which he had washed the car.

The bare house in which we met was really one room, with partitions breaking it up into a bedroom, and a bedroom/kitchen. On the kitchen table was a cross, with a lighted candle on either side. Over his open-necked shirt, Bill placed a 'yoke' or stole and was ready to start. About ten neighbours pressed in, some bringing their own chairs or stools with them. For a good part of the service, two of the children of the household were crying intermittently; occasionally one would get up to pull back the curtain and gaze at us. Outside dogs barked and howled, competing with a transistor radio. I shared with an older man a couch whose middle had the flock showing through. Most of those who took part were in their twenties or early thirties.

There was an introductory section in which people sang and gave responses. Then a passage from the Acts of the Apostles, used throughout the parish that week, was taken for study. Practically everyone participated in building up an understanding of the passage. At one point Bill seemed to be pushing them too strongly in emphasising God's presence in the midst of life. They would not have it.

'We know God is in the thick of things where we are,' they said. 'We believe that. But that is not all. God is also beyond us. We don't know how he can be with us and beyond us. But that's just the way it is.'

After about forty minutes of Bible study, those who took part were asked to offer prayers and all but two responded. Another song was sung, there were one or two more responses, and the service ended.

Ian M. Fraser

NON-VIOLENCE AND PEACEKEEPING

Power of Love: What can non-violence say to violence?

Over the past decade I've had the unusual experience, for a Quaker pacifist, of being asked to address annually 400 senior military officers at the Joint Services Command and Staff College, Britain's foremost school of war. Typically I arrive at Shrivenham the night before and dine with army brigadiers, wing commanders and naval commodores. The next morning I share a platform, and twice now it's been with Lord Deedes, the retired editor of the *Daily Telegraph*.

He warms things up nicely as he tells the brass, assembled from sixty different countries, about the virtues of fox hunting! 'You see, it gives a young man an eye for country,' he says, 'and if you're going to run a tank through a battlefield, you need to develop a good eye for country.'

My job is to follow that! 'Ladies and Gentlemen,' I begin diffidently. 'I am the sort of person you're more likely to meet on the other side of one of your fences at Faslane – or, if you are very unlucky, perhaps through a hole in one of your fences!' The place erupts with laughter and a buzz comes into the air. You can palpably feel the metaphorical 'tally ho!' as 400 uniformed riders surge forwards after their darting pacifist quarry.

Officially my brief is to speak about 'the influence of non-governmental organisations on government'. I'm here to share case studies of campaigning, such as Scottish land reform and the anti-corporate battle that stopped the Harris super-quarry. But really, I've come to talk about what's deep behind the lines on that long front that is about peacemaking in a world of fractured social and ecological justice.

'You're here to make us think,' says the Course Director. 'We're all here because we want peace. Our men and women seek peace just as deeply as you do. The challenge is how you achieve it.' Well, just as the Countryside Alliance maintains that the fox only survives because the farmer gives it cover, so many of the military think that pacifism only thrives under the protection of their nuclear umbrella.

Yet time and time again I get told, 'We *need* people like you to remind us of the limits.' And that's what makes this exchange so interesting. You wouldn't think the military would care much about what peace campaigners think, but many do. Their implicit objective is to emerge from the chase reassured that, even if they are 'sinners', they are 'justified' ones.

My objective is to show that non-violence is a force for change that engages effectively with power but has nothing in common with cowardice. I reciprocally let them challenge my comfort zones, conceding that, yes, it is just possible that we are all occupying different posts on a long front that's about peace. It's just possible that without their nuclear umbrella, the freedom to challenge their ethics would never even have arisen.

Who knows, maybe in the deep and mysterious working of things, the world needs both: the fighters and those who are totally committed to non-violence. Maybe there's a more complex interplay between war and peace than meets the eye. When on occasion a soldier comes up afterwards and asks if I think they should leave the forces, I recount what George Fox told fellow Quaker William Penn. Penn was vexed as to whether he should continue wearing a sword. Fox counselled, 'Wear it as long as thou canst.'

'When we first joined the services it was simple,' many an officer has told me. 'The Russians were over there, we were over here, and it was our job to keep it that way. Nowadays it's often less clear what we might be fighting for. That is why we're open to people like you.'

One cannot fail to be touched and impressed. These are people of dignity and integrity. Yes, in the heat of war, decent people can do terrible things. But the thrill

of 'having a go' is not, quite emphatically, not, why ninety percent of them are here.

As rapport builds and my presentation draws to a close, the missiles start raining in. It's a kind of friendly fire, but the metaphorical fox has to twist and turn on his wits' edge.

'So, what would you do about weapons inspections?' asks a senior military policeman.

'Set them to work first at Faslane – our own nuclear submarine base.'

'And Saddam?' demands an army major.

'A "monster", of our own making,' I suggest, adding, 'but where were you when the West armed him and he gassed his own people? What were you doing when people like me were writing our Amnesty International letters to Number 10 and getting fobbed off?'

'And what would you do if somebody attacked your home?' enquires a Kuwaiti naval officer.

'I've been there,' I'm able to say. 'They cleaned the house out while holding a knife to a friend sleeping downstairs with our children. If we'd kept a revolver, as did many expatriates, she'd likely have got her throat slit.'

'What about rape?' asks a pilot.

And so I tell a real-life non-violence story. It was 1995, and I was living in a beautiful but violent Third World country. I was close to the family of an Australian professor at the university – fellow Quakers. One night his seventeen-year-old daughter found her car surrounded. Fourteen young men from the nearby squatter settlement abducted and gang raped her.

Normally the police would have sorted it out in eye-for-eye fashion. They'd have trashed the squatter camp and beaten folk up. Not so on this occasion. The daughter trenchantly asked her father to find a way that might 'touch their hearts'. Rape can only happen in the absence of empathy. The capacity to feel has to be restored if the cycle of abuse is to be broken.

The family asked the chief of police that there be no retaliation. The father and I then walked into the squatter settlement and requested a meeting with its leaders. They said they were really sorry about what had happened. It was hard to control their young men who had become embittered by poverty and hopelessness. They were relieved not to have been roughed up.

We said that the girl wanted softening and not a hardening of hearts. She wanted whatever, in their culture, would be an appropriate ceremony of confession and reconciliation.

So it was that we subsequently stood at the university gates as the entire squatter community turned out to apologise amidst much bearing of token gifts and beating of drums. Fourteen young men headed the procession. Many had tears in their eyes. They had not expected such humanity.

You just knew that, whilst the re-offending rate might not be zero, it would be very much less than had they been treated in kind. Hearts had indeed been touched. It also suggests a very important contrast between violence and non-violence. They operate on different timescales. The logic of violence only makes any sense in the short run. Non-violence, however, is a long-term and big-picture approach.

Some of the military just shrug off this sort of story. 'I admire your courage,' they'll say, 'but very frankly, I think you're mad. Maybe in heaven, but it's just not a realistic way to face the world.'

Others see that non-violence is actually a different way of engaging with power. It's about the love of power yielding to the power of love. It's ultimately about preferring to die than to kill. It's about saying, yes, you have a right proportionately to retaliate in self-defence, but also, you have the option of renouncing that right. We're talking here about a power that may be greater than coercive force or the psychology of fear. We're talking about the psychology of convincement. We're talking, even, about the spirituality of transformation.

In my experience, and I've now addressed in total some 4,000 senior officers, the military can and do respect this. They can't relate to cowards, but they do have time for those who, like any true warrior, will look death in the jaws. They too know that any fool can live in conflict but it takes guts to live in peace.

I conclude by emphasising that the similarity between us is a mutual willingness to die for our beliefs. The difference, however, is whether we will also kill for them.

In my line of work as a writer and activist for social and environmental justice, I've several times faced people who have threatened to kill me. It has been my experience that if you seriously renounce the option of violence and don't even prepare for it, then a whole new range of tactics can come into play.

The truth is that there's nothing more disconcerting when trying to pick a fight than being told, 'Well, you can hit me if you must, but I won't strike you back.' It kind of puts the rationale of violence on to a wobbly. Violence, it is true, only understands violence, and it gets confused and has to think twice when faced with the opposite.

I remember once, sitting in Iona Abbey at the Tuesday night healing service. Mindful of all the spiritual abuse that's gone on in the name of religion, and dubious of the hocus-pocus that can surround 'healing', I sat diffidently at the back. Nearby were two men, big guys: one, a white Glaswegian; the other, a black American.

During the first hymn, the Glaswegian started singing loudly and erratically. When silence fell, he took the opportunity to hurl obscenities, including some pretty spot-on abuse about the hypocrisy of the institutional Church. His embarrassed American friend drew him outside. I followed them, conscious that the disturbed guy had maybe come to the healing service because of mental illness. I

went up and said, 'Look, if you've come for healing, go back in. There's people in there who'd help you.'

'And who the fuck do you think you are?' he said, spitting the words in anger and agitation as he measured me up. Within minutes, he was challenging me to fight, shadow-boxing within a shave of my face to try to provoke an instinctual response. He threatened to kill me and it really felt like he meant it: he seemed crazy and strong enough to succeed.

I managed to stand my ground. I told him he could strike if he wished, but I was not going to reciprocate. I'd been bloodied like this before and could be so again. At this point, something very strange happened in my consciousness. I was pretty scared and increasingly out of my depth. But suddenly, it was as if a wonderful force-field had swept down quite literally from the stars. It was like some great scooping hand, and it was holding me now in a state of perfect transcendental calm.

I had an utter conviction that 'all shall be well, and all manner of thing shall be well', no matter whether he attacked me or not. Had I been struck, I do not think I would have felt the blow in a normal way, at least, not right then. The answer that non-violence offers to violence is not retaliation in kind, but the taking-on of suffering. However, as evidence from contexts like South Africa's Truth and Reconciliation Commission suggests, that suffering may, sometimes, carry a transcendental reconciling property.

Later on, my would-be assailant ended up

munching toast with Helen Steven, the Iona Community's Justice and Peace Worker, and playing Bach far into the night on the Abbey piano. The next day he told her he had 'never known such love', and had decided to join the Church.

'And do you know who that was, Alastair?' Helen asked me. 'It was R.D. Laing, the great but crazy psychotherapist!' Sure enough, an obituary in *The Guardian* of 8th January 1990 reported, 'There is disagreement over Laing's religious beliefs, and a clergyman at his funeral claimed that he joined the Church in his last four years, which rather surprised his relatives.'

I'm certainly not suggesting that joining the institutional Church is the necessary objective of non-violence! Neither am I suggesting that my role that night was more than a small part in a larger process, in which others like Helen played a much more conclusive role. What I do suggest, however, is that non-violence can open the doors to experience and powers not normally of this world. There is a path here that we discard at our peril.

I should add, too, that in retrospect, I had probably been in no real danger. It was just a real-life psychodrama such as Ronnie Laing, of *The Divided Self* and *Knots* fame, was adept at creating. Given his phenomenal psychological knowledge, he proba-bly did a pretty good job at making it more scary than the real thing! Whatever, the experience certainly felt like a testing and it left me with something precious.

It showed, and it has not for me been a unique event in this respect, that Mahatma Gandhi was right when he said that non-violence is an active and not a passive force. Gandhi said that *satyāgraha*, as he called it, or 'truth force', is nothing less than the sword of divine love. Non-violence, then, is about seeing ourselves in true relation to the whole, to the rest of life with which we are interconnected. If violence is the absence of love, non-violence is about the presence of relationship. It is the means of connection with that which gives life.

That is why it's hard to explain in prosaic language why non-violence matters and from where it derives its power. It's why many of those who argue for peace have difficulty in completing their arguments. The argument starts in this world, but doesn't end there. The suffering that we voluntary take on is a birth pang, and you have to trust to life beyond life to get to full delivery. You have to remember that the greater part of our being can never be killed, and that God is always on the side of the suffering.

Like Jesus on his cross; like Gandhi, wounded by a bullet, many will lose their physical lives through non-violence. In this the risks are the same as using violence. But equally, there's mounting evidence that non-violence can be effective. Consider India's independence struggle, the Philippines' revolution, the liberation of several former Eastern-bloc countries and South Africa's Truth and Reconciliation Commission. All these demonstrate non-violence as a credible force in the face of tyranny.

Finally, back to the fox hunt. How ought we have dealt with Iraq? We should have refused to appease death, and insisted only on actions that gave life. Saddam would have gone the same way as other once-implacable dictators like Marcos and Ceausescu. Yes, it would have meant massive suffering. But it would have avoided, as John Major warned, sowing the seeds of an ongoing Armageddon.

Alastair McIntosh

Lord Deedes passed away at the age of 94 as this book was going to press.

INTERFAITH

Across barriers created by religion

There is a Sufi story about four travellers – a Persian, a Turk, an Arab and a Greek – arguing about how they should spend a single coin they possessed amongst themselves. The Persian suggested buying *angur*, the Turk wanted *uzum*, the Arab wanted *inab*, while the Greek suggested buying *stafil*. Another traveller, who was a linguist, asked them to give him the coin and promised to satisfy the desires of all of them. When he was given the coin, he bought grapes, which the Persian recognised as *angur*, the Turk as *uzum*, the Arab as *inab,* and the Greek as *stafil*.

In *The Sufis,* Idries Shah points out that the grape is the raw form of the wine, while wine is the essence of that fruit – the linguist shows the travellers that the basis of all religions is the same. He does not impart the 'wine' or essence, 'which is the inner doctrine waiting to be produced and used in mysticism'. [5]

St Paul says that he has only received partial revelation, and only 'sees through a glass darkly'. We have only partial understanding of that partial revelation. It is presumptuous of followers of one religion to claim that theirs is the only way to approach and revere the Divine. We may see the action of the Holy Spirit at work in and through those who practise other religious beliefs, and, hopefully, they will see the Spirit at work in us as we travel our faith journey.

In *Open Christianity*, Jim Burklo writes: 'There is a big difference between respectful politeness and an open-hearted, open-minded approach to people of other religious beliefs. There is a profound contradiction in claiming to have faith in a God who is greater than our ability to fully comprehend, and at the same time claiming that traditional Christianity is the only true faith in that God … We are called to worship God, not Christianity. What is divine is our encounter with God, something that is available to Christians and non-Christians alike.'[6]

God's love for all people was revealed through, and by, Jesus Christ. Jesus reaches out across barriers created by religion (Jesus and the Samaritan woman at the well, John 4:7–26); we can be his true disciples by doing the same. As Christians, we are called to share God's love by loving our neighbour. We cannot do this unless we are willing to build bridges to aid understanding and appreciation of people of different beliefs. This is a collaborative and cooperative activity which is reliant on mutual respect. In interfaith dialogue we affirm hope and seek to build a society based on justice and peace. Let us leave the task of judging others to God: the Creator God who created man and woman in His own image and saw that it was good.

Sharing of faiths prayer

Almighty, ever-living God, Lord of the universe and Lord of our lives, we praise You. You have created us to be Your people, drawn from all the rich variety of the world's families and the world's faiths.

We confess that we are prisoners of prejudice, bound by the chains of yesterday's wrongs and tomorrow's fears. We pray that You will forgive the wrong that we have done and set us free from our fear of one another, free to celebrate our beliefs and our liberty as one universal family under God.

Andrew Sarle, Inter Faith Education Officer, Churches' Agency for Inter Faith Relations in Scotland (CAIRS)

COMMITMENT

Invitation to the great adventure: A meditation

Read *John 21* and use your imagination to picture those disciples on that early morning – tired and hungry, dispirited and discouraged from a hard night's labour with no results … And then use your imagination to see a stranger on the shore. See the surprise on the disciples' faces as they make that amazing catch, and then the joy, as recognition dawns and they know it is Jesus.

Listen to Jesus's words of invitation: 'Come and have breakfast.' The charcoal was glowing and the smell of fish was enticing – an invitation to much more than breakfast for these tired, dispirited men. What is Jesus offering?

This is the last recorded time that Jesus invited the disciples to 'Come'. But remind yourself of other occasions when Jesus invited those around him to 'Come' …

The most famous invitation of all, 'Come, follow me' (*Matthew 4:19*), were words that changed the course of the lives of all who responded. 'Come, follow me.' Ponder how you have responded to that invitation in the past and what it means to listen to it today.

Following may also imply a cross to be carried (*Matthew 16:24*). Are you aware of carrying a weight at this time? Offer your faithfulness to Jesus, and ask for help with anything which is a burden.

'Come and see' (*John 1:39*) – the invitation offered to two of John's disciples when they approached Jesus. It is an invitation to intimacy – an invitation to come closer and get to know him. What time and space do you give to cultivating this intimacy?

'Come … and Peter stepped from the boat' (*Matthew 14:29*). How often have you been in and out of the boat with Peter? Jesus says, 'Come' – leave your boat, your safety, your security; don't look at the depths of the waves – walk on water. How has this been an element of your discipleship?

Not all of Jesus's invitations are as daunting. He invites us to come to him in our need and receive from him. Hear Jesus say, 'Come to me all you who are weary and burdened and I will give you rest' (*Matthew 11:28–30*).

So hear that word addressed to you: 'Come.'

What is Jesus asking of you and offering you in that word today?

Prayer

Lord, you hold out your hands to me, beckoning in love. Help me to accept what you offer and to respond to your call.

Lynda Wright, Tabor Retreat Centre, Key House, Falkland, Fife

THE REDISCOVERY OF SPIRITUALITY

Life in all its fullness

'Leave the beaten path to find happiness. Take your mind over uncharted terrain – it might just change your life for ever.'

Just the advice I needed in the newspaper yesterday morning. In the bookshops, too, the shelves are full in the 'Body, Mind and Spirit' sections. The whole area of self-improvement, personal growth, health and well-being – and, of course, diet – has become an industry in itself; people are queueing up to join gyms and health clubs.

And the politicians are at it too. We are promised policies that will increase everyone's prosperity – although more than likely we shall not read the small print that tells us that that really means that the rich will get richer and the poor will be left as far behind as ever. A recent book by a leading economist asks why, although average incomes have doubled, people are no happier than they were fifty years ago, and argues that happiness should be at the heart of public policy.

Of course we all know that you cannot buy real happiness – it does not come automatically with material prosperity. And the harder you try to be happy the more difficult it is to achieve. In the Bible we find Jesus talking of fullness of life – the kind of joy and deep inner contentment that comes from living a life that seeks to be generous, faithful, compassionate, just and self-giving. Centuries ago St Augustine wisely said that 'our hearts are restless until they find their rest in

God'. How can we but be restless in a world that is so full of suffering and need, conflict and injustice? Somehow it is in caring and striving to change things for the better that happiness and contentment are to be found. And some of the happiest people I know are those who have come through sorrow to know grace and joy and to give thanks for all the good things of life. I find this wisdom much more healthy and helpful than all that the latest lifestyle gurus have to say.

Norman Shanks

THE THIRTY-FIRST DAY

The desert of that single room

I believe it is vital that carers have their own place of security and strength from which to launch into the desert and to return to for their own strengthening and inner renewal … It is scary going into the desert to experience some of the 'lost-ness' of the forlorn traveller. We need a place of safety to which we can return. But it is taking the risk of abandoning our security and entering into the desert for a while that makes spiritual care a reality. So, in order to accompany the lost and dislocated traveller, there has to be a commitment to listen and not to offer instant solutions; to hear the cries of anguish and not to judge or condemn; and to be aware of the struggle for direction and purpose, and to wait with patience until it is time to move on.

I recall Sam and his family. Sam was in a single room in our Centre and, while I knew him a little, I had never met his wife and two children, as they always seemed to have been around when I wasn't. Sam had taken a turn for the worse, and his wife, son and daughter had been called in during the night. When I came in the following morning, they were sitting quietly by Sam's bed. His wife had red eyes. His daughter was sobbing. His son was staring blankly out of the window. They were dignified and caring, but obviously distraught. I knew all of this because I could see them through the open door of the room as I walked by. And having seen the distress, I did the only thing I felt I could do – I went to our coffee-room for a cup of tea!

I did not want to enter that room, so I walked right past it many times that morning. I was simply frightened to go in because I had nothing to say. I ratio-nalised it by telling myself I did not want to intrude on the privacy of a family or that I had other pressing things to do. In actual fact, I ducked it because I felt so useless. I had nothing to offer. The nurses were superb. They couldn't duck it. They were in and out, doing what they do extraordinarily well. But it wasn't for me.

Eventually I realised this could not go on. There was that little voice in my head asking me how I could live with myself if I did nothing. So, later in the day, I took a big deep breath and in I went. I said hello. I put a hand on a shoulder. I said I wished I could say something really clever, but I wasn't going to try. But I assured them we were around when we were needed. I was there for five minutes or so. I did that a few times that day. Each time I felt awkward. I felt I had achieved nothing, only the satisfaction that I could go home knowing that I had not ducked it altogether.

Sam died that night. The following morning when the family returned to collect the death certificate and Sam's belongings, his wife asked to see me. She asked me to conduct Sam's funeral service. I agreed to do so, and we arranged to meet the following day to go over the details. As she was leaving, she held my hand and said thank you for my support – and specifically for my help the previous day. I mumbled something about not giving very much. And she said, 'But you did. You came into our room, and I know how hard that must have been for you.'

I was floored! But, you see, whatever had happened, a family had known that the chaplain, with all his inadequacy and tearfulness, had met them in the desert of that single room, and they took more peace and comfort from that than I could ever have realised. They genuinely felt that along with all their practical needs their spiritual needs had been cared for too – simply because the threshold had been crossed.

Tom Gordon

MONTH 3

NEW WAYS TO TOUCH THE HEARTS OF ALL

Bridging the Gap

For over ten years now, Molly and I have been worshipping as part of the little Church of Scotland congregation in Gorbals in Glasgow. This has been very much a return to our roots. When we married in 1963, we joined the Gorbals Group Ministry, a ground-breaking approach to Christian presence in what was then a decaying inner-city slum. We lived and worked there, as part of the Group, for eight years; three of our four children were born there; and for the last three years of our stay, I served as minister of the local parish church.

But most of our time was involved with the children of Gorbals; in playgroup and nursery school and holiday scheme and youth club and football team, using our home, an abandoned school, an old upstairs warehouse, and, more often than not, simply the streets.

Now, forty years later, I have found myself involved again with Gorbals' children, in the ecumenical project there, 'Bridging the Gap'.

Bridging the Gap was the initiative of Iona Community member Ian Galloway, the present parish minister, and Brian McGrath, who was the local parish priest at the time. In 1998, they got together, determined to give practical expression to their common desire to show a united Christian face to the emerging 'new Gorbals'.

Initially, they began by enabling joint working in the local schools. The Local Authority had closed all the secondary schools in the area, leaving three small primary schools and a special school behind. In the chaos of the new situation, the local children were therefore also having to cope with leaving their own area to go to secondary school; and Ian and Brian saw the importance of seeking to support them, as together the children faced an uncertain future.

Two part-time workers, Christine Carson and Lyn Ma, were the first staff members of Bridging the Gap. Working from a cupboard (literally!) in the Catholic church hall, and from home, they pioneered innovative work, in the arts and with music, bringing the children together across the denominational boundaries for festivals and special events – and drawing in, naturally, their parents and grandparents as well. Their work very quickly attracted attention outwith Gorbals – indeed, the Church and Nation Committee of the Church of Scotland praised it as 'a model of anti-sectarian practice for the Church to follow'.

Within a few years, the work of Bridging the Gap began to expand. What happened first was that Lyn introduced a Peer Tutoring project, which she had borrowed from inner-city Chicago, and from Tower Hamlets in London. This project – which now has two full-time workers, involves five schools, has an annual budget of nearly £90,000, and is managed in part by a locally formed Youth Steering Group – was an immediate success. Each year, some 35 fourth-year pupils from the two secondary schools – some of whom are in danger of dropping out – are trained by the Bridging the

Gap staff to tutor – or mentor – some 35 primary school pupils in P7, about to move up to the 'big school' – some of whom are in danger of not making the transition very successfully. The latest development, for which new funding has been found, is for the staff to work with previous tutors, who have wanted to maintain their involvement with Bridging the Gap – training and supporting them in volunteering, and in preparation for entering the world of work.

The other side of Bridging the Gap is the work with the local asylum-seeker and refugee community. Since 2000, when the Home Office and Glasgow City Council made an agreement whereby thousands of asylum-seekers were dispersed to Glasgow from the South of England, Bridging the Gap has been the body nominated by the local Community Forum to welcome those who come to Gorbals, and to support them during their stay. This has meant a further increase in the staff complement and of course in funding, some of which has been coming from the Scottish Executive. Bridging the Gap offers daily support and case work, training sessions, English classes and a weekly drop-in. Three part-time workers and twenty volunteers undertake the hard work of accompanying sometimes quite traumatised families and individuals as they try to negotiate the complexities of the UK's asylum system.

Bridging the Gap is of course one amongst a number of voluntary bodies working in this part of Glasgow – and we network with many of them. But it still sees itself as an expression of the ecumenical outreach of the whole Christian community in Gorbals; in the Iona Community's terms, another expression of our continuing commitment to try to find 'new ways to touch the hearts of all'.

John Harvey

John Harvey was Chairman of the Management Committee of Bridging the Gap from 2003 to 2006.

Prayer of the Iona Community

O God, who gave to your servant Columba
the gifts of courage, faith and cheerfulness,
and sent people forth from Iona
to carry the word of your gospel to every creature:
grant, we pray, a like spirit to your church,
even at this present time.
Further in all things the purpose of our community,
that hidden things may be revealed to us,
and new ways found to touch the hearts of all.
May we preserve with each other
sincere charity and peace,
and, if it be your will,
grant that this place of your abiding be continued still
to be a sanctuary and a light.
Through Jesus Christ.
Amen

From *Iona Abbey Worship Book*

ECONOMIC WITNESS

Part of the five-fold Rule of the Iona Community calls members to 'sharing and accounting for the use of our money'.

On accounting for the use of money

My parents belonged to the generation that lost everything
twice in their lives.
They brought me up on generosity,
but there was never a spare penny in our house
that could be lost
to yet another bankrupt dictator.
I learned to share freely but I
did not learn saving.
I find it difficult to make lists of what I earn
and what I need,
what I spend and what I share.
I live from hand to mouth, I'm in the red every so often,
and sometimes
I don't know whether or not I am squandering my money.
(Shouldn't I know?)
Yes, it is useful to make lists
and tell each other
what we earn, and need and give away.
And why!

Reinhild Traitler

Economic discipline

The discipline bit for me
is doing the arithmetic.
I am 'dyslexic' with numbers.
The posh word for it is dyscalculia,
but basically
I struggle with sums.

And then, there are the questions.
What counts as necessary to life?:
Good food? Broadband? Keeping warm in winter?
And what about air miles relating to food,
my used time in ratio to the speed of my computer,
and should I install a fuel-efficient boiler this year?
Plus, the biggies:
Can I justify hanging on to my capital?
And is it OK to retire next year at sixty?

Nobody can sort this lot out on their own;
that's why we belong in community.

Ruth Burgess

YOUTH CONCERN

Joe (a poem from Camas)

Originally quarry-workers' cottages, then a salmon-fishing station, the Camas Centre on the Isle of Mull is run by a staff group with specialist skills, helped by several volunteers. Young people from the city and elsewhere, and other groups too, come to Camas for an adventure holiday with outdoor opportunities for canoeing, walking, swimming and camping, a visit to Iona, and the experience of exploring issues, building relationships, and facing new challenges through living and working in community.

Rachel McCann, a former Camas Coordinator, writes: 'Camas is a place of encounter and exchange where walls are broken down and we discover ourselves in the other. Certainly Joe brought some beautiful moments and found a sense of place at Camas:

Joe

Lights flicker in the bay,
always the same,
always in change.
Joe meets me,
the same wide grin on his face,
only this time his hands are softer,
his hug more tender,
and the scars are healing.
He has a new home now, he announces – his home.
Pride guides me around the kitchen:
cupboards full of food, and plans to decorate.

He says he never meant to scare me
the first time we met when
he waved a big knife.
I laugh and tell him
I knew from the off he was a teddy bear.

Rachel McCann

Month 3 Day 3

THE WORD

'The Human One'

… During a bible-study role play on Iona, I came to experience something profoundly revealing about the power which Jesus had, which has remained with me ever since as a challenge and an inspiration.

The passage which we were studying was from Matthew's Gospel, the story of the paralysed man being lowered through the roof by his friends for Jesus to heal. We were a large group of about 40 people, and we began by reading the passage through carefully. We were then offered a choice of groups – a disciples group, the man's friends, a group of 'paralysed people', a Pharisees group, onlookers, and a Jesus group. We were encouraged to pick the group that most interested us. I found myself in the Jesus group. Each group was then given a short task to help us into our roles. The paralysed people just lay on the floor; the Pharisees were given various legal passages of scripture to study; the Jesus group that I was in was asked to think quickly about what our message to the crowd was going to be.

After we had done this we were given some questions about our characters, and were asked specifically to use our imaginations to think about how we were feeling at the time, still in our role as Jesus. My imaginings really surprised me. I found myself thinking that I was young, a bit of a country lad, speaking in a broad local dialect, inexperienced, not at all sure of my authority, and, yes, frightened. Totally real, totally human feelings. And yet completely at odds with all I had previously believed about Jesus as 'Son of God', somehow special, untouched by everyday worries, going through life knowing it would be 'all right in the end'. Here suddenly was a human being, a frightened, fallible person, just like me. It bowled me over!

Almost immediately in the role play we were given our next task, which was to go over to the Pharisees group and ask them in what way we were causing them offence. By this time we were so afraid that we drew straws for the task, and I was one of two detailed to go. It was like stirring up a hornets' nest! We were bombarded with legalistic jargon about why we should not be healing the man, and we were repeatedly asked the very question we weren't sure about: 'On what authority can you do these things?'

We suddenly found ourselves blazingly angry that such legalism could prevent an act of mercy, and we both found ourselves quoting passages of Micah and Amos we had forgotten we ever knew. It was a gloriously liberating experience of holy rage.

As we gathered together to make peace with each other and reflect on what we had learned, I felt as if I had received a profoundly exciting revelation – one which I am still processing today.

Firstly I learned that Jesus was as fully human as I am, subject to all the same joys, fears, triumphs and limitations. In fact Jesus was often described as the 'Son of Man', and I had always given this title a somewhat exalted, mystical meaning. But it can be quite simply translated as 'the Human One' or 'everyman'.

But if this Human One, who was like me, was also endowed with special power – was also the Son of God – then by extension I too am a Daughter of God, also able to lay hold of that special power. For a few moments I had experienced a power and outrage beyond myself, and this showed that that special power which Jesus had is also available to me. This is the power

that inspired the prophets, Gandhi, Martin Luther King, Rosa Parks, Dorothy Day – and me. It was an extraordinarily exciting discovery.

I went back to the Gospels and read them through again in the light of this discovery, and I found many passages where Jesus seemed to be emphasising this very message to his listeners. He said things like 'The kingdom of God is *within you*' (Luke 17:21), or 'Greater things shall you do' (John 14:12); he sent the disciples out in pairs in the full expectation that they could carry out his mission just as effectively as he could.

Then I began to reflect on the word 'Messiah'. Messiah means the 'anointed one', and there is a very real sense in which we are all anointed with the Spirit to do the work of the kingdom. 'You are the One we have all been waiting for.'

This was exciting stuff, and as I tried to explain it to people, just as I am doing here, I discovered the inadequacies of language to express deep spiritual experience. Some friends would say to me, 'Oh, so you've been born again', or 'You've taken the Lord Jesus Christ as your saviour and lord', and I would react vehemently, 'Oh, no, nothing like that.' And yet how do I really know what others mean when they use these words, or how do I put my feelings into words?

It sounds supremely arrogant and even blasphemous to say that I can experience the same kind of power as Jesus, and of course it was precisely this very question of authority and source of power that constituted the offence of Jesus to the religious leaders of his time. Such claims led him directly into conflict with church and state.

And this is the sting in the tail. Just as, in the role play, I felt fear when going to speak with the Pharisees, so now it came to me with blinding clarity that claiming this power and letting it drive where it must, leads straight into trouble. As Douglas Steere once said, 'A Christian should be without fear, happy and always in trouble'!

Helen Steven

HOSPITALITY AND WELCOME

Beyond the barriers

In September I had a phone call from Ghana telling me that my friend Kofi Anafo had died in hospital after injuries sustained in a car accident. We had kept in touch with Kofi for over 35 years and had tried to help him occasionally when he was out of work. He was the keenest member of my youth football team in 1971 and, since he lived next door working as a cook for an Italian engineer, he came to a Ghanaian 'outdooring' ceremony in our house when our daughter was born. It was a custom for guests on these occasions to give money to help support the new child. But for us, as comparatively 'rich' missionaries, to receive money from a poor young lad seemed ridiculous, even immoral. I squirmed as the collection bowl was passed round and Kofi put several hard-earned *cedis* in it. I thanked him with an embarrassment which clearly showed a bad conscience. I had yet to learn the difficult lesson of receiving from the poor and being enriched by the generosity of those who appear to have so little.

Another Ghanaian friend was entertaining two African-American teachers from New York. Kwabena, himself a teacher, offered local food in his home, which had equally local bathroom and toilet facilities. The Americans found it impossible to resist the hygienically safer facilities of the local international hotel and later asked me to explain why my friend was deeply offended and upset. Kwabena told me that he thought they were snobbish and fastidious, but in reality they hadn't been able to cope with the juggling involved in making authentic connections across cultures. They were uncomfortable at the lack of privacy and personal space, something cherished in an individualistic society. To accept what is on offer can be a health risk

(I once saw maggots towing the cheese from which I had eaten in an Egyptian village!) but it is a huge risk to the dignity and self-esteem of others not to find ways of sharing what is provided. Many of us feel more comfortable when simple fare or token gifts are presented. But when those with little means go to excess it is an affirmation of their love and respect. Enthusiastic and understanding acceptance will cement friendships and enable the barriers to come down in a dignified way.

Jesus taught that 'it is more blessed to give than to receive' but his life of service was also about receiving – a meal from Simon the Pharisee and a tomb from Joseph of Arimathea, water from an unnamed Samaritan woman, loaves and fishes from a young peddler, rest in Peter's boat, excessively costly ointment from Mary of the streets, help with the Cross from African Simon, and fussing over from the Bethany sisters. Many a time he must have had reservations and the gospel accounts record his sacrifice of privacy. But he found fulfilment in simple friendship offered and received beyond the barriers of gender, race, income disparity and social acceptance. And it was in accepting an evening meal with strangers in a village near Jerusalem that he became real to them in the sharing of bread.

Prayer

Generous giver of the earth and its people, enable us to be generous towards others in our use of resources and our offering of hospitality, but help us to be equally generous in our acceptance and appreciation of what others have to offer. Give us the enjoyment of true sharing and the fulfilment of friendship that values the gifts of the other. So may we know together true companionship across cultures when we break bread together.

Iain Whyte

Month 3 Day 5

THIS IS THE DAY

Sometimes we need help
to walk more slowly
to feel what it is like to have a wondering, wandering child
hanging on to our hand
hanging back.
It is not easy to listen to someone
to hear the story of our companion
when they have to run to catch up.

When the child within us
points to the old man selling poems
or stares with wet eyes at the weeping homeless woman
or sways to the solitary melody of a saxophone outdoors
let us forget our destination
for a moment.

Emily Walker

THE IONA EXPERIENCE

How will I find you?

Lord, on this sacred and beautiful isle, it seems so easy to find You.
But how will I find You when I am gone from here, back to my world?
How will I find You
when the children plague me?
When work seems hard, mechanical, soulless?
How will I find You
when tiredness and opposition
smother my resolves?
How will I find You
when sin and oppression stifle my spirit?

Child – dear, most beloved – do you still not understand?
You will find me because I am with you;
we are together;
my life entwines in yours.
Your world *is* my world.

Open your eyes;
open your ears;
open your heart.
I am with you always!

Pat Bennett

A blessing for an Iona pilgrim

May you have the integrity of the high cross
  – weathered wisdom reflecting a sacred connection.
May you have the ability of the ferry
  – to ride the currents and waves of life, yet also to know one's limits
    and when to cancel.
May you have the freedom of the nunnery
  – bringing forth life in unexpected places and open to the world
    and all that life brings.
May you have the character of the Sound
  – embracing the ever-changing light and transforming it into inner beauty.
May you have the presence of the Burg
  – strong and grounded.
May you have the peace of the cloisters
  – open, yet contained
  – enfolding and embracing.

Rowena Aberdeen–de Voil, a member of the Resident group on Iona

LIFE IN COMMUNITY

Home to the heart of God

They know not what they do,
nor do we,
in our search
for comfort
while millions can't find bread.

They know not what they do,
nor do we,
in our obstinacy
to change direction
as the planet cries in pain.

They know not what they do,
nor do we,
in our conviction
that bombs will defend us,
and that violence will triumph.

They know not what they do,
nor do we,
as we pray that God will bless
our addiction to possess,
while kids eat from garbage dumps.

They knew not what they did,
but you
you knew
and transformed them,
by offering
a gift without price
in the moments of your dying.

It's known as 'forgiveness'
and, in an instant, it
brought them home
to the heart of God.

And that word
is still on offer
in our confused times,
but we,
perhaps,
are unwilling
to be transformed.

Peter Millar, Good Friday, 2007

Prayer

O Jesus, you weren't only crucified 2000 years ago.
You are being crucified today –
here and now …

We pray for those who are being crucified here and now:

We pray for those being crucified by poverty:
in Sudan, in Easterhouse in Glasgow …
For victims of capitalism and other powers;
for those struggling under the burden of unfair debt and trade,
unfair debt and trade we profit by.

We pray for children being crucified.
Children working in sweatshops around the world.
Children who make the clothes we wear, who help to harvest the food we eat.

We pray for women being crucified.
Women working in the sex trade in London, in Bangkok …
Women who suffer abuse in our neighbourhoods
and in the neighbourhood of the world.
Women who suffer while we look away, deny, remain silent.

We pray for those being crucified by disease,
by AIDS, TB, malaria …
Diseases which might be cured if only we'd choose life;
if only, as a nation, we didn't spend 29.9 billion pounds every year on the military;
if only, as a world, we didn't spend over one trillion dollars U.S. a year on death.

We pray for those being crucified in jails around the world,
in Saudi Arabia, Indonesia, Guatemala, Guantanamo Bay …
in countries and by countries whose governments
our government is happy to do business with
and to call good friends.

Month 3 Day 8

And we pray for this good earth we stand on,
this precious, fragile planet
we pay mock homage,
give poisoned streams to drink,
bind with fences,
strip and beat and flog,
pierce with spears until the blood and water pours out.

Jesus Christ,
we confess our complicity in all these crucifixions,
and in others.
Forgive us, Lord, we know not what we do.
Or do we?

We give thanks for individuals and organisations working to bring healing and hope in your world:

Church Action on Poverty
Oxfam
Save the Children
Christian Aid
Médecins Sans Frontières
Amnesty International
Earth First!

We give thanks for their passion and commitment.

Spirit of love, help us to do all that we can to support them in their work;
help us to do more to ease suffering and to bring healing and hope,
in our neighbourhoods and in the neighbourhood of the world.

_____

Month 3 Day 8

Christ has no other hands but our hands:
No other hands but our hands
to do God's work in the world.

Christ has no love but our love:
No love but our love to share
with the imprisoned, the silenced,
the persecuted, the marginalised.

Amen

Neil Paynter, Biggar Kirk Stations of the Cross, Good Friday, 2006

WOMEN

Remembering Iona's sisters – the abbess's farewell

It is the end.
The last evening on Columcille's Isle,
before the sword, the killing comes.

We three, who alone remain of our ancient sisterhood,
will make ready our few possessions:
the Word of God,
the Cup of blessing,
our salves,
some food.

Then, shawl-clad,
in the wool from mountain sheep we've tended,
we'll row away from Iona of our hearts,
Iona of our love,
and in a far-off cave we'll sit,
and pray,
and think on what is to come.

Who will remember our sisterhood?
Shall we be minded on?
For eons our joys, our lives,

have been a living witness
to God's presence,
in the rocks and stones,
the wildness of the waves and winds,
the lonely hillsides.

As our Brothers followed Colum's hallowed memory,
and Adomnán's Rule,
we sisters,
faithful to the triune God of Wisdom, Love and Justice,
opened our doors to the orphaned child,
broken men
and homeless women.

We gave refuge to the wounded soldier fleeing battle,
to the violated girl whose child we'd love;
through tending plants we sought the earth's healing wisdom.

And all the time we listened,
listened to the heartbeat of God,
whose name is Justice.

And shall we be remembered?

It may be that the very stones enshrine our prayers,
our hopes,
our dreams.

It may be that when pilgrims come to Colum's blessed Isle,
they will stop,
and pause amid our ruined stones,
and know that veilèd sisters lived a ministry
faithful to God's little ones,
and faithful to this sacred earth.

And let them know that in the presence of the Triune three,
of Wisdom, Love and Justice,
our sisterhood prays on, dreams on, that pilgrims find peace.
My sisters, let us go.

Mary Grey, Iona Abbey, 1998

Mary Grey is a theologian and an author, formerly of the University of Wales, Lampeter and Sarum College, Salisbury, now at St Mary's University College, Twickenham. She is a friend of the Iona Community. In 1998 she led a week on Iona during which this poem was written, and read out at the Friday evening Communion service. The poem is still often read out during the weekly pilgrimage around Iona, in the ruins of the twelfth-century nunnery.

PRAYER

Using imagination

We can enter more fully into a gospel narrative by using imagination to bring it alive and to let it speak directly to us. The historical details of the story become unimportant as we let the Holy Spirit guide us in our imagination, lifting the story out of the pages of history, and making real an encounter today.

Here is a guided meditation based on the story of the feeding of the five thousand. Allow the Spirit to guide your imagination, that you too may be fed in the sharing of the bread.

A meditation on the story of the feeding of the five thousand

First become still and present to the Holy Spirit …

Let the scene take shape in your mind's eye. Don't worry about whether it is historically or geographically accurate: let your imagination create the scene for you.

Picture the Sea of Galilee – see the beauty, smell the air, listen to the sounds. When the scene becomes real to you (don't just picture it from a distance) be there in it yourself.

On the hillside you see Jesus sitting with his disciples. They are resting. They have been working hard, meeting the needs of the crowd; Jesus has healed the centurion's son and the lame man at the pool of Bethesda, and many others.

So they are enjoying these moments of peace, this space away from the crowds, but the quietness doesn't last long.

A large crowd is coming to find Jesus – the sick who want to be healed, those who want to listen to his stories and those who are simply curious. All sorts of people. As you look at them notice who is there.

Now join the crowd, become one of them. Allow to happen what will – why are you there?

What do you want of Jesus?

Notice the reaction of the disciples as they wonder where they will get bread to feed all these people.

Listen as Philip says: 'It will take more than 200 silver coins to feed these people.'

Watch Andrew as he draws a small boy from the crowd who is offering his five barley loaves and two fish.

Look at the loaves and look at the size of the crowd.

Hear Jesus tell everyone to sit down.

When everyone is settled, watch as he takes the loaves and blesses them.

Perhaps you can hear the words he says.

Now the bread is being passed around. What is the atmosphere in the crowd? Are people saying anything or are they silent?

What is their reaction as they take some of the bread?

Now it is your turn to share the bread.

Hold it in your hands – look, smell, taste …

How do you feel?

Listen as Jesus says to you: 'I am the Bread of Life.'

Lynda Wright, Tabor Retreat Centre, Key House, Falkland, Fife

JUSTICE AND PEACE

Breaking the chains: Making the links

He shall judge between many peoples and shall arbitrate between strong nations far away; they shall beat their swords into ploughshares, and their spears into pruning hooks; nation shall not lift up sword against nation, neither shall they learn war any more; but they shall all sit under their own vines and under their own fig trees, and no one shall make them afraid; for the mouth of the Lord of hosts has spoken.
Micah 4:3–4 (NRSV)

I have always loved these famous verses from the prophet Micah, but it is only very recently that I have realised that not only are they about making peace, but also show us the essential link between justice and peace; one a prerequisite for the other. When will the weapons of war be seen as an anachronism and turned into tools to build rather than to destroy? When all can sit without fear in a place in which they have a real stake; under their own vines and their own fig trees – in other words, when we move to a more just world; no longer one dominated by the rich and powerful controlling the land and lives of the poor majority. This is a vital connection between issues that it is easy to miss in our reading of this famous text.

As a campaigner I've been thinking a lot lately about connections. The oppressive networks of power and money that fuel wars and keep the poor in chains (economic and all too often literal). But also the positive connections between the seemingly disparate work of millions of justice and peace campaigners and grassroots activists around the world. The way that each small step of progress in one apparently discrete area of campaigning so often has much more far-reaching repercussions in the bigger struggle to build justice, make peace and protect the fabric of this beautiful planet than those involved in the hard work of that particular campaign ever realise.

When I first started to get involved in justice and peace issues in my late teens, I tended to see each issue in its discrete box. UK poverty. Poor-country debt. Nuclear weapons. The arms trade. Environmental destruction. Each an issue to be campaigned on, but each a separate issue. So much to do – so little time! Well, I still feel the pressure of time and the desire to do more, but I think I understand better now that the bit that I am able to do on one or two issues is part of a much bigger picture and complements, supports and enhances what others are able to do on the interrelated issues that I would like to get my teeth into if only there was time!

Most of the big justice, peace and environmental issues of our age focus around the unholy alliance of money and power. Behind the arms trade, behind trade injustice and the free trade movement, behind the resistance to tackling climate change, let alone acknowledging it, behind the scandal of the global AIDS lottery – behind all these are the transnational global companies: worth more in dollars than many countries' GDPs and with vastly more power than most of the governments whose strings they pull on the stage of global politics.

The impacts of the activities of powerful companies and countries are interlinked too. The arms trade not only kills poor people directly; it kills them through diverting money from healthcare and other essential services. Trade injustice not only keeps billions of people in absolute poverty but also fuels militarism in the rich countries determined to keep, by bullying and force of arms, that unjust advantage that they have stolen through centuries of violence and oppression.

This should not have come as a surprise to me in my journey of life and faith. Again and again the Bible makes connections between these big issues that have faced every society in history. The prophets emphasise repeatedly that justice to the most disadvantaged in their society (the widow, the orphan, the stranger and the foreigner) is a prerequisite to the peace that ancient Israel clearly yearned for but so seldom found, either within its own society or with its neighbours. Many of the psalms too make the connection explicit, for example Psalm 55:9–10: '… I see violence and strife in the city … Iniquity and trouble are within it … Oppression and fraud do not depart from its marketplace.' And Jesus himself in the Sermon on the Mount: 'Blessed are the poor … Blessed are the peacemakers … Blessed are you who are persecuted.'

This realisation of the interconnected chains of injustice and violence forged by those determined to keep power and wealth can feel very disempowering. I remember years ago sitting in a campaign meeting on global poverty issues at which we decided to write down our objectives. We started to list local things: raise awareness, get signatures on a petition, write letters, hold a meeting. But that's not really enough, we said. So then we started to write our wider ambitions: Get debt cancelled. Make trade fair. Reduce the power of multinationals. But what do we need to make that happen, we asked? We ended up writing 'the ending of global capitalism'. And then we felt hopeless. Well, we're not going to achieve that, are we?!

Now I think that we went about it the wrong way round. We should have started with the big picture. We should have recognised our awareness-raising and our petitions and our letters as one small but significant contribution to that picture: a tiny but essential piece of the jigsaw. That way we would have felt empowered and inspired to continue doing what we could in the place where we were, heartened that we were part of the activity of millions, all interlinked around the world to bring about the global change that we were longing for.

Recognising the links has given me real hope. I do believe a more just world is being built; incrementally through the millions of grassroots campaigns and community actions around the world. Whatever campaigning work each of us is involved in has a vital role to play. We need to realise that our small part is an important part of the process of transformation. And to believe and hope that one day those who come afterwards will see a very different big picture: a just world, a world of peace, a cherished creation: the Kingdom of God amongst us.

Helen Boothroyd

The world belongs to God,
THE EARTH AND ALL ITS PEOPLE

How good it is, how wonderful,
TO LIVE TOGETHER IN UNITY

Love and faith come together,
JUSTICE AND PEACE JOIN HANDS.

If Christ's disciples keep silent
THESE STONES WOULD SHOUT ALOUD.

Open our lips, O God,
AND OUR MOUTHS SHALL PROCLAIM YOUR PRAISE.

Responses from the Iona Community's morning service, *Iona Abbey Worship Book*

THE INTEGRITY OF CREATION

Alternative vision

'I struck you with burning and scorching, and withered your gardens and vineyards; the locusts devoured your fig trees and olives; and yet you never came back to me.' …

'Since you have trampled on the poor man, extorting levies on his wheat – those houses you have built of dressed stone, you will never live in them; and those precious vineyards you have planted, you will never drink their wine.'

Amos 4:9; 5:11 (Jerusalem Bible)

'Sir,' he said, 'I had heard you were a hard man, reaping where you have not sown and gathering where you have not scattered; so I was afraid, and I went off and hid your talent in the ground. Here it is; it was yours, you have it back.'

Matthew 25:24, 25 (Jerusalem Bible)

Radio broadcast, April 2106:

Breathless voice shouting over background of strong winds, roaring sea, taut sails snapping

'Today, on our weekly visit to different parts of the Scottish countryside, we've chartered a boat to take us on a tour around the historic isle of Iona, where the Irish monk St Columba is reputed to have landed in the year 563. The island was inhabited right up until the end of the 21st century: the last residents being evacuated after the great storm of Christmas, 2097. By then, the population on the island had been declining for centuries, although it did enjoy a peak of temporary visitors from the wealthiest parts of the world during the last decades of the oil age.

The area we are passing now is a large shallow cove, so for safety the boat is keeping well out from the shore. Fifty years ago, this was dry land, and was known as the Machair. It was used by islanders for cattle grazing and even for golf, and was known for its wealth of wild flowers. Now, since sea levels have risen, it has become shallow salt marsh, though parts of the Machair are still visible at very low tides.

As we reach the northern end of Iona, the highest point of the island, Dun I, is clearly visible, and the Isle of Mull is coming back into view. During the last twenty years of habitation Iona became increasingly remote from Mull as oil depletion reduced access. Residents had to rely on sail and rowing boats and even then could only land when the sea was calm enough.

As we sail back into the Sound of Iona, on the east side of the island between Iona and Mull, you can see the ruins of the 13th-century Benedictine abbey, which was rebuilt in the 20th century by George MacLeod and the pioneers of the Iona Community, but then destroyed in a storm in 2048. This storm effectively led to the closure of the Iona Community's operations on the island, although a vigil was kept by community members until the evacuation in 2097 …'

I wrote this after hearing a similar programme, which was followed by a familiar news item: It was reported that Sir David King, the British government's Chief Scientist, at a news conference, stated that, even by the most optimistic estimate, carbon dioxide levels are set to rise to double what they were at pre-industrial levels, which will lead to a three-degree centigrade rise in temperature. If this happens, few ecosystems will be able to adapt and up to 400 million people around the world will be at risk of hunger, as between 20 million to 400 million tonnes of cereal production would be lost. In Britain, the main threat would be flooding and 'coastal attack' from rising sea levels. Even if international agreement could be reached on limiting emissions, climate change is inevitable, he said. [7]

Such a radio broadcast will only be heard by the once-rich survivors. The effects of human-induced climate change are global, unpredictable and devastating, and are already affecting the poorest most. The G8 countries are cumulatively responsible for 60% of the emissions of carbon dioxide, the main greenhouse gas. To prevent climate change, carbon dioxide emissions need to be reduced to a global per capita level of one tenth of the current UK levels – i.e. a 90% cut. We can be forgiven for feeling helpless.

We do our bit. We drive less, buy locally, use energy-efficient household appliances. We bury our 'talents' because we feel bad about this exploitative system. Meanwhile, the exploiters flourish and the global logic of destruction continues. And we, a tiny minority, are the beneficiaries – and can't help it. Despite our intentions, we collude with, and benefit from, the corrupt, talent-multiplying system of the landowner. We are complicit in destroying the climate and we can see no way out, no way to reach the radically different society which is needed.

Walter Brueggemann writes that 'prophecy is born precisely in that moment when the emergence of social political reality is so radical and inexplicable that it has nothing less than a theological cause'. [8] The prophets Amos and Jesus were both living through a time of rapid (for its time) intensification of ecological resources, driven by, and resulting in, deep social inequalities. They didn't come up with alternative technology or progressive policy but simple condemnation.

However, we also know that Amos's Yahweh does present a vision of a restoration. And Jesus of course announces the Kingdom of God. Brueggemann again: 'The prophet does not ask if the vision can be implemented, for questions of implementation are of no consequence until the vision can be imagined. The imagination must come before the implementation.' [9]

We're not short of lifestyle choices, technological solutions and policy mechanisms. We're short of vision. Visions which come from God appear in odd places – a shepherd from Judah, a Nazarene wanderer.

Imagine an alternative vision of Iona in 2106. It won't be the same as it is today.

Eurig Scandrett

COLUMBAN CHRISTIANITY & THE CELTIC TRADITION

Heirs of Adomnán (A liturgy)

This service took place in Iona Abbey in 2000.

Introduction

This service reflects the Iona Community's concern for issues of peace and justice through the recalling of Iona's past, in particular, Adomnán's seventh-century *Law of the Innocents*.

Abbot Adomnán of Iona is best known to us today for being the biographer of St Columba. Indeed, we would know next to nothing about St Columba were it not for Adomnán's biography/hagiography *Life of St Columba*.

In the year 697 AD the ninth Abbot of Iona, Adomnán mac Rónáin, devised and promulgated the *Law of the Innocents*. Known as 'the first law in heaven and earth for the protection of women', Adomnán's *Law of the Innocents* extended to children and clergy as well, and was enforced throughout Ireland, Scotland and Pictland. This law was an early attempt to limit the effects of war by protecting non-combatants, and it is the precursor of the Geneva Convention, the UN Declaration on Human Rights. It is an early sign in these islands of that fundamental Christian vocation to stand alongside the weak and vulnerable, to oppose injustice and oppression. [1]

In this service, we are invited to look again at this law in the light of our present circumstances, globally and locally, and to ask ourselves: who are today's innocents?

The congregation are invited to discuss among themselves the question of who, for them, are the innocents of today (for example, child soldiers, women who are trafficked for sex, victims of landmines …)

'Adomnán's Bell' is rung from the nave of the church to bring people out of conversation. (For the Iona service we borrowed a copy an early Irish hand-bell, known as 'Adomnán's Bell', from Kilmartin House Museum in Argyll.)

Introduction to the bell:

Leader: It is written that Adomnán did not carry a sword with him into battle, but the bell of Adomnán's Anger, [2] which he rung out against the tyrants of the day, [3] and proclaimed against them:

Reader:

'My own wee true-judging bell
by which Irgalach is made childless,
I beg the true-judging King
that there may be no king from Irgalach …

The bell of truly miraculous Adomnán
has laid waste many kings.
Each one against whom it gives battle one thing awaits:
it has laid them waste.'

From Adomnán's Law of the Innocents *(p. 12, paragraph 21), translated by Gilbert Márkus, Blackfriars Books, 1997*

Month 3 Day 13

Leader: Iona was the promoter of the law and the spiritual 'enforcer'. Following Adomnán's death, the abbot would travel the land with the relics of the saint, and renew the Law. [4] The power of God was present in the saint, and the power of the saint was present in the relics, and particularly in the ringing of the bell. [5] God would use the bell to oppose injustice and violence, and to thwart the plans of the oppressors. [6] Bells were not only instruments of confrontation, however, they might also have healing powers. [7]

Adomnán was said to have rung his bell in anger against injustice. Later, we will invite you to come ring out 'Adomnán's Bell' once again, in defence of the innocents of today.

The congregation stand to say the following:

Call to worship

NOW IS THE TIME TO LIVE,
TO COME TO THE CREATOR,
TO DANCE AND SING TO THE LORD WHO FREES US FROM FEAR,
TO HELP CREATE A BETTER WORLD WITH THE SPIRIT OF LOVE. [8]

The bell is processed from the nave of the Abbey to a table in the crossing, led by a candle and an open bible, to the ancient chant 'Iona Gloria' (Common Ground 64). (Incense is lit beforehand, at the beginning of worship before folk come in.)

Month 3 Day 13

Invocation

Leader: Surrounding Trinity, be with us gathered here tonight.
Help us to celebrate and explore God's word in story and song.
Open our ears, that we may understand.
Strengthen our voices, that we may speak out for justice.
Make us more ready to act, that we may make our hopes for peace into reality.

How the law was made:

(Adapted from Adomnán's 'Law of the Innocents', Cáin Adomnáin: A seventh century law for the protection of non-combatants, *translated with an introduction by Gilbert Márkus, Blackfriars Books, 1997)*

Reader one: This was the beginning of the tale: once Adomnán and his mother were travelling on the road by Áth Drochait, and they came upon a field of slaughter. This is how thick the carnage was on which they came: the two feet of one woman reached to the headless neck of the next one. Of all they saw on the battlefield, they saw nothing which they found more touching or more wretched than the head of a woman lying in one place and her body in another, and her infant on the breast of her corpse. There was a stream of milk on one of its cheeks and a stream of blood on the other cheek.

Reader two: 'This is touching and pitiful to me,' said Ronnat, Adomnán's mother, 'what I see at your feet, O dear cleric. Why do you not let me down to the ground, so that I may give my breast to the child? But it's a long time since my breasts ran dry. Nothing would be found in them. Why do you not prove your clerical skill for us on that pitiful body to see if the Lord will revive it for you?'

Reader one:	At the word of his mother, Adomnán turned and set the head on the neck, and he made the sign of the cross with his staff over the woman's breast, and the woman rose up.
Reader three:	'Alas, O my great Lord of the Elements,' she said.
Reader one:	'What makes you say alas?' said Adomnán.
Reader three:	'My having been put to the sword on the battlefield, and then my having been put in the pains of hell. I do not know anyone, either here or there, who would do a kindness or a mercy for me except for Adomnán and the Virgin Mary urging him on to it on behalf of the community of heaven.'
Reader two:	'Well then, Adomnán,' said Ronnat, 'it has been given to you now to free the women of the Western world. Neither food nor drink will go into your mouth until women have been set free by you.'
Reader one:	'I will not rise,' said Adomnán, 'until women have been freed for me.'

Scripture reading: Ezekiel 37:1–10

Song: Inspired by Love and Anger (*Inspired by Love and Anger,* John L. Bell and Graham Maule, Wild Goose Publications)

Prayer of confession

Forgive us, God,
for times when we were deaf to the cries of the innocent,
when we had come upon injustice but
passed by on our journeys;

when we were unmoved
by the cries of children,
the tortured screams of women,
the cry of your beautiful and precious creation
being rent and broken and violated.

Forgive us for times when we were dumb,
when we did not sound out
because we believed you were deaf to our cries [9]
and to the cries of poor.
When we took your silence for absence, [10]
when our tongues lolled in our mouths, [11]
or sounded excuses, reasons, rationalisations, empty promises.
Justifications instead of justice.

Forgive us our complacency,
and our complicity, God,
in this distantly divided but deeply interconnected world
where all actions and choices have their reverberations.

God, free us of all doubt and guilt and fear
and help us now to ring out:

To ring out in protest and praise,
in love and anger.
To strike [12] out against tyranny,
to sound out an alarm and wake up the world,
to announce Christ's good news of liberation and life,
to proclaim your justice until the Day of Judgement. [13]

Help us to summon our courage God
and give us voices –

brave, clear and strong.

Voices that clang and disturb
    create a stir
make waves
    charge heavy, dead air,
touch hearts and souls with their passion and honesty.

Voices that clonk [14] and clank like the sound of hammers,
like the sound of hammers beating swords into ploughshares.
Voices that ring out and stubbornly keep on ringing out until

the whole of your creation is free from bondage,
everybody is fed,
all innocents are protected and held in respect …

O God, we have no power but the power that comes from you.
No strength but your strength. [15]
Come, fill us with your Holy Spirit
and hear our prayers as we call out to you
in our need and longing. [16]
Amen

Scripture reading: Ezekiel 3:17–21

Introduction to action:

People are invited to come to the crossing of the Abbey, and to ring out the bell of 'Adomnán's Anger' against situations in the world where they feel the *Law of the Innocents* is being violated, or in support of organisations and individuals working to protect the innocent and to bring peace to the world.

At the end of the service, the bell remains in place, so that there is a chance for folk to come ring the bell with less 'exposure'. There is also an opportunity for anyone to write down their concerns in the 'Book of the Bell'. [17]

Leader:	The Annals of Ulster in 727 state that when the relics of Adomnán are returned the Law is renewed.
	So, having brought this bell back to Iona, now is the time to renew the law and to proclaim justice for the innocents again.
All readers:	When the relics are returned, the Law is renewed.
Reader 1:	Now is the time, for the law is still violated.
All readers:	When the relics are returned, the Law is renewed.
Reader 2:	Now is the time, for people still suffer.
All readers:	When the relics are returned, the Law is renewed.
Reader 3:	Now is the time, for innocents perish.
All readers:	When the relics are returned, the Law is renewed.
Reader 4:	Now is the time to proclaim liberty.
All readers:	When the relics are returned, the Law is renewed.
Leader:	Now is the time to ring the bell, and uphold Adomnán's Law.
All readers:	Now is the time *(readers stand up to go ring the bell)* for the Law to be renewed.

Month 3 Day 13

Bell ringing:

Each person rings the bell three times, facing the congregation, proclaiming: 'I ring this bell against …'(e.g. the trafficking of women, the exploitation of children by big business …) 'I ring this bell for …'(e.g. Amnesty International, Save The Children, Women In Black …)

The ringing is rounded off by the ringing of the Abbey bell, rung three times in remembrance.

Leader: We bring together all our prayers and concerns in the ringing of the Abbey bell.

We ring the bell once for the innocents who have suffered or died in the past.
Once for the innocents who are suffering and dying today.
Once in the hope that God's Law will soon be fulfilled,
and that God's Kingdom of peace will come on earth.

The Abbey bell is rung three times.

Silence

Affirmation

Leader: In the presence of the Father, the Son, the Holy Spirit, the community of heaven and the saints of earth: [18]

WE, AS HEIRS OF ADOMNÁN OF IONA, COMMIT OURSELVES
TO FULFILLING THE SPIRIT OF ADOMNÁN'S LAW,
ACCORDING TO OUR STRENGTH AND ABILITY. [19]
WE VOW TO RENOUNCE VIOLENCE,

AND THE INCESSANT PURSUIT OF MATERIAL WEALTH. [20]
TO PROTECT THE INNOCENT,
TO RESPECT ALL OF GOD'S CREATION,
TO WORK FOR JUSTICE AND PEACE,
AND THE HEALING OF CHRIST'S BODY ON EARTH.

TO LOVE JUSTICE, DO KINDNESS AND WALK HUMBLY WITH GOD.

Leader: Like Adomnán,
who went into battle armed with only a bell and a book,
we go out into the world:

WITH VOICES READY TO RAISE IN PROTEST AND IN CELEBRATION,
YOUR WORD TO GUIDE AND SUPPORT US,
AND THE STRENGTH OF YOUR MERCY
WITH WHICH TO CONFRONT THE TYRANNIES AND MONSTERS OF
OUR OWN AGE. [21]

Song: I Waited Patiently (*Psalms of Patience, Protest and Praise*, John L. Bell
and Graham Maule, Wild Goose Publications)

Closing responses (Universal Prayer for Peace)

O God, lead us from death to life,
FROM FALSEHOOD TO TRUTH.
Lead us from despair to hope,
FROM FEAR TO TRUST.
Lead us from hate to love,
FROM WAR TO PEACE. LET PEACE FILL OUR HEARTS, OUR WORLD, OUR
UNIVERSE. AMEN

Month 3 Day 13

Blessing

The eye of the great God be upon you.
The eye of the God of glory be on you.
The eye of the Son of Mary Virgin be on you.
The eye of the Spirit be mild on you.
To aid you and to shepherd you;
oh, the kindly eye of the three be on you,
to aid you and to shepherd you.

From the *Carmina Gadelica*

Jane Bentley and Neil Paynter with contributions and inspiration from Gilbert Márkus, The Adomnán of Iona Trident Ploughshares Affinity Group, Leslie Griffiths, the Wild Goose Resource Group, and the Kilmartin House Museum, Kilmartin, Scotland. www.kilmartin.org

Footnotes

1. The introduction to this service is taken from/drawn from *Adomnán's 'Law of the Innocents', Cáin Adomnáin: A seventh century law for the protection of non-combatants*, translated with an introduction by Gilbert Márkus, Blackfriars Books, 1997.

2. 'Adomnán did not carry a sword with him into battle, but the bell of Adomnán's Anger' – Ibid: See p. 11, paragraph 17.

3. 'Rung out against the tyrants of the day' – in the article 'Ring out your Prayer: early Irish hand-bells', *Spirituality* magazine, Spirituality 16, January 1998, Gilbert Márkus writes: '… bells often appear in opposition to the power of kings'. And: 'Such aggressively confrontational use of the bell is not unusual. The saint is portrayed defending his churches or his monks against aggression.'

4. 'Iona was the promoter of the law … renew the law.' – In his introduction to *Adomnán's 'Law of the Innocents', Cáin Adomnáin: A seventh century law for the protection of non-combatants*, Gilbert Márkus writes: 'The community which first promoted the law and received the *cáin* payments was Iona …' 'Promulgation of the Law involved the abbot or his representative travelling around the country with the relics of the patron saint …' See also p. 20, paragraph 43.

5. This sentence is drawn from 'Ring out your Prayer: early Irish hand-bells', Gilbert Márkus, *Spirituality* magazine. Gilbert Márkus also writes: 'God's power and the power of their original saintly owners dwelt in them …' And: 'The power of the saint's curse is present in the bell itself.'

6. 'God would use the bell …' – Ibid: Gilbert Márkus writes: '… that God will use that relic to oppose injustice and violence, to drive away the devilish snares of the enemy.' And: 'They must rely on God's aid against oppressors, and the bell is the concrete expression of that divine assistance.'

7. 'Bells were not only instruments of confrontation … healing powers.' – Ibid.

8. 'Call to worship'– from 'An Adomnán Liturgy of Celebration to mark "Carnival" at Faslane Nuclear Base, 13 May 2000', by the Adomnán Affinity Group. Complete liturgy published in *This Is the Day*, Wild Goose Publications, 2002, Neil Paynter (ed).

9. The first three lines of this stanza of the prayer of confession were inspired by the R.S. Thomas poems 'No Truce with the Furies' and 'Counterpoint'. Poems quoted in *At the far side of the Cross: The spirituality of R.S.Thomas*, an unpublished lecture by Leslie Griffiths on the poetry of R.S.Thomas.

10. This line inspired by R.S. Thomas, and the unpublished lecture by Leslie Griffiths (Ibid). In this lecture Leslie Griffiths writes about D.Z. Phillips' book on R.S.Thomas subtitled, *Poet of the Hidden God*, and discusses and quotes several R.S. Thomas poems which deal with the subject of God's absence and silence. Leslie Griffiths also mentions and quotes the philosopher Wittgenstein in relation to this.

11. This line taken from, or inspired by, the R.S. Thomas poem 'No Truce with the Furies'. 'My tongue lolled, clapper of a disused bell … 'Poem quoted in *'At the far side of the Cross: The spir-*

ituality of R.S. Thomas', by Leslie Griffiths.

12. 'Strike' – See *Adomnán's 'Law of the Innocents', Cáin Adomnáin: A seventh century law for the protection of non-combatants*, p. 11, paragraph 18.

13. 'Day of Judgement' – Ibid: See p. 17, paragraph 29.

14. In 'Ring out your Prayer: early Irish hand-bells', *Spirituality* magazine, Gilbert Márkus describes the 'clonking sound' of one of these 'prayer-machines'. He writes: 'That pathetic sound is the sound of real prayer.'

15. Ibid: Gilbert Márkus writes of the bell being rung in contemporary services by people 'whose help is in the name of the Lord rather than in their own strength'. He writes: 'To ring out … is to enter into a tradition of prayer … which seeks to transform the world not by getting power over it but by entrusting ourselves to God in prayer.'

16. 'The sound of need and longing' – Ibid.

17. See *Adomnán's 'Law of the Innocents', Cáin Adomnáin: A seventh century law for the protection of non-combatants*, p. 14–17. Gilbert Márkus has incorporated the 'Book of the Bell' idea into the services he has led.

18. Ibid: See p. 17, paragraph 30.

19. 'according to strength and ability' – Ibid: See p. 17, paragraph 31.

20. In 'Ring out your Prayer: early Irish hand-bells', *Spirituality* magazine, Gilbert Márkus writes of the ringing of the bell being 'a prayer of the heart uttered by men and women who have renounced violence and wealth'.

21. Ibid: Gilbert Márkus writes of the bell being rung 'to confront the tyrannies and monsters of our own age'.

RACISM

The dance of life

For several months after I returned from Ghana last summer, I felt a sense of loss. Those who have worshipped with African Christians often comment on the power and exuberance of the singing, the heartfelt nature of the prayer, the conviction of the preaching. The dancing, however, was a completely new experience for me. It's not that we don't dance in Scotland; no social occasion is complete without the Dashing White Sergeant or the Eightsome Reel. But we don't dance in church!

What I experienced in Accra was something that felt entirely natural, whether it was in the General Council worship, or in a local church where the whole congregation danced the offertory, or in the outdoor service where 15,000 people were swept to their feet and into dance again and again. To be among people worshipping with their whole being was dynamic and uplifting.

One aspect of the dancing made a particular impression on me. After every service had ended, the musicians would strike up again. A moving circle would form and the dancing would recommence. At first the circle would be joined only by Ghanaians, other Africans, and those few adventurous souls who will always try anything new. But as time went on, I noticed that more and more people were joining in, not just the young and extrovert but the self-conscious Europeans, the stiff North Americans, the reserved Asians, those who had thought dancing was something for the exhibitionist, those who were angry or sorrowful, those whose lives encompassed huge loss and tragedy. By the end of the Council, everybody was dancing, including some people in wheelchairs, and the circle was like an ever-changing kaleidoscope of movement, shape and colour. It seemed to me like the dance of life.

I observed that when people got up to join in, there was no fuss, and no judgement. The circle just made space for them. Not everyone was in step, but that didn't matter either; within the dance there was room for a bit of diversity. People who were in deep disagreement danced in the same circle. And gradually I saw how much the dance was responsive to context. We had visited the slave fortresses, had come face-to-face with the terrible racism and brutality that had trafficked 15 million Africans into bondage in Europe and the Americas. We had been confronted with the extent to which this commodification of human beings had profited or impoverished our own countries. We had been shamed that all of this had been done by believing Christians, and been forced to consider the extent of our own complicity in the continuing dehumanising effects of globalised markets, debt bondage, trade injustice and environmental degradation. The following day, the dance was sombre and anguished, the drums sobbed. In contrast, on the day of covenanting for justice in the economy and the environment, the dance was joyful and energetic – and the drums ecstatic.

I thought then that the dance reflected the kind of inner as well as outer journey that those of us who had come to Africa, particularly from the West, had made. We had had the opportunity to see the world through the eyes of those who live in it unprotected by wealth, power, status or any of the myriad insurances we have to defend ourselves from what is reality for most people. What they had shown us was the power of hope in the midst of suffering and the absolute value of human kindness.

We had had the opportunity to see ourselves through the eyes of the world, and put Western whingeing and mean-spiritedness in a clear, and not flattering, perspective. What they had shown us – who so often appear like overindulged children, prone to tantrums if we don't get our own way (which we sometimes confuse with freedom), good at making messes but not so good at cleaning up after ourselves – was the nature of real care, a generous and sacrificial commitment of time, energy and interest.

And we had been invited to see God anew. To be part of the Body of Christ in the dance of life is to recognise that my profligacy with energy, my polluting, my increased share profits, is another's dangerous working conditions, environmental catastrophe, debt burden. It is to really experience that when one part of the Body suffers, all the others suffer with it. But it is also to experience the truth that when one part rejoices, the other parts share its joy. The joy of being invited to covenant together with people who have no particular reason either to be grateful to or to trust the West, an invitation to a new relationship, a new solidarity. The joy of knowing that we too have gifts to bring to the dance of life, that we are all needed. The joy of a shared faith that transcends barriers of race, class, culture. The joy of being reminded that even in the midst of huge problems and challenges, of profound sorrow and loss, the dance of life goes on, and the decision to go on celebrating that life in all its beauty and tragedy and ambiguity by joining the dance is the most tremendous affirmation of the love of God, in whom is our only true security. And the resurrection joy of knowing that somewhere in the dance of life, moving through the circle, Jesus is dancing with us.

Kathy Galloway

Gabi, Gabi
Bash' abazalwan'
Siyoshiywa khona
Sidal' ubuzalwan'

Praise the Father
Liberator Lord
He frees all the captives
And gives the hungry bread

A song from South Africa

Month 3 Day 14

COMMUNITY

Celebrating hope and unity in diversity and despair

Every Sunday at 6pm a very special worship event takes place in a traditional Reformed Church in an industrial area of a town in Switzerland. Where there is only a small congregation at the morning worship, before 6pm most of the benches in the church are filled by women, men and children from many nations and denominations. They meet to pray, to sing and to celebrate community. The focus of the worship is the biblical message, presented as drama/role play. The preparation for worship is done in an open meeting every Thursday evening: those present choose and discuss the story for Sunday. Some of the actors are asylum-seekers, or persons without permits living and working illegally. There are Africans, speaking French or English; people from Central and South America – Guatemala, Ecuador, Bolivia – speaking Spanish; folk from Sri Lanka and Vietnam – and they feel safe and at home in the church where they meet. We Swiss people are a small minority. All are welcome.

I feel deeply moved by this diversity, and feel ashamed that my home country does officially so little to help these people to be safe.

This multinational and multiracial worship has been celebrated for more than 15 years; and it has influenced the poorer area around the church, where at least 50 percent of the population are foreigners. The warmth of the singing and praying has given voice to despair and hope, has fostered understanding and acceptance – and is a counter-event to the official policy and our country's laws. The Spirit of the living God is present and fills the atmosphere with Her love.

For the final blessing, sung or spoken to one another, those present form a circle by holding hands around the whole church. Once I was next to a man from Ecuador who was holding his baby girl in his arms. Later, I learnt that his father had just been arrested – our peace prayer and shalom was urgently needed.

After the service many stay for a simple meal shared in the basement of the church. This worship event reminds me of Jesus eating with the outcasts of his time.

Why is it so difficult to transfer such encounters into our everyday politics? Do we lack the deep connectedness with the Divine?

Prayer

O God of all nations,
you welcome any person in need:
you embrace them with your warm love.
Guide the rich and safe citizens
to open doors and hearts to strangers
who seek safety, work and hospitality.
Enable us to walk with our sisters and brothers
and to stay with them in times of distress and exclusion.

Elisabeth C. Miescher

PILGRIMAGE

A different journey

When I was in school, one of the chief bullies was a French teacher. Like all bullies, she was much feared. Then, one day, in the assembly hall, on the anniversary of the Second World War, she told us her story.

She had studied in England in the 1930s and with the outbreak of war she had been stranded.

For five years she had witnessed at a distance the fall of France, and lived through the loss of contact with her own family. She knew, as did everyone, of the hunger, the repression, the destruction of the Jews; the danger to those who put their country above their own lives. In time she had been approached by the secret services, and asked if she would be willing to work as an agent in France.

'But,' she concluded, her face returned to her hostile, riveted audience, 'I was not the stuff of which heroes are made.' And so she declined.

After the war she returned to France, for a time, to her family. They had suffered so much hardship, loss of neighbours, limitations so much more severe than rationing – and she had been so far away. Now she no longer belonged. 'And so,' she concluded, a quarter-century of bitterness in her voice, 'I returned home, to England.'

I learnt her language when I was free of her anger and her loss. However, her moment had been not in the classroom, but in that hall, among those who had protected themselves by rejecting her. For a moment, something broke open, and we stared into the eyes of the enemy and found there the companionship of compassion.

Sometimes, it is in acknowledging our failure that we touch greatness – and transmit the everlasting romance, the pursuit of greatness, to others.

The greatness of Christianity comes from that it seeks not a supernatural remedy for suffering, but a supernatural use for suffering. Simone Weil, 1909–43.

Rosemary Power

Mustard seed

A mustard seed
is full of possibility
there's a tree in there
somewhere

reach into the sky
little seed

what possibilities lie dormant in us
ready to grow into being
when we let go
and open ourselves
to the light of the sun
to the refreshing rain
to the hidden depths of
the mothering earth
solid beneath us
yet soft to shelter our sprouting

reach up to the sky
let yourself grow
and one day you will
find the birds of the air
resting with their heads under their wings
waking and singing the dawning of hope
sheltering in your branches
a soft nest
perhaps
a pale blue speckled egg
waiting to be born
and to fly

let yourself be grown
your life is full of possibility
you are the seed
you are the bird
and you are also the tree

Lotte Webb

SEXUALITY

A group Bible study

Justice for same-sex couples

'You have neglected the more important matters of the law – justice, mercy and faithfulness. You should have practised these,' said Jesus.
Matthew 23:23 (NIV, amended)

'Why do you try to test God by putting on the necks of the disciples a yoke that neither we nor our fathers have been able to bear? No! We believe that it is through the grace of our Lord Jesus that we are saved,' said Peter.
    Acts 15:10,11 (NIV, amended)

'My parents never went any way towards accepting my sexuality. I came out to them at 18. They pleaded with our GP to refer me for psychiatric help and tried to report him to the General Medical Council when he refused. They then had me interviewed by the local CID [Criminal Investigation Department]. My parents never visited any of my/our homes and there was never the slightest possibility of my partner, or my partner's son, whom we are now bringing up, visiting them. Despite everything I did feel an obligation to keep up the relationship with my parents. My father died two years ago and my mother died recently. I stopped work to look after her for the last couple of weeks and it was a very special time, which was completely ruined when one of the last things she managed to whisper was "promise me that you'll never bring James (my part-

ner) or anyone like that to the house after I've gone" My imperfect relationship with my parents will always be the greatest sadness of my life.'

A gay man, from Equal as Citizens, Stonewall, 2001

There are some who simply cannot accept that an enriching, loving, faithful and committed same-sex relationship can be part of God's good plan for a couple.

There is no doubt that the Bible condemns any act which is an expression of lust, exploitation or abuse, whether homosexual or heterosexual. Those who condemn any form of same-sex relationship rely on a number of biblical texts which refer to male rape or cult prostitution, which no one would defend, but there are two – and only two – isolated passages in the whole Hebrew Bible which appear to offer a blanket condemnation of all sexual acts between people of the same sex:

You must not have sexual intercourse with a man as with a woman. This is a hateful thing.

Leviticus 18:22; 20:13

… They must be put to death.

Leviticus 20:13 (NIV)

Laws which were regarded as of central importance for the maintenance of a just and compassionate society were repeatedly reaffirmed in Hebrew scripture. There must always be a question mark set against any isolated legal requirement. If a biblical law relating to intercourse between people of the same sex is to be regarded as universally legally binding, this should equally apply to the related death penalty, but few, if any, would argue today for such a provision. Jesus for his part clearly states that some matters of the law are weightier than others.

So what are the weighty commandments and what is justice?

In giving advice to the churches St Paul explained what things are wrong and what are right, what acts are just and what are unjust. (Included in brackets in the following text are transliterations of the original Greek words which have the common root word *dike,* which means 'justice'. It is possible to see from this how vigorously St Paul is grappling with issues of justice.)

How dare one of your members take up a complaint against another in the law courts of the unjust (adikon) instead of in the community of God's people? ... Why, it is already a fault that you have lawsuits with each other at all. Oughtn't you to let yourselves be wronged (adikeisthe)? Why not rather let yourselves be cheated?

But you actually treat one another unjustly (adikeite) and cheat one another, and members of the Christian community at that. You know perfectly well that those who are unjust (adikoi) will not inherit the kingdom of God? Make no mistake! Neither the sexually immoral, nor idolaters, nor adulterers, nor sexual perverts, nor male prostitutes, nor thieves, nor the greedy, nor drunkards, nor slanderers, nor robbers will inherit the kingdom of God. And that is what some of you were. But you have been washed clean, you have been sanctified, you have been justified (edikaiothete) in the name of the Lord Jesus Christ and by the Spirit of our God.

1 Corinthians 6:1,6–11

St Paul makes a number of allusions to the basic code of the Hebrew people, the Ten Commandments, and it is helpful to compare this code with St Paul's list:

The Ten Commandments	Paul's list
'You shall have no other gods before me.'	Male (cult) prostitutes
'You shall not make for yourself an idol.'	Idolaters
'You shall not misuse the name of the Lord your God.' 'Remember the Sabbath day by keeping it holy.' 'Honour your father and your mother.'	
'You shall not murder.'	
'You shall not commit adultery.'	Adulterers, sexually immoral
'You shall not steal.'	Cheats, thieves, robbers
'You shall not give false testimony against your neighbour.'	Slanderers
'You shall not covet.'	Greedy, drunkards, sexually immoral

Exodus 20:3ff (NIV)

Discussion

1. Discuss in the group the criteria that members would want to use for establishing the weight of any particular law.

2. Discuss the nature of the injustice done to other people in: not keeping the Sabbath holy; stealing; sexual immorality; not honouring father and

mother; giving false testimony; committing murder; coveting; committing adultery; drunkenness. Be selective. It will not be possible to discuss all of these issues.

3. Just supposing that sexual relations within an enriching, loving, faithful and committed same-sex partnership were included in this list, who is being treated unjustly?

Graeme Brown

HEALING

This song, by John L. Bell, is often sung at the Tuesday evening healing service in Iona Abbey.

Take this moment

1. Take this moment, sign and space;
   take my friends around;
   here among us make the place
   where your love is found.

2. Take the time to call my name,
   take the time to mend
   who I am and what I've been,
   all I've failed to tend.

3. Take the tiredness of my days,
   take my past regret,
   letting your forgiveness touch
   all I can't forget.

4. Take the little child in me
   scared of growing old;
   help me here to find my worth
   made in Christ's own mould.

5. Take my talents, take my skills,
   take what's yet to be;
   let my life be yours, and yet
   let it still be me.

John L. Bell & Graham Maule

SOCIAL ACTION

'Everyone talks about the cost of the Millennium Dome. It will cost 700 million but that will be a one-off cost. We spend 900 million on these [nuclear] bases every year and that's just the MOD figure – the CND [Campaign for Nuclear Disarmament] estimate, a more likely figure, is one-and-a-half billion! Let's be clear, to waste resources on such a scale for such an obscenity is sinful – all the churches recognise that.'

Maxwell Craig, General Secretary of Action for Churches Together in Scotland, at a demonstration at Faslane Naval Base (from the Trident Ploughshares website www.tridentploughshares.org)

Trident is capable of destroying most of the northern hemisphere in 10 minutes. 30 million men, women and children would be wiped out. The effect of radiation would make much of the earth uninhabitable. I would be failing my children and my grand-children if I did not make a stand against it.

The cost of Trident is equivalent to spending £30,000 a day since the birth of Christ. Is this what we, as a so-called civilised society, really consider to be a responsible use of our money? I work in partnership with families living in poverty and social exclusion in Glasgow. I would be failing these people, whom I feel privileged to call my friends, if I did not make a stand against this obscene expenditure.

Molly Harvey, from the article 'Diary of a Jailbird'

Jesus Hates Bombs

One day I had a theological discussion with a man called Robert. Over a period of two hours I argued that Jesus hates bombs. In the end he agreed wholeheartedly and decided to reconnect with his faith community. As is often the case in life, the journey that led to the arrival was much more interesting:

Dusk had fallen when Barbara and I set out. Our friendship has lots of room for comedy: an age gap of 29 years; crippling disability and matching bags full of prescription medication; Barbara's mischievous announcements when she is about to fart; and a habit we both now have, but she started – a tendency to spit (metaphorically) on all that ails or annoys us. And there we were, hirpling into a wee van with our medication and books and a couple of cans of spray paint. A short time later the driver stopped the van near Coulport Armaments Depot, home to all of Britain's nuclear warheads. We tumbled from the vehicle with absolutely no style or panache. A battle ensued between adrenaline and coordination. My limbs as usual were on the wayward side and I was relieved I'd opted for my wheelchair. We made our way towards Coulport, shrouded by the dense tree cover. My heart rate was fairly high by then and I concentrated hard on my breathing. What we were doing seemed daft. It was too late to turn back though.

We approached unseen. Barbara wanted to do some work on the roundabout next to Coulport and I'd opted for the concrete bollards next to the main gate. I was unable to get the lid off my can of paint. In a forlorn voice I shouted to Barbara for help. She came hobbling in my direction, shaking her head and smiling. We were, and probably still are, the worst anti-nuclear activists in Scotland. Cap off, I set to on those bollards. The surface was square and flat. I chose to slide from my chair and work from the ground. The statement we'd agreed to write was JESUS HATES BOMBS. The bollards were in two separate groups of three. I finished the first three bollards and noticed that Barbara was being arrested. I crept back into my wheelchair and proceeded to skite down the hill to the next set of bollards. The police hadn't seen me. I managed to paint another two-and-a-half blocks before my arrest. And that's where I first met Robert.

He'd just hauled the can of paint from me. I would have given it to him happily but he hadn't wasted time asking. And then he saw what I'd written and got very angry indeed. Robert was, and still is, a Ministry of Defence policeman. His reaction intrigued me and I was keen to learn what was behind it. There's a lot of dead time when you are under arrest, with procedures that must be followed. It can be very boring. Barbara was processed first and that left me in Robert's company in the holding pen. A policewoman, Sheila, was there too but she didn't say much. She knew that Robert and I needed to talk.

It turned out that Robert was a Catholic, a rather lapsed one. I don't know if it was guilt or panic that hit him first on reading our paintwork. I spent the next hour explaining that God's love transcends jobs, fences, bombs and even the barriers we put up ourselves. With few well-paid jobs in the area, a young child to support and a mortgage Robert had to work in a place that compromised his faith. He was seriously upset by this grim reality. With my usual lack of subtlety I got him telt: God loved him NOW. God wanted that relationship to be restored NOW. It was one of those 'let those without sin cast the first stone' moments. With none of us perfect and free of sin, God is still interested in us and that is the bottom line. I know it's going to sound coercive, but I threatened him towards the end of that conversation. It felt like the right thing to do. He was frightened to be answerable to God so I figured I'd do instead. I used what I had. I knew I'd see him again – at my trial, when he'd be giving evidence against me. I told him I'd ask him if he'd been back to Mass when he was on oath.

Some months on, the day of the trial finally came. I knew how I was going to run my defence. I decided not to use the standard pieces of law but to use only theology. I went to court that day to defend the statement and not the action. I knew I was going to lose anyway so it didn't matter. What mattered was proclaiming to anyone who would listen that the God I believe in loves, and is entirely opposed to the behaviour prevalent in the world at present. I would allow myself a minor rant on the ills of Bush and Blair – more metaphorical spitting, I'm afraid to say. The prosecution had to make their case against me first though. The MOD police officers were brought in one at a time and questioned by the Procurator Fiscal. I was allowed to cross-examine them and took the opportunity. When it was Robert's turn to answer my questions I kept them fairly sensible so I'd be allowed to continue without interruption. My final question was the crucial one. I took a deep breath and asked if he'd been back to Mass. He said YES! I felt like doing somersaults around the courtroom but instead we beamed grins at each other. Everyone else was confused but that didn't matter.

Robert and his colleagues chose to stay and watch the rest of my trial. The court was freezing and they were shivering but they wanted to stay. I baffled the poor soul prosecuting me. Theology was not what they had anticipated. In the end, having dodged about six objections, I'd made my arguments and felt happy. The Justice of the Peace (Magistrate) agreed completely that Jesus did indeed hate bombs but wasn't convinced that Jesus loved graffiti. He retired to make his final judgement and the court adjourned for a few minutes. I went to have a blether with the MOD police, who were by this time extremely cold. I was found guilty a few minutes after that and given a small fine. I continue to this day to view Robert and Sheila as my friends.

I've always been of the opinion that God has a cracking sense of humour and that even the silliest of activities can become sacred. I'm writing this on the very day that the UK Parliament takes the decision about the future of nuclear weapons in this country and it's not looking good. I will remain true to my belief that Jesus hates bombs and will continue to resist in my own eccentric manner whatever the result of the vote.

Morag Balfour

Shadows on the pavement

In March 2007, the British government voted (409 for to 161 against) for the next gener-ation of Trident nuclear missiles. I was at the demonstration in Parliament Square on the day of the vote in the Commons.

Can we not see
the shadows of the dead
on those silent Hiroshima streets
and hear their shrieks
of unimaginable pain?

And yet, and yet,
we vote
again – in the name
of self-defence.
Trident will save us
in the hour of attack
and keep
our democracy alive –
intact
to build yet more of the same.

Yet these shadows on the pavement
will not be silent,
reminding us
of our
collective insanity
and our
empty morality;
that bankruptcy of spirit
incapable
of halting global violence
as the planet weeps.

Peter Millar

CHURCH RENEWAL

The ministry of the Church

On Iona this last summer we were, specifically at our regatherings of members of the community and generally at our visitors' weeks, discussing the ministry of the Church. We discussed the basic ministry of the whole Church in the world – that ministry which is essentially of service in the name of Him who came 'not to be ministered unto but to minister', which is for the sake of the world and which is prepared to suffer for the world: which seeks not to build up itself but to build up the world. We discussed the recovery of the ministry of the total members of the Church, corporately and individually, in this service of the world – what we now call the ministry of the laity. We discussed the ministry of those ordained to 'the ministry of word and sacrament' inside the Church for the nourishment and training of the Church for the work of its total ministry. Those three topics raised questions which demand answers in action. For the difficulty in all of these is not that there is anything new to be discovered in theory but that our practice in the Church is so removed from our teaching that words without action become dangerous.

'The ministry of the Church' means little to the members of the Church because the main aim of the Church, as revealed in the discussions and decisions of its solemn assemblies, is seen above all as being to preserve, uphold and develop the institution, authority and influence of the Church. To make service of the world the determinative factor in all its discussions and decisions would be a revolution which would affect its whole life and worship. Our conception of the ministry of the members of the Church – of what we now so often call the laity, and of the

ordained ministry – depends on our idea of the purpose of the Church itself. So when we accept the idea that the Church's purpose is its own self-preservation, we inevitably regard the ministry of its members as to serve this self-preservation. This can be accepted as reasonable in the case of the ordained ministers of the Church who are ordained to serve the Church. But when this becomes the pattern for the ministry of the members of the Church, we distort all that the New Testament has to tell us about ministry and land the members of the Church in frustration. In nothing have we more distorted the teaching of the New Testament about the ordained ministry as in our emphasis on it as an individual affair: in the New Testament it is always corporate. We have denied to the members of the Church the sense that they are called to the immediate service of their Lord in the world which was the mark of the early Church.

The result is that the members of the Church are bewildered and frustrated because at one and the same time they hear themselves called by the Gospel and know that they are called by the demands of the world to immediate tasks in the service of the world – the abolition of the threat of nuclear war and the feeding of the hungry, for example – and yet they feel that all that the Church offers them is to sing in the choir, or to teach in the Sunday school or to help in the upkeep of the Church's property. No one will deny that these are things that have to be done. But equally no one will deny the frequency with which discussion on the task of the Church or the meaning of salvation ends in a discussion of the need of religious education, the need for younger office-bearers or the inadequacy of the worship.

This blockage in the thinking of the Church – for the effective thinking of the Church is the thinking of its ordinary members not of its doctors – has somehow to be blown up if Christians are to do anything effective in the world, in the matter of the bomb or of anything else, and if the Christian faith is to be understood and regarded as relevant in the world today …

T. Ralph Morton, Former Deputy Leader of the Iona Community, from 'Worship and Daily Life', *Coracle*, 1963

Prayer

O Christ, you are within each of us.
It is not just the interior of these walls:
it is our own inner being you have renewed.
We are your temple not made with hands.
We are your body.
If every wall should crumble, and every church decay,
we are your habitation.
Nearer are you than breathing,
closer than hands and feet.
Ours are the eyes with which you, in the mystery,
look out with compassion on the world.
Yet we bless you for this place,
for your directing of us, your redeeming of us,
and your indwelling.
Take us outside, O Christ, outside holiness,

out to where soldiers curse and nations clash
at the crossroads of the world.
So shall this building continue to be justified.
We ask it for your own name's sake.
Amen

From *Iona Abbey Worship Book*

WORSHIP

Specialists in living

The interpretation of scripture is often taken to be a matter for academic specialists. Boundaries based on competence may be placed between them and ordinary members. But the members are also specialists in many forms of living which give competent access to scriptural truth. They are, moreover, Spirit-gifted. All kinds of knowledge need to be drawn upon to get to the heart of scriptural texts. It is in community, where different perceptions can support and challenge one another, that we get nearer to the truth.

On one occasion I was asked at short notice to prepare something on homelessness. I fastened on 'Foxes have holes and birds in the air have nests, but the Son of Man has nowhere to lay his head'. I consulted two commentaries and found that the scholar-authors were preoccupied with the phrase 'Son of Man': what did Jesus intend by using it here?, what did it convey to others in his time?, why did he not just say 'I have nowhere …'?, etc. It was clear that the scholars needed another specialist, a rough sleeper or migrant, to get them to the theological heart of the saying. Those who have instruments of scholarship to enable them to interpret scripture and those whose experience provides effective means to do so need one another.

There are some who simply reject the need for scholarship and scholars. For them the Bible speaks 'directly to the heart'. They take it literally. They may say they believe in the Bible from cover to cover. If so, they deceive themselves. We cannot take together both the psalmist's verdict that the way to treat enemies is to get hold of their little ones and dash them against a rock (Psalm 137:8,9) and Jesus's command to love enemies and do good to them.

On the road to Emmaus Jesus helped two disciples who knew by heart their scriptures (the Old Testament) to discern 'the things concerning himself'. It is clear that they had to sort these out from other things which were not to his mind. That is also our responsibility.

In 1984, a group from Britain established relationships with Italian basic ecclesial communities from Milan in the north to Naples in the south. There we came across three Roman Catholic communities that had taken journeys in seeking to understand the scriptures. These journeys had distinctive features (due to differences in members' situations and characters) and yet had a common thread running through their experience.

The Council of Trent (1545–63) had forbidden ordinary members to have access to the scriptures other than by official licence. Vatican II Council (1962-65) changed all that. The starting point of these three basic Christian communities could be stated thus: 'We were brought up to believe that this is the priest's book to be interpreted his way. Now we find it put in the hands of the whole church. We do not need a priest.' So they set to working directly on scriptural texts.

After some time they said: 'This is the wrong approach. The Bible was written in different ways at different times. We are treating it as if we could get to the heart of it today without taking account of that.' So they looked out different commentaries and divided them among the members to get better understanding.

Again after some time they said: 'We are not there yet. We are no longer sitting at the feet of a priest. But we are sitting at the feet of commentators! There is a job still to be done to figure out what *we* make of the biblical texts so that we are helped to work out the way we should live in our time.'

At this point they sought out a non-dominating male or female scholar who was prepared to be attached to each group, who would listen and learn as well as contribute. Failing this, they looked for such a person who could be with them once a month. Insights of scholarship met up with insights drawn from experience …

Ian M. Fraser

The work of the people

'Liturgy' means 'the work of the people', I'm told. That's how it was on Iona most of time. We all did services – not just the ministers – the cooks, the shop staff, the maintenance team … Different people had different gifts. Some were good at writing prayers, some were good at music, some were good at leading, some were good at seeing how the whole would hang together. You know, like that bit in Corinthians. In the churches it's hardly ever like that. No wonder they're empty. Who wants someone talking down to them from a box. What is this, 1666? When I left Iona it was so disappointing going back to church. It was really depressing. Someone told me I might get to read a Bible passage if I stayed long enough. 'I did sermons on Iona,' I wanted to say.

It's not that I'm proud or conceited, it's just that on Iona I felt valued – my life and experience had worth. I didn't have to be a lawyer or a doctor or a pillar of the community to get up in church and tell a story. Iona was a place where, most of the time, people were welcomed, included, challenged, held. I remember one time ten of us did a service together; it took a week to plan. We wanted to take our time because we cared about what we were saying. Leaders, ministers had faith in us, encouraged us. We got together in a cottage in the evenings after work to plan it. It was so exciting, the way we listened to each other. We were full of dedication and passion. Walking down the road after our meetings the stars seemed close. Some nights I couldn't sleep. Not everything we did in the service was great – but it was sincere. A lot of it *was* good – we moved people, touched people, because it was human.

When will the churches change? If liturgy was really 'the work of the people' the churches would be full. What are they afraid of? Losing their jobs? Iona is a model. But, to me, change is far too slow. I've given up on the church now. 'Church' to me is a much wider word. There are a lot of people who feel like I do. It's sad really – because there are so many people who are hungry for the spiritual – for more than is being offered in the malls and shops. And to act effectively in the world you need to root yourself, be fed, connect.

The churches don't know what to do to attract people. It seems obvious to me.

A volunteer with the Iona Community, 2000

CALLED TO BE ONE

Vulnerable people matter more than theological difference

The most telling expression of poverty in our land is homelessness. The figures tell it. In Scotland last year, over 50,000 households applied to local authorities to be registered homeless. That means some 80 to 90,000 men, women and children – more than the population of the city of Paisley. The same distressing proportions apply in England and Wales, and in other countries of the developed world. 'In Denver,' writes Jim Wallis of the Sojourners Community, 'I learned that you had to work 144 hours per week at minimum wage in order to find any kind of housing in that city. Other cities are even worse. That's America, the world's richest country.' Wallis goes on: 'We now have record prosperity and rising inequality at the same time.' [10]

So who are the homeless in the developed world? There are those who sleep rough – in doorways, under bridges and on park benches. But they are the tip of the iceberg. Most do have a roof over their heads, but it's a roof that leaks – or they're overcrowded, or in condemned property, or imposing for too long on family or friends. They have no permanent address, so many of the comforts the rest of us take for granted are denied them.

Why are they homeless? There is a host of reasons. Each homeless person, family or household is unique. The break-up of family units is one of the causes; and this can be the result of widely differing, often tragic family problems. A person leaving an institution, a children's home, a prison, even the armed services – these situations may often lead to homelessness, simply because some of these people have no experience of caring for a home or obtaining one. Yes, sometimes the underlying cause can be drugs or drink; but there are other reasons. Take Jim, for instance. Jim signed on to join the army. After two years, he decided he'd made a mistake. Because he had signed on for seven years, he had to buy himself out. After he did that, he was penniless. A school friend had often said that if he was needing a bed, he'd only to give him a ring. So he went and stayed with his friend and his wife. Two weeks passed; then three. He still had no job, no money, but was fit and had no family responsibilities. He realised that he was imposing on his friend. So he left and was homeless.

What can we do? Scottish Churches Housing Action (SCHA) was launched in 1995, because it became clear that homelessness was not going to disappear, even though the Scottish Parliament has provided the necessary legislation and many local authorities and housing associations are doing a great deal to improve the supply of rented homes at affordable prices. In 2005, the Scottish Executive declared that it is the Executive's aim to provide a permanent home for every homeless applicant by 2012. SCHA is a small organisation, with a long reach. It is maintained by eleven Christian denominations and also includes the Evangelical Alliance and the Iona Community, unaccustomed bedfellows. This wide embrace recognises that the needs of vulnerable people matter more than theological difference.

SCHA, under the leadership of Alastair Cameron, its Chief Executive, is in touch with more than a hundred church groups throughout Scotland, from Orkney to Dumfries, from Arbroath to Stornoway. Each group is encouraged, first, to see what is already being done in their community, and then to identify the gaps. Start-up schemes, for example, provide crockery, kitchen utensils, bed linen, furniture, toiletries – all the things which can transform a house key into a home. Our 'By My Side' initiative aims to supply the friendship that can be helpful in tiding a family over during those first difficult weeks and months after getting a place of their own. In addition to these practical tasks, SCHA is at the forefront of lobbying the Scottish Executive to persist in its aim of banishing homelessness by 2012. We also encourage churches which have underused or redundant buildings to ensure that whatever development takes place includes social housing at affordable rents, as is being done in Leith where the Duke Street URC congregation, in partnership with Port of Leith Housing Association, now has 18 flats for people in need and a new church building.

Your own congregation may be involved in a local group's work for the homeless already. If it is, why not join it? If it's not, why not be the person to find out what the needs are in your area and then encourage your fellow members to form such a local group? Take a look at our website, www.churches-housing.org, or telephone the office in Albany Street, Edinburgh. Finally, become a Friend of Scottish Churches Housing Action. Micah tells you why. At this time of growing fear across God's world, the prophet has a vision for us: 'They shall sit every man under his vine and under his fig tree, and none shall make them afraid: for the mouth of the Lord of hosts has spoken' (Micah 4:4).

Prayer

O God, our Father, we remember before You the thousands in our land and throughout the world, the men, women and children, who today are homeless. They have no place of their own, no hearth on which to rest. Spread the shadow of Your gracious wings over them, we pray; grant them the dignity which our nations have denied them. Protect and save them in their suffering and need. Fill us, O Father, with a lively sense of the responsibility we owe them as our neighbours; and give us the grace to value more highly the comforts and care which we enjoy. Hear our prayer in the name of Jesus Christ, who had no place to lay his head. Amen

Maxwell Craig, Chairman of SCHA, 2000-2006

Homelessness is you, homelessness is me

In this litany use many voices.

Leader: Homelessness is you, homelessness is me
Voice: Homelessness is Dan who was a miner
Voice: Homelessness is Eric who was a computer programmer
Voice: Homelessness is Emily who was a student
Voice: Homelessness is Brian who worked packing meat for a while,
and worked picking fruit for a season,
and works construction when they can use him
Leader: Homelessness is you, homelessness is me

Voice: Homelessness is Jack who fought in the Falklands War
Voice: Homelessness is Harry who fought at Normandy and in Korea
and in the east end of Glasgow
Voice: Homelessness is Jane who fought and survived the mental health system
Voice: Homelessness is Maggie who says:
If there's one thing she's learned – it's she's a survivor
Leader: Homelessness is you, homelessness is me

Voice: Homelessness is David who sees guardian angels in the trees;
seraphim perched on fences
Voice: Homelessness is Sarah who sees no way out
Voice: Homelessness is Eric who jumped from a bridge in London
Voice: Homelessness is Chan whom they found frozen in a dumpster
Leader: Homelessness is you, homelessness is me

Voice: Homelessness is Ewan who has travelled to South America and China
and Alaska, and has so many stories he could fill a book
Two books!

Month 3 Day 22

Voice:	Homelessness is Victor
	who has a tattoo of a butterfly he reveals –
	like he's baring his soul
Voice:	Homelessness is Jenny who is dying of AIDS,
	and whose last wish is to travel to Skye,
	to sit on a beach near Portree
	and watch the sun setting
Leader:	Homelessness is you, homelessness is me
Voice:	Homelessness is Mohammed who sleeps in his car,
	and has to keep moving on when the cops come
Voice:	Homelessness is Ray who sleeps in the graveyard
Voice:	Homelessness is Vernon who lives in a tidy squat where he likes to read
	the *Evening Times* and cook sausages
Leader:	Homelessness is you, homelessness is me
Voice:	Homelessness is Sittina who escaped the war in Sudan
	and is scared of being deported by the Home Office
Voice:	Homelessness is Susan who escaped her husband in Manchester
	and is scared of being found and killed
Voice:	Homelessness is Jessica who escaped her stepfather
Voice:	Homelessness is Curtis who works at a charity shop and can fix anything
	– radios, TVs, bicycles, washing machines …
	Homelessness is Curtis who has lived for forty years with the labels –
	stupid, defective, disabled, broken …
Voice:	Homelessness is Neil who loves to sit and talk about 60s' music –
	and knows his stuff
Voice:	Homelessness is Nicola who loves the ballet
Voice:	Homelessness is Sylvester who plays joyful, jangly ragtime piano in the
	shelter chapel
Voice:	Homelessness is Paul who writes the most sensitive, beautiful poetry

---

Month 3 Day 22

Leader: Homelessness is you, homelessness is me

Voice: Homelessness is Craig who never speaks or smiles
            and has an abused, collie dog he takes excellent care of
Voice: Homelessness is Ian who wanders the streets looking for a hit –
            and has a distant light in his eyes when he remembers:
            playing football with his mates, walking in the hills, fishing for salmon …
Leader: Homelessness is you, homelessness is me

Voice: Homelessness is Chaz and Barry and Lynne,
            who spent their childhoods in and out of foster care,
            their teenage years in and out of institutions,
            and all of their adult lives inside either jails or night shelters
Voice: Homelessness is Albert who spent 10 years in Belmarsh,
            where he learned to hate
            and how to play
            the whole, dirty rotten game
Voice: Homelessness is Dave who wants to work with children
Voice: Homelessness is Lewis who can't pay his council tax
Voice: Homelessness is Norma who can't pay her electric
Voice: Homelessness is Elizabeth who is eight months pregnant
Voice: Homelessness is Miles who misses tucking his kids in
Voice: Homelessness is Robbie who says:
            when he wins the lottery he's gonna buy his own tropical island,
            and give what's left to the nuns –
            who accepted him for who he is,
            who treated him like a human being again
Leader: Homelessness is you, homelessness is me

Month 3 Day 22

Voice:	Homelessness is Dick who says:
	'I was staying with friends but they get sick of you.'
Voice:	Homelessness is Chris and Nina who take good care of each other
	and make love where
	– and when –
	they can.
Voice:	Homelessness is Matt who says you feel like 'the invisible man'
Voice:	Homelessness is Vincent who says:
	'It could happen to anyone, people don't realise –
	lose your family, your job, your mind …
	People have no idea –
	how close to the edge they're walking.'
Leader:	Homelessness is me
	Homelessness is you

Neil Paynter

The phrase 'homelessness is you, homelessness is me' is taken from a story by Ed Loring of the Open Door Community.

Month 3 Day 22

MISSION

Revelation

China gave me insight into the basic truth of Christianity. If I had stayed at home I would, I hope, have come to know why I believed. Fortunately one believes before one gains the conviction of knowing why. And such conviction comes through life. Sometimes it comes slowly and inevitably. Sometimes it needs the shock of the unfamiliar to shed new light on what we have known for long. We see this in the experience of the twelve disciples of Jesus. It is perhaps what we mean by revelation.

Certainly China gave me moments of revelation. One happened in what must have been one of the few ugly spots in China. It had none of the beauty that catches you unexpectedly in almost any other corner of China. It was simply a dusty narrow street of little mud houses opening onto a swampy, empty patch of mud with a derelict little temple on one side and the school compound with our house in it on the other. There was not a tree to be seen or a hill. The drabness was relieved only by the width of the sky, the light of the sun and the fact that it was our home.

I was coming home. I had come down the street. I can still see it in all its detail. I can still hear the drumming sound made by a woman crouching by a doorway, thumping with a stick the clothes she was washing. Some children were playing around her. I didn't know her. Nothing happened. She went on washing. I walked on. But something had happened to me. The revelation came to me that this woman was the centre of God's world; that God's creation was this woman; that her work, so monotonous, so unending, was in some way what God was doing; that her life and the lives of all the other people of the town and of China and of the world were somehow linked with God.

Of course I had believed in God, or thought I had. I had even imagined that by training and ordination I had some divine right to talk about God, or thought that other people thought I had. But in that place, on that evening, I knew for the first time something of what it really meant. The ordinary world of ordinary men and women was God's world and their most ordinary work his business.

You do not have to go to China to find the ordinary world of ordinary men and women – the world into which Jesus came. But some of us have to go abroad to have our eyes opened. At home in our familiar place we cannot see the ordinary world of men and women as God's world – in other words we cannot see it with imagination or concern – because we take that world for granted and take for granted that it is dull, and so we build for ourselves little citadels of privacy in which we feel at home and think we find God. It can be our family or our circle of friends or our church or just ourselves. We don't want to ask questions about the ordinary world because we are afraid of the answers. We don't want to seek because we are afraid of what we might find. We don't knock because doors might open that would take us into new worlds. The poets and the artists sometimes make us see this ordinary world. And it was what Jesus was showing his followers. But theology and the life of the Church have tended to put blinkers on us and to force us to look not at God's world but at a lost world of abstractions. We need the shock of some surprise to awaken us. It's in our experience of the ordinary world that there can come to us the surprised awareness of God.

But China taught me more.

This revelation of God in the ordinary world of men and women brought a new sense of the unity of all mankind …

T. Ralph Morton, Former Deputy Leader of the Iona Community, 1976

Month 3 Day 23

WORK

Those 'greater things' required of us (John 14:12)

Those 'greater things' required of us
who follow in your way –
how get the courage to say 'Yes',
and love like yours display.

You healed the sick, the hungry fed,
confronted powers-that-be,
raised and were raised up from the dead,
set those in bondage free.

Yet you were given a narrow place
some years in time's expanse –
can our restricted time and space
your Kingdom's growth advance?

Transnationals and superpowers,
arms dealers fuelling strife
point to new mandates which are ours
to urge your way of life.

We're in our world, not ages past,
and global is our task:
then live in us – that, to the last,
we do great things you ask.

Ian M. Fraser

THE POOR AND DISADVANTAGED

The stonecutters' struggles

Sholinghur is an old weaving and market town in southern India. It has been a place of human settlement for thousands of years and has been part of different kingdoms down through these long centuries. High above the crowded town, approached by a thousand magnificently carved stone steps, stands an ancient Hindu temple – a place of pilgrimage for thousands of devotees every year. From the precincts of this place of prayer, one looks down across the plains where green paddy fields (thanks to electricity and pump sets) alternate with vast tracks of thorny scrub – the home of hundreds of wandering animals such as goats and sheep, cows and water buffalo. In the wet season, in a hundred fields, bullocks plough in preparation for the rice planting – part of the timeless cycle of rural India. To see these bullocks at work, against a backcloth of tall palmyra trees, is to witness a scene unchanged in centuries.

In years gone by, many of the roads surrounding Sholinghur were only narrow sandy tracks – an unmapped maze of lanes reaching out across these seemingly limitless plains. But now things have changed and the town can be reached by fairly good tar-sealed roads. The road from Sholinghur to the neighbouring town of Pallipet is busy with regular buses, some private cars, many lorries, thousands of cycles and the ubiquitous bullock carts. And it is by the side of this road that a community of stonecutters live and work. The community must have one of the least enviable jobs in the world. Day after day, they cut rocks from the granite hillside and then, by hand, break these huge boulders into smaller stones. They then load these stones into lorries which carry them to different parts of Tamil Nadu.

To say that the lives of these stonecutters is hard is an understatement. Their life is exceptionally hard; they are appallingly exploited and oppressed; their living conditions are terrible and it will take at least another generation to free these workers from this dreadful bondage. Their daily working conditions are unspeakable – hewing granite in temperatures which are usually between 85°F and 105°F – the heat coming off the hill face is always intense, with very little seasonal change. The actual breaking of the stones, by men, women and children with small hammers, is a job which would kill most people within weeks.

The stonecutters live in small communities – perhaps up to 30 families in one place – and it may take them several years to 'work' the hillside. At night, they shelter in fragile thatched huts, more like thatched tents than the traditional sturdy mud and thatch huts of rural India. These tiny homes cling precariously to the hill slope. There is no water available, and the mothers walk a kilometre to find even a single drop. What must it be like to come back after a day amidst the stones and then search for a pot of water for washing and cooking? Once a week, a group from the community go to Sholinghur bazaar for rice.

The hillside itself is owned by the Tamil Nadu government, but the granite areas are let out to various 'owners' who are absolute landlords. These bosses are totally ruthless as far as the workforce is concerned and even today, at the end of the twentieth century, they pay a tiny amount for a full lorry of broken stones. If they are 'fortunate' (hardly an appropriate word in such a context), the family as a whole takes back £1 at the end of a day's labour. If they are lucky. Often it is less. The hold which these owners have over the workers is complete, because through the years they have loaned money to them, and this financial obligation creates a kind of cementing of the bondage – a sad reality everywhere in the developing world. The dark satanic mills of Victorian England seem, in comparison with this situation, like paradise.

Because they regard themselves as a nomadic group, none of the children go to the local government school in Sholinghur. The parents prefer the children to work on the hillside, ensuring a little more daily income. Most of the children work hard, helping to break and carry the stones, and the infants sit close by their mothers on a boiling hot pile of stones. It is little wonder that all kinds of illnesses are found in the stonecutters' community, not least among the children, many of whom die at an early age.

Recently in some areas of South India, development workers have tried to fight along with the stonecutters for their basic rights. In a society where millions live below the official poverty line, this is not an easy task and very little headway has been made in such places like Sholinghur where oppression reigns. The injustice is so deep and the bondage so pervasive that it is difficult to know where to enter this whole cycle of deprivation. An obvious solution would be to create stoneworkers' cooperatives, but the formation of such cooperatives in this part of the world faces all kinds of official, bureaucratic restrictions. Nor are such groups given encouragement by government departments.

At Sholinghur, some local Christians have started a small informal 'evening school' for the stonecutters' children. Many of the parents, all of whom are illiterate, join in drawing the Tamil alphabet on the sand. The fact that some outside people care about their plight seems to be just as important as any formal learning – a lesson which is often lost sight of in the million dollar 'development schemes' which come from the drafting committees of the World Bank and many others.

If there was an easy answer to the situation of the stoneworkers on the Pallipet Road, such groups would not be in the terrible plight which they face. There are no easy solutions, and among certain groups in India today, exploitation is increasing, though in other communities the fight for justice has brought

benefits. Despite the dreadful plight of these particular stone-workers, the situation in rural India is not static, and awareness about basic human rights is growing.

I can never forget the little community on the road just beyond Sholinghur. In that dry and rocky place, amidst these fragile houses, you will find families who must be among the most exploited in India. They seem to be totally powerless, and even their fight for water seems only to bring them more oppression. But as we look into the tired faces of the stonecutters, we find laughter, intelligence, hope and deep compassion. These people are alive to life perhaps much more than I will ever be. And through them, God offers an amazing gift – the uprooting of my easy assumptions about my own priorities.

Peter and Dorothy Millar

Prayer

Lord God, you humble me before the poor.
The more I have the more I want to cling to.

Jesus Christ did not grasp at divine equality but laid aside his glory,
stripping himself of privilege and security
to live life with the conditions we live under;
he was a vulnerable child, a refugee;
he was found alongside the lowest, the least, the lost;
he gave all, even life itself.
Yet I hesitate to part with some of my abundance.

Lord God, you humble me before the poor.

Ian M. Fraser

Basic Christian Communities

An advert in the local paper

What makes church church has to be continually discovered. What exists has to be continually reshaped. Jeremiah provides an illuminating illustration. He is told to go down to the potter's house. He finds the potter working at his wheel. Jeremiah is instructed by what he sees.

The vessel he was making of clay was spoiled in the potter's hand. He reworked it into another vessel as seemed good to him. Then the word of the Lord came to me: 'Can I not do with you, O house of Israel, just as the potter has done?' says the Lord. (Jeremiah 18:4–5)

The basic material is not discarded. It is reshaped. In the reshaping the original intention may be better realised – even improved upon when fresh imaginative possibilities are brought to bear.

If I find that some people are giving up on church, I do not try to dissuade them. Their action may cause the church, as a prodigal, to come to itself. But I do urge them to get together with others to bring a small community into being and to join them on a journey of discovery about life's meaning and purpose.

Something like this is what had happened when my wife, Margaret, and I participated in the first European Congress of Basic Christian Communities in Holland in 1983. The congress lasted for four days. For three of these, those who came from outside Holland were allocated to different basic Christian communities to share life experiences. Our group, the Salland group, had come about in the following way. One person had contacted a few acquaintances and had put an advert in the local paper to this effect: 'I want to find what it is to live the Christian faith today. It seems to me that the official church is hindering rather than helping me. Any others willing to join me in this quest?' In no time thirty people had responded. By the time we arrived the number had risen to over seventy. Two small communities had to be formed to cater effectively for those keen to go on such a pilgrimage.

Grow into fullness (Partitions)

The partitions of Japanese houses can be removed to provide a substantial meeting place in even quite small houses. One Sunday morning, some forty or fifty people gathered in such a home. Most of them were young adults. Some Western hymns were sung and some of Japanese origin. The readings were followed intently, and people really worked on the exposition of four different Bible passages, although they did not discuss the interpretations with the young pastor. I did not need to know the language to be part of a vitalising and refreshing act of worship.

'A pity about that,' said my guide as we left.

'A pity? Far from it! An exhilarating experience – even for a foreigner!'

'I mean, it's a pity that this church grew as it did.'

'How did it grow then?'

'Well, a few Christians moved into this area and discovered one another. They started to meet for Bible study and worship. Then the quality of their life began to attract others. Most of the people you saw there came from Shintoism, or some other faith, or no faith at all. It was the sheer quality of life of the original group which produced this church.'

'But that is all good – what worries you?'

'Well, you see, the original group was simply the church of this place, the Christians who happened to be here who were drawn together by the common faith they were living out. But, unfortunately, they were all kinds: Roman Catholics, Baptists, Salvation Army, the lot.'

'But isn't that a good thing?'

'In one way. But, we have not only learned the gospel from you Westerners, we have received your divisions. The people who have joined this house church cannot be baptised. There is no one tradition into which they all may enter. The church cannot grow into its fullness.'

Ian M. Fraser

Non-Violence and Peacemaking

Mediation

Is it possible that there is nobody among you wise enough to judge a dispute between believers?

1 Corinthians 6:5–7

I see this passage as an advertisement by Paul for mediation. He was horrified that some Christians, prompted by greed and in their desire for gain, were taking other Christians to the Roman law courts to settle disputes.

Paul emphasised that this behaviour was contrary to the teaching of Jesus – throughout the Sermon on the Mount Jesus maintains the need for individuals and groups to treat one another fairly and in love. Jesus set a higher value on goodwill and friendly relations than on the successful assertion of rights.

Paul said that the very fact that they sought legal redress against another showed that they had failed as Christians. 'Do not take revenge on someone who wrongs you' (Matthew 5:38).

This principle of finding someone or some body to facilitate in the settlement of disputes and disagreements can extend into many areas – from mediation in marriage breakdown to the resolution of international conflicts.

So many conflicts could be avoided if parties were persuaded to talk and listen to each other before pursuing a course of action which could make the possibility of agreement impossible or considerably more difficult to achieve.

It should be the aim and purpose of each one of us as Christians to deal fairly with each other, even though relationships may have broken down for some reason and we feel hurt or angry, or both.

In situations where it has been too painful or acrimonious to deal with the issues without involving independent help, by using mediation we have a method or process which enables us to speak to, and to listen to, those with whom we are in dispute. Thereby we can avoid diving straight into a conflict which may become more and more difficult to resolve as time passes.

The words of the folk song 'Elsie Marley' summarise beautifully one way to resolve a conflict: 'We gathered up our differences and threw them in the air and gave them to the wind that shakes the barley.'

Mediation is not about revenge, gain, power or self. It is about fairness, consideration, sharing.

It should be the aim of all of us who care passionately for reconciliation and peace in the world to encourage or call for mediation wherever it is clear that the issue or dispute would benefit from impartial involvement.

In this way we fulfil the teaching of Jesus.

Hostility, suspicion, blame.
Stiffness in demeanour.
Hurt, anger, pain.
Warring parties
apart, but together.
Unwilling, yet willing.

Present with a stranger.
Impartial but within reach.
Listening, understanding,

equally attentive to each.
Peacemaker, enabler,
encouraging respect, openness,
focusing minds.

Protagonists
shifting, turning towards the other,
seeing new viewpoints and needs,
amid moments of anger, occasional laughter.
Finding common ground.
Moving in the same direction.

Katherine M. Rennie

INTERFAITH

Jamila, Amir and Paddy

Jamila was distraught. Her husband, Amir, had just been admitted to the hospice and, while the nurses settled him into his bed, she sat alone in the conservatory. She was unmistakably Muslim, in her hijab and traditional dress. She looked lost, and the fact that she could not converse in English made her even more isolated. She cried openly, and in those stressful early times none of the staff knew quite what to do. The usual words of comfort weren't understood and it would be a while before an interpreter would arrive. And I, the hospice chaplain – male, Presbyterian and not at all well-versed in the etiquette of dealing with Muslim women – was unsure about what to offer.

In time, with Amir comfortable, Jamila took her place at his side and began a long bedside vigil. We learned later that Amir was a postgraduate student at the local university, and that he and Jamila had come from Egypt the year before. The cancer had been rapid and devastating, and Amir's time in the hospice was to allow his distressing symptoms to be better controlled. Jamila, in her devotion as a faithful wife, would sit for hours in silence beside his bed.

Paddy, one of the two other men in the ward, was a bit of a rogue. He had lived a pretty dissolute life, and had been thrown out of more pubs than Glasgow Celtic had celebrated victories at Parkhead. Paddy wasn't an easy man to like, and he didn't like me much either. He was a lapsed Irish Catholic, and any clergyman of whatever denomination was to be viewed with great suspicion. So this chaplain wasn't in that room much: awkward with a Muslim woman, and not flavour of the month with an Irish Catholic.

One morning I stood, unnoticed, at the door of Amir's ward and wondered at my failure. Amir was asleep, and Jamila was in her usual place by his bed. She had her head in her hands and was clearly weeping. Across the ward, Paddy sat on his bed and gazed intently at her distress. Then, to my surprise, without a word, he got to his feet and moved slowly across the room. With creaking bones, he knelt down by Jamila's side and put a big labourer's arm around her shoulders. No etiquette, no protocol, no words, just a big arm comforting a woman in distress. Jamila lifted her head from her hands, turned towards Paddy, and laid her head on his shoulder. He spread his arms around her and gave her a huge hug as Jamila sobbed in his embrace. In time the sobbing subsided, and, his job done, Paddy returned to sit on his bed and Jamila went back to her faithful vigil.

Tom Gordon

Month 3 Day 28

COMMITMENT

Prayer becomes the very mainspring of action

Part of the worship cycle on Iona includes a weekly service of commitment. In this, people have the opportunity to re-dedicate their lives, sometimes quietly in personal prayer, sometimes by going to the front of the congregation and kneeling, while the worship leader pronounces a saying of Jesus over each person. For me this became almost a routine, as I would recommit myself at the end of a summer season before going back to work on the mainland. On this particular occasion, I went forward as usual, and the words for me were, 'Ask and you shall receive.' I went away considering these very familiar words, when suddenly it occurred to me that I was asking the wrong person. What I ardently prayed for was an end to the nuclear arms race. Why then was I asking God to deliver what was the province of the military and the politicians? Thus was born the first of the 'Options for Defence' conferences to which military generals, defence experts, campaigners and church leaders were invited. These dialogues are still continuing in the regular Rhu Consultations, where there is still a really deep exchange of views and concerns.

Thus if we are seeking an answer to prayer we may be led into direct engagement with the social and political structures of power. As William Penn famously said, 'True Godliness doesn't turn men out of the world, but enables them to live better in it, and excites their endeavours to mend it' (Quaker Faith & Practice 23.02); or in a more contemporary context, Gordon Matthews wrote: 'We need both a deeper spirituality and a more outspoken witness. If our spirituality can reach the depths of authentic prayer, our lives will become an authentic witness for justice, peace and the integrity of creation, a witness which becomes the context for our prayer' (Quaker Faith & Practice 23.10).

Thus prayer becomes the very mainspring of action. It was in response to inner leadings of prayer that Friends campaigned against slavery, that they dared to travel to Russia to speak with the Tsar during the Crimean War, that Amnesty International was formed, and that Mary Dyer was driven back to Massachusetts to her death. Prayer that is real can have the most unexpected results and almost inevitably leads us into action in ways we might never have dreamed of. Prayer is essentially practical and political.

I once stayed with a group of nuns in a convent in St Louis. Part of their daily prayer involved either watching the news on television, or else reading a daily newspaper in an attitude of awareness and openness to action in response to current events.

George MacLeod used to say that it was no use praying for a woman to be cured of her TB if we were not prepared to work politically with government and local authorities to provide adequate, damp-free housing. One of the inspirational groups arising out of this essentially practical philosophy was the Gorbals Group. This was a group of young Church of Scotland ministers and committed lay people who decided that rather than praying for an end to poverty in Glasgow, they were going to live as an intentional community in the Gorbals, one of the poorest areas of the city, well-known for its violence and deprivation. Their houses were open day and night and people knew that they could find a listening ear, a cup of tea or a bed for the night. But their actions went beyond neighbourliness to an active political engagement to tackle some of the roots of endemic poverty ...

Helen Steven

THE REDISCOVERY OF SPIRITUALITY

An epiphany in Antarctica and a communion in Guguletu, South Africa

Everything is one

'Here were the imponderable processes and forces of the cosmos, harmonious and soundless. Harmony, that was it! That was what came out of the silence – a gentle rhythm, the strain of a perfect chord, the music of the spheres.'

Richard Byrd, 1934

In December of last year I was privileged to visit the Antarctic. There were many remarkable things about that trip but one in particular continues to arise in my mind on a regular basis.

From an Antarctic mountain I looked down and stretching away into the distance was the Ross Ice Shelf, a stretch of ice that is permanently frozen and is fixed to the continent of Antarctica. This is a land of extremes – the highest, coldest, driest, windiest place on earth – and this ice shelf is no exception: we were told it is the same size as France. I simply had to move away from other people and sit down wordlessly as my mind tried to process this sight; and I wanted to laugh and cry at the same time. I was completely overcome by this pristine, trackless wilderness stretching off endlessly into the distance. Then I had something of a 'eureka' moment.

For most of my adult life I have been concerned with finding 'the way'. You know – the blueprint for life, the Maker's instructions, the truth. I have built, and then have huffed and puffed and blown down, more houses than I care to remember, some of which had taken a very long time to construct. But I have no regrets, for it is only with the walls flattened that I can begin to see the vast horizons all around and to realise that actually there is no 'way', there is just being. I have been like the proverbial fish, charging around frantically, looking for the sea.

Perhaps by letting go of hope, of something better, of something other, of a direction, we will come into the fullness of life as it is available to us right now, without anything, absolutely anything, added. This is not a barren, anodyne place devoid of symbolism and story. It is one full of the amazing richness of the present moment, and the diversity of those with whom we share our remarkable incarnate journey. In doing this we might fully appreciate that everything truly is one, and that there may be peace and justice.

Communion (from the Guguletu web journal)

Last Sunday, during the service, Spiwo, the minister, called all the children to the front of the church, and then summoned me. I had received no warning of this and so was a little uncertain as to what was going on. He then said that I had some special magic to show them and instructed me to do my finger tricks! I had foolishly shown him these in an idle moment the day before, in an attempt to demonstrate just what amazing gifts I had brought with me to Guguletu.

Those of you who suffered these on Iona for three years will now be groaning … Anyway, I did my stuff to gasps from the children, some indulgent smiles, and a couple of grimaces and shaking of heads. So, for the next two days, I had children running up to me and tying their fingers in knots trying to emulate my magic. I also had one parent who told me off because her child had done nothing else but this for a whole day until told that that was enough. This could be part of my legacy to the township: when I went on a visit recently I found the car surrounded by several enthusiastic youngsters, all keen to demonstrate their trickery to the *mfundisi* (teacher).

Month 3 Day 30

This, and the rule I broke. Well, this bit isn't funny. I was asked if I would share Communion with an elderly member of the church who was HIV positive and too sick to attend. I reflected on this considerably. Several years ago I was ordained as a deacon into the Anglican Church, yet I declined to go through with ordination as a priest a year later – for many reasons. This meant that I could perform magic tricks, but I could not do the magic of administering Communion. Yet here was such a profound need; how could I refuse? And my understanding of this sacrament as a celebration of life – body and food – of being incarnate, of being loved, of one body one flesh, given by all to all – enabled me to enter into it wholeheartedly. And I felt able to do so without a backward glance at the formal structures of church which may have complained or argued about whether I was ontologically equipped to do such a thing. And so I found myself in a shack in Guguletu – with the sun beating on the corrugated iron roof, sweat pouring down my face, a sick man on a bed – administering Communion for the very first time.

I am having many different types of experiences here. Some ordinary and everyday, many full of laughter, some scary, some joyous – much singing and music – and some profound moments that are almost impossible to put into words. This experience of administering Communion falls into the last category. At that moment, the church was that shack, the congregation the family and youngsters who wandered in and watched this strange spectacle with interest. And it was a sacred place, at least it felt so for me. It was a place where life and death came together in a real and immediate way, where there was a wonderful human connection between us, despite our profoundly different circumstances. For a moment we were one flesh, fully alive at that moment, sickness or no sickness, yet with the knowledge that we are all born to die. It was overwhelming, it was life-affirming; I felt privileged to be there; and then it was over, and I stepped into my smart hire car and disappeared to another world …

Nick Prance

THE THIRTY-FIRST DAY

After Alzheimer's disease (A prayer)

Let us share the quiet of this place …

> Are you with us, Lord?
> Were you with the one we mourn today?
> You who, to enter the pain of our world,
> were broken in your body,
> shattered in mind.
> You who suffered on the Cross.
> Sharp pain for tortured hours,
> but only hours, and you gave up the ghost.

Are you there? Is there anybody there	Yes, for there,
when lucid moments grow rarer	in our grasp and in need of our care,
and stillness is no peace?	is the one who promised
When there is nothing but	we would meet him
endless endless endless	in the hungry and the naked
confusion and emptiness?	and those imprisoned.

> Even in those locked deep in what they have been.

David Coleman

MONTH 4

NEW WAYS TO TOUCH THE HEARTS OF ALL

Four sketches about working as an aide in a nursing home:

Grace

The nurses were dolling everyone up for the Christmas party. Putting on make-up. Giving manicures. So I grabbed an emery board, and sat and filed and shaped Grace's jagged, cracked, thick yellow fingernails that had been soaking soaking … Not bad. We had a good chat.

'And, so what about a little Christmas glitter on those nails, Grace?'

'Oh, no thanks, dear – I've never been the flashy type.'

Everyone was having a good time. I gave a facial. Smoothed and massaged Pond's cold cream into a ninety-one-year-old woman's tired, dry wrinkles. She closed her eyes – it must have felt good. I wondered how long it had been since somebody had touched her (not counting turning her to change her, not counting wiping her rear). How long had it been? How long since someone had touched her? It felt good. I wondered if she remembered a lover; a son; the summer breeze – fragrant as Pond's cold cream? Or nothing: just a relaxed, full, soothing feeling sinking in …

Amazing grace

Jane is far away in her interior landscape. She sits in her room all day. Locked in her wheelchair. Hums and sings to herself. Loudly sometimes, as if saying: 'I'm still here. I'm still fucking here.'

I glanced at her case file. A hell of a life – deaths, deaths, alcohol …

There's a piano in the Alzheimer's unit. I played 'Amazing Grace' – and Jane sang along.

Amazing how someone who can't remember their daughters' and sons' and spouses' names – their own name some days – can remember all the words to some old song. Music is holy. Music is the voice of God.

I played Jane 'Summertime'. And she sang along – her voice rough and broken and sore and beautiful. Tears in her throat.

Kate

Helping Kate get dressed. Talking about stiff things – the weather, current events …

'Did you hear about the two hunters up in Red Bay?' she suddenly asks me.

'No. No, I haven't.'

'Yeah, two hunters up in Red Bay. And the one was going hunting – for bear or deer, I guess – and was saying to his friend that what if he got bit by a rattlesnake up there? 'Cause he was feeling a little perturbed about it, you know. What to do.'

'There are a lot of rattlesnakes up there I've heard.'

'Right, a lot of rattlesnakes. So his friend told him no problem, that it's no problem – you just slit it open with your hunting knife and suck the poison out. Suck out the poison.'

'I've heard that –'

'Right, no problem. So his friend goes out hunting – for bear or moose, I guess – and comes back and his friend asks him, when he sees him, so how'd it go? How his hunting trip

went. "Did you have any problem with rattlesnakes?" he asks him. "Oh good – no, no problem," his friend tells him. "Oh, I got bit when I was out." "Oh yeah? Where?" his friend asks him. "In the backside," he says, "but, no problem, I did what you told me. And gosh, you sure know who your friends are'."

And Kate laughs and I smile and she beams up at me – a roguish, lopsided smile. And I think: she's paralysed all down one side but still full of flowing spirit. And I stop trying so hard and relax. Take it natural. And from then on the conversation flows easy. Easy as a good joke.

Emily

Helping Emily to wash her hands and face after lunch.

'This always reminds me of being a child,' she says.

'Why?' I ask, thinking it's because I'm *treating* her like a child – washing her hands and face for her.

'Peanut butter and jelly sandwiches,' she smiles. 'When you eat them they're sooo good. And you get it all over your hands like that. Remember?'

'Yes, yes – I remember picnics.'

'Oh yes, picnics!' exclaims Emily, and we giggle. And I glance up and the whole room is looking over at us – like we're crazy.

Neil Paynter

Month 4 Day 1

ECONOMIC WITNESS

Fair play!

'We were robbed!' they shouted when England lost in football over a split-second judgement by the referee. Every child will know what they mean. 'It's not fair!' gets said every day in the school playground, and is often true.

World trade isn't fair. Wealthy countries get the best deal, and can make demands on the poorer, setting the rules which favour themselves.

The fair trade movement is a way ordinary people can do something to change things. It is not about charity, but about changing the rules to make the world fairer.

For Christians, how we treat our neighbour is vitally important. 'Neighbour' in the gospels means everyone we meet, or those whose lives touch ours. Today, when we get news from all over the world, a neighbour can live anywhere.

Wealth matters. How we use money, to give people a chance, is the most common subject of the stories in the gospels.

The fair trade movement started small, with ordinary people. Now goods with the independent, international fair trade mark can be bought in supermarkets and cafés. When we buy fair trade, the producers – family farmers and village cooperatives – get a guaranteed price. We get their best produce or handicrafts. Their children get to go to school, and sick people get medicine. They are likely to use organic methods to grow food or dye clothes, so the environment gets less damaged. They get a say in world markets. We get a fair deal.

Rosemary Power

Prayer

Between friends
for my family
about politics
when I'm alone
in the supermarket
shopping for clothes
leisure time decisions
choices abound
my actions affect
my desires influence
my direction matters
I do not choose in isolation.
God, let me choose you.

Ewan Aitken

Youth Concern

A visit from the School Inspector

Back in the dark ages of 1960s-education, our class always had a test on a Friday afternoon – mental arithmetic, spelling and Bible knowledge. The results determined the seating arrangements on the Monday, and there was always great excitement as the class positions were appropriately readjusted at the start of the week – the bright ones at the back, in the cosy corner of the room, down to the dimmest ones. Some of us were fortunate always to be at the top of the class. But the bottom seat – the final, draughtiest seat right by the door – was always occupied by – Marion Thomas.

Marion had no friends, and she was bullied too. There were various names the other kids had for her, but 'Daft Marion' was the most common and cruellest. After all, she was always bottom of the class, wasn't she?

One Friday Mrs McDougall made an important announcement. On Monday the school was to have a visit from the School Inspector and we were to be on our very best behaviour. 'We don't want anyone to let the school down, now do we?' was the final warning.

The class arrangement having been sorted as per normal first thing on the Monday, we settled down to a morning's work, barely able to conceal a mixture of anticipation and terror. Eventually the time came for the School Inspector to come to the class, and it wasn't nearly as scary as some of us thought. Questions were asked on sums, spelling, geography, Bible stories, and the like, and, in response to each, a veritable forest of hands shot up. Someone – usually one of the ones at the back – would get the answer right. The class was doing its stuff. Mrs McDougall

looked suitably delighted.

The School Inspector, looking pleased too, announced that the inspection was almost at an end – and that we had done very well. 'But let's finish with some singing, just to confirm how good you are,' he announced. 'Who knows The Bonnie, Bonnie Banks O' Loch Lomond?' Again, a forest of hands … 'OK, let's sing it together – one, two, three …' and off we went, the whole class in great voice, singing with gusto. Mrs McDougall, conducting discreetly from the side, looked fit to burst with pride.

We'd lustily got through one verse when the School Inspector waved his hand. 'Stop, stop just now,' he ordered. 'Let's have someone sing the next verse on their own.' Once more, a forest of hands, especially from the back, for the brightest of us believed we had the best voices too.

'I wonder,' pondered the School Inspector, looking round the class, 'I wonder …' And then, after what seemed an age of pondering, he announced, 'I know, we'll have you,' and he pointed right at Marion Thomas.

There was a corporate intake of breath, followed by barely concealed whispers, 'Daft Marion, oh no …' 'Mrs McDougall will stop him …' 'This will be terrible …' Marion looked stunned, and glanced round to see if the School Inspector wasn't really pointing to some- one else.

'Yes, you, right by the door, you come up and sing a verse for us.'

Slowly Marion rose from her seat. The class held its collective breath as Daft Marion stood beside the School Inspector. 'OK then,' he announced, 'I'll start you off, and you sing the rest on your own … one, two, three …' and the School Inspector and Marion Thomas started to sing. After a few notes, the School Inspector stopped, and Marion carried on … singing … unbelievably … beautifully … This girl had the most gorgeous voice we'd ever heard.

When she was finished, there was a long silence, broken by the School Inspector saying, 'Well done, little girl. You've done your class proud. Your school is very fortunate to have as good a singer as you. I hope you don't waste such a special talent. Come on, children, let's give this girl a great, big clap.'

It was the loudest cheer I'd ever heard – and, do you know something else? I'd never seen Mrs McDougall cry before.

Prayer

God, help us seek and find again the gifts a child is given.
Help us know and celebrate what treasure store from heaven
is bestowed on any child whom others might deride.
Help us offer hope to those who are always cast aside.

Tom Gordon

THE WORD

Biblical Truth?

Last Community Week on Iona, I was invited to introduce a session entitled 'Reading the Bible from the margins'. I'm sure such a session would have been both fascinating and challenging: there has been a global explosion of engaged biblical reading and interpretation from standpoints which could be called 'marginal' to the mainstream, the privileged and the powerful in church and society. But I'm afraid that isn't what the community got from me last October, because I wanted to raise, and to share, a more personal and basic question of integrity for me as a member, and for us as a community. It's a question which has confronted me with a nagging persistence over the past few years – and especially when I give an undertaking each year that I am 'with the community' in commitment to its Rule. The first part of our five-fold Rule (and its position may indicate some notion that it is foundational for the other parts) asks us 'to read the Bible on a regular and frequent basis'. I confess here, as I have done over the years to various leaders, and as I did to my fellow members on Iona last October, that I do not read the Bible very frequently or regularly. The problem is not that I endeavour and fail to do so, but that I resist (you might say reject) the injunction to do so. As you'll appreciate, this wilful and persistent failure to keep the Rule presents a rather serious challenge to my membership of the community, and I've been waiting for years to get the boot!

I've been a member of the Iona Community for 22 years, and in that time we have discussed in Plenary and Family Groups the rationale and practice of all the other elements of the Rule. But I cannot recall any time when we have engaged seriously and corporately with some basic questions about reading the Bible:

- What constitutes 'the Bible'?
- How did it get to be 'the Bible'?
- Why should we read it?
- How should we read it?
- What criteria help to shape our reading?
- What outcomes should follow from reading?

There has been an apparently unquestioned assumption that the Bible is central, normative and privileged in our lives as Christians and as a community. I simply want to place a question mark, to interrogate the apparently obvious, to highlight some of the problems in leaving that assumption unchallenged: not 'reading the Bible…' but 'reading the Bible?'

I tried to articulate my concerns as part of the accounting process, in a letter to the leader:

'I value the texts of the Christian Bible as a rich store of stories and insights, of central importance in shaping our culture and worldviews – both dominant and resistant. Historically, the texts themselves, in all their complex wonder and glory, contradiction or horror, have been invested with a power to shape people's lives, and not always for the good … Is it possible any longer for an inclusive Iona Community to avoid accusations of imperialism if we claim the viability of reading off an exclusively Christian template, or primarily from the collection of texts we know as 'the Bible'?

If we continue, without even talking about it, to hold fast to the apparently normative boundaries of a bible-based ethos in our Rule, we might keep out explorers and strugglers for an incarnational life of faith and justice-seeking. Could we reflect more on this? I would find that helpful, and maybe other members would too.'

I was relieved to have those questions, and the desire for open reflection, so warmly affirmed and endorsed at Community Week.

But perhaps I should say more about the problem with the Bible from my current context. I have been active in campaigning and struggles to name and overcome the pervasive sexual violence and profound gender injustice which have blighted human history, and which continue to constrain and damage possibilities for fullness of life in every part of our world. In this struggle for female rights and opportunities, the Jewish and Christian scriptures are not the most obvious resource! In fact, you have to work bloody hard to extract useful nuggets of empowerment and transformation for women from these male-centred texts. The womanist theologian Delores Williams has described them as telling 'a male story populated by human males, divine males, divine male emissaries, and human women mostly servicing male goals'. The narratives are overwhelmingly driven by male concerns and agency, and incorporate some overt and extremely violent accounts of the mistreatment, degradation and destruction of women, who are used, abused, discarded, silenced and forgotten. In places the personal God is represented almost pornographically as a hyper-masculine jealous divine male, and the church or people of God as faithless harlots or submissive wives. The bodies, lives, desires and sexuality of women are seen almost entirely through male lenses (and that goes for the gospels too). The fragments of their stories are parts of larger, much more cohesive stories of men, which biblical scholarship and interpretation has traditionally taken as *the* Story. So what can we discover about the authentic lives and concerns of the women portrayed – especially when they are often made by the creators of the text to speak and act against their own interests? Perhaps biblical texts reveal more about male fears, desires, power games and prejudices. To be sure, they are full of beautiful poetry and surprising twists; ethical challenges and potent visions; 'parables and patter'. But these are inescapably embedded in an androcentric ideology of social, cultural and gender relations. In this the scriptures are of their time. All of human life is *not* in the Bible – at least it's reasonable to say that the laws, histories – yes, even the prophecies of resistance – are based on the privileged perspective of certain ethnic groups, classes and interests in the history of the Ancient Near East, to the detriment or exclusion of other standpoints. Thus the Bible can be used as a tool against values and visions which we claim to derive from the gospel. For slaves, for Palestinians, for abused women, it has too often operated not as good news, but as bad news.

Many other literary sources, both ancient and more modern, share these characteristics, and we nevertheless value and enjoy their cultural riches. But the Bible is more than literature, however profound. Because it has been invested with sacred power as Scripture – the Word of God – it has given divine legitimacy to those who have assumed the authority to interpret and practise its injunctions. So the Bible has been used to shape and influence the social structures and attitudes which have enabled patriarchal social control over gendered roles, practices and identities. In short, injustice and violence against women has traditionally been explained and justified in the Christian West as part of God's order and intention for humankind. Certainly, movements to resist and liberate have also found powerful support from scriptural sources, but as leading biblical scholar Elisabeth Schüssler Fiorenza has said: 'because the Bible and Christian tradition have contributed to abuse, injustice and silencing, we cannot trust or accept them simply as divine revelation.' She has pioneered a rigorous 'hermeneutics of suspicion' to expose and critique the social and historical construction of that collection of texts we call 'the Bible'. It has no intrinsic core of meaning or authority, but only through its functions: what is ascribed by different people in diverse situations. And the ascription of meaning cannot be separated from locations and relations of social power in human history. At the heart of my problem is not the collection of literature which constitutes 'the Bible', but the concept of *canon* which has selected, ordered and maintained the boundaries of

Month 4 Day 4

'sacred scripture'. Who made these decisions, and whose interests have they served? What was left out, and why? Which writings and voices have been excluded, anathematised or suppressed – and why? Who has organised and controlled translation and rights of interpretation – and to what ends? Who uses 'Truth' (especially scriptural 'Truth' as Word of God) to regulate behaviour? What has happened when challenges have been made to these rights (the Reformation, the Enlightenment, liberation theology, Zionism …)? These are questions about function, use, power: and if we take them seriously, they radically destabilise the canonicity of the Bible. In simple terms, it is not a closed or finished book. I welcome the many, often conflicting subversive strategies for reading by those seeking to discern the Word of God in dialogue with the scriptural texts. Another feminist theologian has said: 'I strive for healing and so must confront what is toxic.' But is there not a case for toxic waste disposal? Instead of devoting energy wrestling counter-intuitively to find constructive readings of bad news stories, might we not simply remove their authority, both practically and symbolically, from our attempts to be faithful to a God of love and justice? Should we not free ourselves to attend more fully to some of the excluded, forgotten voices, bodies and lives around us – the testimonies and sacred texts which have never been part of the canon of the religious and political powers-that-be?

In her fascinating book *Changing the Subject: Women's Discourses and Feminist Theology* (1994), Mary McClintock Fulkerson argues that truth is situational, not absolute, and that different Christian communities create their own canonical systems for the practice and performance of scripture. They develop *reading regimes* (both dominant and resisting) which provide norms for using biblical texts in their endeavours to practise faith and extend the realm of God. In these situated, ever-changing engagements, biblical narratives are not simply retold, but remade. It's a creative, dynamic and corporate activity. At Community Week, I posed the question: what is the Iona Community's reading regime? What are the goals and values which give us authorisation, so that we create our own performances of living sacred text, and invest them with meaning? According to page 1 of *Coracle*, the magazine of the Iona Community, we are 'committed to the gospel of Jesus Christ, and to following where that leads, even into the unknown'. We are 'engaged … for justice, peace and the integrity of creation' and 'convinced that the inclusive community we seek must be embodied in the community we practise'. Are these intentions the hermeneutical keys which allow us to challenge any absolute claims and rigid canonical boundaries of 'the Bible'? Do they allow us, by the Spirit, to reject the binding authority of texts long past their sell-by date? Do they open our eyes and hearts to the living bible beyond ancient written, fallible words? Do they call us to account for 'the Bible' – not to assume that it provides the normative archetype for Christian communities with words of inherent significance or value, but always to ask how it can bear meaning for survival and justice in a broken world?

Belonging to the Iona Community is vital for me, because it helps me engage with a 'talking book' which shifts authority from written text to incarnated struggles to be faithful to a God of love. And let me conclude here, as I did during our Community Week discussion, by appealing to our own canonical tradition: the gospel according to George MacLeod:

We must honour the Bible. It was most certainly not originally designed to be read just as literature. (But) if the Bible is to be relevant to our daily rounds and common task, we must remember that God is not speaking only in the Bible. He (sic) is speaking in the world and through history … God does not just speak from a book. (Coracle, 1947)

Lesley Orr

HOSPITALITY AND WELCOME

Just a cup of tea

For many years I have accompanied a Kurdish couple, Leila and Hasan. They came to Switzerland seeking asylum, because Hasan had been politically active and was going to be put in prison. They have two boys now, a permit to remain – which must be renewed every year – and still many problems.

I visited them in times when they lived in shabby housing with many other asylum-seekers; when they were hiding with another family. Now, finally, they have their own apartment. Over all that time, they have always offered me hospitality – a cup of tea, many cups some days, and, if there was an oven to bake with, some homemade bread or biscuits.

I have tried to explain official letters written in German, and we have discussed next steps; I have been to court with Hasan. I have tried to use my contacts and have sometimes been successful. So I have learnt about the many hardships in the lives of 'asylum-seekers' – yet my most profound experience during these years has been their warm hospitality: sharing simple meals, stories and even laughter. I feel deeply rewarded for my small efforts to befriend one family. I am convinced that our laws and restrictions would change if more people made an effort to meet refugees.

Every Christmas Eve begins with a visit to Leila, Hasan and their boys. Last Christmas Eve, Hasan played his flute for me for the first time, a herdsman's flute – simple and moving songs. An angel passed through the kitchen as we sat round the table.

It seems so easy to offer hospitality, to share and to live community. But how often do I miss the chance, living in a comfortable house in suburbia?

Elisabeth C. Miescher

It's not rocket science

It's not rocket science,
is it, Lord?
Making others feel welcome,
I mean.
If they show up
(like John)
barefoot,
we can just slip off our shoes
and get more comfortable;
if they come
(like John)
speaking in a way
we don't understand,
all we have to do is listen;
if they invite us
(like John)
to try a different way
of doing things,
we can jump into the water
and see what it's like.
It's not rocket science,
is it, Lord?
After all,
you welcome us
to your heart
just as we are.

Thom M. Shuman

Month 4 Day 5

THIS IS THE DAY

Sensible

Most of the time we sleep
in a world of comfort
and sensible ideas,
where slippers
and an early night
are wise
and not rocking the boat
is the best
course of action.
But occasionally
there are blinding moments
when the scales fall
from our eyes
and we wake up.
When all the
dullness of our
sheltered existence
falls away
and we see the
vibrant wild luminous
world as it is.

And we throw off the
habits of security
and remember that
we have wings
and feet
and power
and we do something
utterly foolish and
wild and
extravagant
and our untamed passion
grasps hold of
the moment
of life itself,
wonderful and reckless,
and walks through a stormy night
or dances naked on the beach.
I don't want to be remembered
for being sensible.
I want to be
remembered
as wild, formidable
and free,
fiery and
fully alive.

Lotte Webb

Wild night

It isn't the stars that call me out.
It's the wildness of the night,
when the wind howls and laps and snorts
around the perimeter walls,
when the wild creature inside me awakes.

The stars are sedate,
dazzling, but dead.
An optical illusion.
Yes, they make me gasp on a clear night,
a celestial scattering of glitter on velvet,
a fire show.

But this night is different.
While others close their windows and curtains,
I throw mine open –
I step outside into the black, wild night
I walk into the darkness,
the familiar paths and trees suddenly
dangerous and untamed
changed and free.
Here they are in their element
just as I am in mine.

I am a wild creature at heart
and the storm summons me out of my sleep
into the wonder of the unknown
wild, intimate night.

Lotte Webb

Month 4 Day 6

THE IONA EXPERIENCE

Praying under my fig tree

It is just about a year since I moved from an isolated, large house with a large garden to a one-bedroomed, ground floor flat with a small garden. I enjoy the ease of caring for a smaller place and the closeness to shops, church and public transport, but there are a few things I miss. I especially miss the nooks and crannies in my former garden, but most of all I miss my fig tree. It is not just the abundant crop of luscious fruit that I long for. It is the 'special place' under the fig tree.

From the moment we planted the tree in 1986, it was special. We planted it in front of a ten-foot-high, south-facing wall where it would get the benefit of the sun and shelter from the cold north winds. The first thing I thought about when I stood back to admire it was the story of Nathanael (John 1). Nathanael asked Jesus, 'How do you know me?' And Jesus answered, 'I saw you under the fig tree.'

I could not go near my fig tree without thinking of that story, so it became, for me, a special place of prayer.

We spend so much time in life wearing masks, playing roles and living up to other people's expectations, that I find that there is something very healing, very peaceful, very consoling, just to be able to sit and be me and know that I am completely loved and accepted by God. That is how I felt under my fig tree.

Most people will have experienced a special place that seems more conducive to prayer and where their physical and spiritual lives become more integrated. For many people, Iona is that special place, but sadly, for most of us, it is not in our back garden. I remember sitting at the north end of Iona with a friend, looking out at Staffa and the cliffs of Mull. After a long time she said, 'How could anyone sit here like this and not praise God?' Her words echoed my own thoughts.

I also remember the closing session when I stayed at the Abbey many years ago. We had had a wonderful week and all the guests were saying how they had found peace, a spiritual uplift and closeness to God. We were told that what we had felt, we had brought with us – within us – and that we would still have it within us. If that is so, maybe I do not need my fig tree. It may be a little more difficult to find that feeling of complete peace, love and acceptance, but it is there to find.

Pat Welburn

LIFE IN COMMUNITY

The late Andy Bennett (A prayer and a half)

The local funeral director phoned me to make the arrangements. The deceased was Andrew Bennett. He had died in a lodging house. He had no family. All the funeral director had was a name. I decided it wasn't enough.

So, later that day, I headed to the last place of residence of the late Andrew Bennett, a run-down lodging house with a dodgy history. I rang the doorbell and waited. After what seemed like an age, the door creaked open to reveal a gorilla of a man. 'Whit? Whit d'ye want? Eh?'

I looked at this large, unshaven lodging house door-attendant, and pondered replying, 'Sorry, I've got the wrong address,' and hotfooting it down the path. But I didn't. Maybe it was the dog collar giving me a boost of confidence, but I pulled myself up to my full five-foot-six and said, 'I'm from the church, and I'm to officiate at Mr Andrew Bennett's funeral. And because he lived here, I wondered if you knew him and could maybe tell me a bit about him.'

The man offered the semblance of a grin. 'Andy Bennett. Aye, he lived here, right enough. But he kept himsel' tae himsel'. So I canne tell you much.' He paused, as if trying to dredge something from his memory. The grin widened. 'Aye, an' he liked his pint did Andy. Aye, right enough, Andy Bennett liked his pint.' And with that, the door creaked shut, the conversation with the somewhat bemused local minister being deemed to be at an end.

So, later in the week, driving to the funeral of the late Andrew Bennett, I regaled the funeral director with the story of my brief conversation with the door attendant. I bemoaned the fact that I knew little about the deceased. 'Not much to offer by way of thanks for a long life, is it?' I complained. The funeral director listened without a word, and we lapsed into a companionable silence.

We were passing through the cemetery gates when he spoke. 'I had a funeral here last week of an old man who'd been found dead in an alleyway, a wino probably, with no identification. We didn't even have a name. The priest did the business well enough, and an unknown man was buried with dignity. And then, before the final blessing, the priest departed from the script. "Lord," he said, "we know nothing about this man. But we give thanks that he was always known to you." Now, that was a prayer and a half, eh?'

A few minutes later I stood by an open grave and looked round at the assembled company – the funeral director, the hearse driver, two council grave diggers and me. As we stood with bowed heads, I offered a prayer of commendation. 'Lord, we know little about this man. His name was Andy and he liked his pint, is all we know. But we give thanks today that he was always known to you.'

I hope it was another prayer and a half, and that Andy Bennett lies in peace.

Prayer

God of our living alone,
you know us as we are,
and always will.
Thank you for our uniqueness,
our lives in your image,
our time in your hands,
our living in your love.

God of our living together,
we know so little of the people around us,
save the odd name,
or the occasional label.
Yet we are quick to judge, and often condemn
their worth and value –
especially if they are not like us.

God of our living in community,
help us to know others as they are known to you,
and to value their uniqueness as we value our own –
their lives in your image,
their time in your hands,
their living in your loving –
and, hopefully, sometimes
in ours.

Tom Gordon

WOMEN

As in the beginning, women and men

This piece was often read at the nunnery on Iona during the weekly pilgrimage.

1.

In the beginning God created the ants.
They multiplied and covered the earth,
and they were as busy as bees –
but a bit boring too.

God needed something better
and so the first human being was made,
who gave names to all the animals,
from A for Ants to Z for Zebra –
but after that it became a bit boring again.

And then God built the best part of the human being,
something totally new: 'woman' –
and what was left behind continued as 'man'.
Building a woman was God's greatest effort,
and God was very pleased to see the both of them
for they did what no creature did before:
they laughed, just for fun,

and simply lived as helpers and partners,
each other's better half.
God must have been laughing, too.

Like the ants, woman and man multiplied
and covered the earth,
walking from Africa to Asia,
to America and to Europe,
even finding paths across the oceans.

But somewhere something went wrong,
somewhere the laughing faltered,
and women had to learn how to laugh anew.

2.

Abram and Sarai could not have a child.
The doctor was unable to tell them why,
but, as with so many women, Sarai got the blame.
So, when an unknown but familiar voice told them
she *would* have a child,
she laughed.
For she knew the facts
men had imposed on her, didn't she?
Guess what happened?
When Isaac was born,
Sarah laughed as she never had before.

Somewhere between heaven and earth
things *do* come right.

3.

Michal fell totally in love with David.
For her, he was her king all night,
as she was his queen every morning.
But in the interest of man's policies
her father simply traded her to someone else,
and Michal did not laugh for long.
When at last she returned to David,
she could only laugh *at* him:
'Are you a king?
So, why didn't you protect me?'

Somewhere things can go so wrong
they can hardly be restored.

4.

A thousand women got the blame
for King Solomon following strange gods and goddesses.
Funny how easily a man
who wanted so much to be a true manly king
was unable to make his own decisions.
In the women's quarters there must have been
quite a lot of laughing.

Somewhere men are very able
to make themselves worth laughing at.

Month 4 Day 9

5.

Yet, the Bible knows better:
wisdom is female.
Lady Wisdom knows when laughing
turns to scoffing.
She reveals the essentials of life,
and therefore she can recognise the rubbish.
When wisdom laughs,
it is the truest laugh you can hear.

Somewhere things *can* come right.

6.

Mary was just a young woman
who became pregnant.
Of course she knew how that had happened,
but she also had the deep wisdom
to accept the unbelievable miracle of it.
No one tells us if she laughed like Sarai
when Jesus was born,
but I bet she did.
As earthly and heavenly
as Flemish painters in the 15th century pictured her,
she must have smiled.
And good Joseph became
what a real man should be:
helper and partner.

Somewhere between heaven and earth
things *do* come right.

7.

Jesus was like his Father
in all aspects.
He was a true partner
to the women who followed him,
to his disciples,
and to everyone who asked him.
For he was a true Helper and Comforter.
And when he died,
the women were most true to him.
In the very early morning of Easter
they dared to face the staggering truth:
death is no longer death.
They didn't dare to laugh,
for joy was too precious.

Somewhere in heaven and on earth
things *have come* right,
and we can start again as in the beginning,
women and men.

Martin Grashoff, Staff member of the Iona Community

Prayer

Filing cabinets

Many years ago I lived and worked in a Christian community. We used to rent out the office space to a charity that worked with sex offenders and their victims. I used to clean the offices and would often pray for the charity as I cleaned. I regularly felt nudged by the Holy Spirit to pray when cleaning one particular group of filing cabinets. I imagined it held the files of the victims of abuse and was shocked at my own reaction when I discovered that, in fact, it held the files of the sex offenders. It caused me to look deeply at my own hidden attitudes. Prayer can take us places we never thought we needed to go!

Polly Burns

JUSTICE AND PEACE

Water

Strike the rock, and water will pour out of it for the people to drink.
Exodus 17:6 (REB)

Water, water, everywhere
Nor any drop to drink.

Coleridge, from The Rime of the Ancient Mariner

The clock is ticking. Tick, tock, tick, tock, tick, tock, seven, eight, tick, tock, tick, tock, tick, fourteen, fifteen …

Fifteen seconds have passed and another child has died from water-related disease. And the clock ticks on. And children die. We tend to take access to clean water and to sanitation for granted. In Britain it is so easy to forget that there are over 1.1 billion people in the world without our privileged access to clean water. We turn a tap and it is there. It is also easy to forget that one in four people in the world do not have access to even the most basic toilet. In such a situation life-threatening illnesses and diseases such as diarrhoea, bilharzia and dysentery are endemic.

Water, essential to life and health, should be a common right for all.

These days news reports of droughts and floods are common. Climate change? Certainly we are aware of changing weather patterns. Water companies in the south of Britain apply for drought orders restricting the use of depleted stocks of water. But these problems are minimal compared to problems in other parts of the world. In spring 2006, Christian Aid launched an emergency appeal to provide aid to the people in the devastating drought conditions in East Africa. Across northern Kenya, southern Ethiopia and south-west Somalia there has been only one year of good rains since 1999. Nearly 11 million people lack food: drought kills livestock; drought means no crops. Starvation follows.

In other parts of the world, flooding and rising sea levels are the life-threatening problem. Dr Atiq Rahman, Executive Director of the Bangladesh Centre for Advanced Studies, a Christian Aid partner organisation and the country's leading environmental research group, says: 'Patterns of rainfall and flooding [in Bangladesh] have changed in the past few years. Severe floods used to come once every 20 years, but now occur every 5 to 7.' In 1988 and 1998 two-thirds of the country was under water at some point. In 2004, terrible floods left 30 million homeless or stranded. [11]

John Harrison

Information for this piece was taken from *Water Aid* magazine (Autumn/ Winter 2005); Water Aid pamphlets, posters and correspondence; Christian Aid magazines (*Christian Aid News*, Summer 2006).

I am thirsty

After this, when Jesus knew that all was now finished, he said (in order to fulfil the scripture), 'I am thirsty.' A jar full of sour wine was standing there. So they put a sponge full of the wine on a branch of hyssop and held it to his mouth.

John 19:28–29

As a deer longs for flowing streams,
so my soul longs for you, O God.
My soul thirsts for God,
for the living God.

As a child in Asia thirsts for clean water
so my soul longs for the God of justice to act.
My soul thirsts for God,
for the living God to show me how to act.

As a family in South America longs for water to flow from a simple standpipe,
so my soul longs for the madness of rich world/poor world to end.
My soul thirsts for God,
for the living God to touch the hearts and minds of presidents and governments.

As the land in Africa thirsts and crops wither and fail
so my soul longs for you, O God.
My soul thirsts for God,
while God hangs on a tree and is thirsty too.

Linda Hill, from Words from the Cross, Biggar Kirk, 2005

Count to fifteen. Be silent for a moment.

THE INTEGRITY OF CREATION

The beauty in the fearsome

Not long ago, and new to Swindon, I was alone in the house one night. I put out the light to hear an enormous buzz – and a creature crashing around my room. When I turned the light back on, the biggest insect I had ever seen – two inches long, black and orange and with huge pincers – crash-landed on my wall. Too scared *not* to act, I trapped it under a cup, expecting it to try to force its way out and attack me. It was actually silent and passive as I got some card under the cup and chucked it out the window.

It took me hours to get to sleep, as I wondered if there were more, and if this monster had come with global warming, or had escaped from some neighbour's collection of live beasties.

It was of course entirely harmless: a native stag beetle, increasingly rare, now a protected species, and only terrifying to northerners like myself who had never seen one. It had been drawn to the light – and may have been more scared than I was.

It's natural to be scared of the unknown. But it's easy to miss the beauty in the world. My visitor *was* very beautiful. As we destroy more and more of our world's resources by living in a way that has caused the climate to change so fast, I may be one of the last to see creatures like this one, creatures that have contributed to life on Earth for thousands of years.

To a Christian, all life is precious. This is why we believe we are called to a simpler, more adventurous lifestyle that respects the rest of creation.

Rosemary Power

COLUMBAN CHRISTIANITY & THE CELTIC TRADITION

The Convention of Drum Cett and the Call to Conversion campaign

Retreat?

'So you're off to Iona again. On retreat, I suppose?'

Well, actually, no. Whatever else Iona is, a retreat it is not – at least not in the way the word is normally understood. Iona is not a place of escape, but somewhere to renew commitment to God's world. The wisdom of Iona points to an engaged spirituality.

Part of the clue lies in its origins. It is a mistaken assumption that when Columba left Ireland in 563, he was abandoning forever the world of power politics. He was certainly present at the Convention of Drum Cett (near Limavady, N. Ireland) in 575, and was in all probability a major player in that great gathering, which negotiated the royal succession – and according to some historians established peace in the region for fifty years.

What Columba left behind when he quit Ireland was the use of violence in the pursuit of political power. As an 'island soldier' he was aligning himself with a different kind of power – a power to heal, reconcile and make peace. In the same way, Cuthbert, wrestling with his demons on the Inner Farne, facing Bamburgh across the water, was a living reminder to the king in his royal stronghold of a higher power to which he was ultimately answerable. In our own time, the Trappist monk Thomas Merton, living an apparently disengaged life at Gethsemani in

the remote Kentucky countryside, was, in his prayer, fully engaged with the world; through his writings he informed and inspired a whole generation of social and political activists.

Once when preparing to return home from some days on Iona I wrote the following:

It's always hard to leave
Iona:
this thin place of sharp
remembering.
But necessary.
Iona is not a terminus, but a stage on
a larger journey,
a launch pad
for earthy engagement.

Prayer

Lord, teach us when we are inclined to forget, that places of retreat are not places of escape; that when we clasp hands in prayer we take responsibility with you for your world; that worship and politics are not separate in your economy, nor should they be in ours. Because it was your Son who taught us to pray for your Kingdom to come in the here and now, in this place and time: for your will to be done on earth as in heaven. We dare to pray in his name, amen, let it be so.

Warren Bardsley

St Columba's Day reflection, 2005

Yesterday was St Columba's Day, and, in acts of worship and other meetings in many parts of Scotland and beyond, Columba's memory was honoured. If Columba and his Celtic monks were alive today I am not sure how many of them, if any, would be on Iona. In 563, when he landed there from Ireland, and transport was mainly by sea, Iona was at a kind of international crossroads, not quite so much on the edge of things as it can seem now.

On Saturday, over eighty Iona Community members gathered in Biggar in South Lanarkshire for a meeting during which we discussed with some local people the economic and social problems affecting rural communities: transport and depopulation, poverty and the need for rural regeneration, some of the difficulties facing farmers at present.

If the Columban monks were around today I believe they would be engaging with some of these issues. Some of them would be working, too, in the inner cities alongside those who experience urban deprivation and are marginalised by social structures. They would be where the action is – at the cutting edge of the churches' mission today. They would also be expressing their commitment to the vision and values of God's kingdom – justice and peace, solidarity with the poor – by involvement in political campaigning.

So I think they would be taking an active part in the Call to Conversion campaign that has been launched by several peace organisations. £763 million of government money goes each year to subsidise the arms trade, providing weapons and military devices that are fuelling wars and violence today worldwide. This public investment needs to be used instead to create real security and to convert the arms trade from military to civil, socially useful production.

St Columba and his monks in their time were experts in a different kind of conversion. But I am sure they would have been sympathetic to this cause.

Norman Shanks

Month 4 Day 13

From Erin's shores

From Erin's shores Columba came
to preach and teach and heal,
and found a church which showed the world
how God on earth was real.

In greening grass and reckless wave,
in cloud and ripening corn,
the Celtic Christians traced the course
of grace through nature borne.

In hosting strangers, healing pain,
in tireless work for peace,
they served the servant Christ their Lord
and found their faith increase.

In simple prayer and alien land,
as summoned by the Son,
they celebrated how God's call
made work and worship one.

God grant that what Columba sowed
may harvest yet more seed,
as we engage both flesh and faith
to marry word and deed.

John L. Bell and Graham Maule

RACISM

What will the Church be saying sorry for 200 years from now?

Like many people in churches up and down Britain, I have been involved this year in planning events to celebrate the 200th anniversary of the passing of the act of the UK parliament that abolished the British slave trade in 1807. The 'Set All Free' campaign asks us to 'remember, reflect, respond' to slavery and injustice, then and now.

Implicit in remembering has been the need to repent. Christians were at the forefront of the abolition movement, driven by their faith to end the appalling evil of the Transatlantic Slave Trade and slavery in the Americas. But it is all too easy to forget that the Church was also very much a part of the apparatus of slavery. Christian scriptures were used to justify the enslavement of millions of Africans and many churches and church leaders reaped huge financial benefit from the slave trade and fought in parliament against its abolition. Recognition of this history has led churches and church leaders today to apologise for the actions of their predecessors, including the Archbishop of Canterbury on behalf of the Church of England.

I welcome these apologies very much. They are long overdue. But it has set me thinking about some of the things that are still defended in our churches, often by church leaders and often by a majority of those in the pews.

In 200 years' time I hope that the churches will be looking back with repentance and apology to the early 21st century, unable to believe that their forebears in the Church demonised, marginalised and excluded people, from ministry and even from blessing, on the basis of their sexuality; unable to understand how many Christians and churches profited from the arms trade at the cost of millions of innocent lives around the world.

Or better still, we could omit the 200 year delay and repent now; apologise now; be where we ought to be – at the forefront of inclusivity and of peacemaking. We have the chance to get it right this time. I pray that the denominations and individual Christians will take that chance. Let us not delay. Remember … reflect … respond.

Helen Boothroyd

COMMUNITY

The Birley Tree

This is a story of a tree which is no longer there. A black poplar, it was known as the Birley Tree because for well over a century it stood in the middle of Birley Fields, a green space in Hulme, at the south edge of Manchester city centre. The Birley Tree, the oldest in Hulme, was a landmark feature visible from major roads – it occupied a fond place in the memories of residents who recalled it standing at the high school gates.

The Birley Tree is no longer there because Hulme was designated for development, and Birley Fields was earmarked for the construction of a hotel. Thus the story of the Birley Tree is a story about regeneration.

I have been on an old red bus today, touring Manchester as a guest of the UHC Collective (www.uhc.org.uk) who for the past three-and-a-half years have been working in various artistic forms 'on the network of power relations currently shaping our local environment, as Manchester swings ever more into regeneration overdrive'. They've been exhibiting their work under the banner 'Incursions In The Knowledge Capital'. (Manchester City Council has rebranded Manchester 'Knowledge Capital'.)

So much of what I saw and heard on the old red bus seemed familiar from Liverpool, where I live: the massive scale of new developments ripping into old established communities; the immense power of the market to dictate the way we use city space (silencing protest, clearing beggars off the streets); the 'thin veneer of democracy' which hardly disguises the huge inequalities of power between the business class – sanctioned and fully supported by city councillors – and the majority, ordinary people of the city – disenfranchised, unrepresented.

Sitting in the bus in the car park of a giant ASDA/Wal-Mart complex, I heard that this monolithic intrusion – for which generations of people were cleared – was called Hulme High Street; that it was built for ease of access for out-of-town motorists, and that pedestrians have to access the place by means of a side security gate. Looking up the road I saw the spiral steel cables of the Hulme Arch Bridge shining in the morning sun and heard that this 'gateway' to the city cost Manchester's people £4 million – twice the amount first quoted.

As the bus chugged up the road I heard the story of the Birley Tree: the protesters' two applications for a Tree Preservation Order, twice refused on the grounds that the tree was in decline, diseased and hollow; the consultant and fellow of the Arboricultural Association who declared the tree to be healthy, an 'important specimen' with at least another 25 years of life; the petitions, the campaign, the strength of local feeling to keep the tree – as a symbol, perhaps, of another way of valuing the city. It all came to nothing, of course, because the power brokers got their land.

However, as often happens, the planned-for hotel investment fell through. The tree went, nothing was built in its place, and the Fields fell into neglect.

Last week I took part in a discussion in which a group of thoughtful clergy mostly agreed that the symbols of our faith were losing their relevance to the people of today. But looking across the scrubby, fallow wreck of Birley Fields it was pointed out to me that someone had created a memorial to the Birley Tree in the place it once stood. Made out of slender lengths of new wood, rising high from the debris of this once public space, there it is, a silent and poignant witness to this story of regeneration – a cross.

John Davies

Month 4 Day 15

Prayer

God, help us to grow
like a garden
like a song
like a tree.
Like a great tree
Like one of those great, old trees
you meet sometimes and hug
wandering lost
or enchanted
in a deep, dark forest
in an empty field.
A great, old tree
with roots that reach down to the heart
roots that reach down but
break through the ground around the trunk and lift
as if the earth can't contain the yearning.
As if the earth shall erode and pass away and
all that shall be left in the end is Spirit.
A great, old tree
with arms that shelter and shade
and house such love.
A great, old tree
with breaks and wounds and scars
but dancing and clapping its hands.
Like a beautiful, old woman at a summer wedding.
A great, old tree still and centred

---

drawing on the living warm core of God
though left stripped of everything.
God, help us to grow
like a garden
like a song
like a tree.
Like one of those great, old trees
you meet sometimes
in a crowded forest
in an empty field.

Neil Paynter

PILGRIMAGE

A liturgy for setting out on a pilgrimage and a prayer for the journey

In this liturgy include many readers.

Opening quote:

A pilgrimage is a journey whose destination is ultimately the same as that from which you set out: through it, you are asking God to show you your life, your home, your place, in a new light.

Call to worship:

God said: 'Leave your country, your family and your relatives, and go to the land that I will show you.' (Genesis 12:1)

Song or hymn

Opening responses:

The day is coming
when things will change.
THE DAY IS COMING WHEN WE WILL SET OUT.

The day is coming to cross the sea,
to touch the earth,

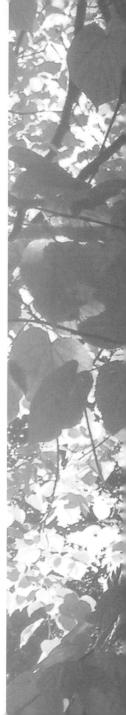

to plant a seed,
to trust … and not look back.
TO TRUST AND NOT LOOK BACK.

The day has come when Christ sets out.
THE DAY HAS COME FOR FOOD AND FRIENDSHIP.

The day has come
not to flee but to embrace;
not to escape but to welcome;
not to shut out but, in safety and in community,
to trust and not look back.
TO TRUST AND NOT LOOK BACK.

The discipline of letting go (Luke 9:57–62):

Along the way, someone said to Jesus, 'I'll go anywhere with you!' Jesus said, 'Foxes have dens, and birds have nests; but the Son of Man doesn't have a place to call his own.'

Jesus told someone else to come with him. But they said, 'Lord, let me wait until I bury my father.' Jesus answered, 'Let the dead take care of the dead; whilst you go and tell about God's kingdom.' Then someone said to Jesus, 'I want to go with you, Lord; but first let me go back and take care of things at home.' Jesus answered, 'Anyone who starts ploughing and keeps looking back isn't worth a thing to God's kingdom.'

Dreaming and not looking back:

Off the top of your head, in small groups, talk about:

– What you need to stop doing

Month 4 Day 16

– What the world needs to stop doing
– What you would like to get round to one day
– One thing which would make the world a better place
– A sign which would encourage you
– A sign which would encourage the world

Soon we will set out.
We will find our ways converge and come together
for no one can always travel alone.
Strangers will cross our path.
But so will angels.
And there's the risk.

Costs and rewards of walking Christ's way (Mark 10:30):

Jesus said: 'You can be sure that anyone who gives up home or brothers or sisters or mother or father or children or land for me and for the good news will be rewarded. In this world they will be given a hundred times as many houses and brothers and sisters and mothers and children and pieces of land, though they will also be ill-treated.'

Soon we will set out.
Not to escape our lives but to catch up with them.
Not to look back at where we have come from,
but, from that distance,
to look forward to where we are heading.
We will travel
in the well-worn footsteps
of centuries of pilgrims,
to find food for our journey
as companions of Christ.

So we take time now to consider a person/people alongside whom we might like to walk in prayer. For them, we give up some time, some effort, some space …

Time for silent prayer

Prayer action: *Passing a stone or cross amongst the group while praying aloud for people or situations, ending with silence.*

God, who brings us together,
re-member us and all we care for.
Add your prayer to ours –
for this land,
this world,
and our daily lives.
AMEN

Song or hymn

Meeting: *practical preparation for travelling and sharing*

Final gathering:

DOWNTRODDEN CHRIST,
AS WE SET OUT
IN SANDALS, BOOTS AND TRAINERS;
ON WHEELS, AND BORNE BY ANGELS;
BE OUR LEADER AND OUR GUIDE,
OUR BACK-MARKER AND OUR PATIENCE,
WITH EACH OTHER,
WITH EACH CREATURE,
WITH OURSELVES,

WITH GOD'S GOOD INTENT
ALL AROUND US
ON OUR WAY.
AMEN

Closing song or hymn

David Coleman

A prayer for the journey

Journeying with you, Creator God,
is to journey in your world,
full of marvels and such beauty.
To glimpse eternity in sky and sea,
to feel the earth and rock beneath my feet.

Journeying with you, brother Jesus,
is to journey with your friends.
To meet and travel a while together,
then part at the crossroads,
knowing you are with us all.

Journeying with you, Holy Spirit,
is to journey with the wind.
To move to your wild music
then try to sing your song
so others may hear.

Chris Polhill

SEXUALITY

A group Bible study

Justified in our same-sex partnership by faith in Christ

An analogy from the meat-eating/vegetarian controversy

Let those who happily eat anything not despise those who do not eat everything, and let those who do not eat everything not pass judgement on those who do, for God has accepted them. Who are you to pass judgement on someone else's servant? It is up to his own master to decide whether he stands or falls. And he will stand firm because his own Lord has the power to confirm him … We should each make up our own minds for ourselves …

Those who eat anything do so in honour of the Lord; they give thanks to God for the food. Those who refuse to eat certain things do so in honour of the Lord and they give thanks to God. None of us lives for herself only, none of us dies for himself only. If we live, it is for the Lord that we live, and, if we die, it is for the Lord that we die. Living or dying, we belong to the Lord … Why then do you pass judgement on your brother? Why do you despise your sister? … Each of us will give an account of ourselves to God …

So don't pass judgement on one another but make up your mind not to make life diffi-cult for your brothers and sisters by putting obstacles in their way.

My union with the Lord Jesus makes me certain that nothing is unclean in and of itself … God's kingdom is not a matter of eating and drinking, but of the justice, peace and joy which the Holy Spirit gives … Happy are those who do not feel guilty when they do something they judge is right!

Romans 14:3–4, 5b–8, 10a, 12–14, 17 and 22b (GNB, amended)

'You are what you eat' is a contemporary slogan of the health conscious. What the earliest members of the Christian Church ate was of supreme importance to some of them. Meat offered to idols was regarded by some as being defiled and was felt to defile them. They feared that they would become what they ate. There are similar feelings around the eating of meat today. The eating of meat would, literally, make some people sick. Most who eat meat do so with a clear conscience. They do not feel guilty when they do something which they judge to be right.

Now you are clothed, so to speak, with the life of Christ himself. So there is no difference between Jews and Gentiles, between slaves and free people, between men and women; you are all one in union with Christ Jesus.

Galatians 3:27–28 (GNB)

St Paul believes that through being united with the Lord Jesus we are liberated from traditional cultural attitudes in relation to food that is clean and unclean, in relation to race, social status and gender.

An analogy from the racial controversy

Peter gave them a complete account of what had happened from the very beginning:

'While I was praying in the city of Joppa, I had a vision. I saw something coming down that looked like a large sheet being lowered by its four corners from heaven, and it stopped next to me. I looked closely inside and saw domesticated and wild animals, reptiles and wild birds. Then I heard a voice saying to me, "Get up, Peter; kill and eat!" But I said, "Certainly not, Lord! No ritually unclean or defiled food has ever entered my mouth." The voice spoke again from heaven, "Do not consider anything unclean that

God has declared clean" … At that very moment three men who had been sent to me from Caesarea arrived at the house where I was staying. The Spirit told me to go with them without hesitation. These six fellow-believers from Joppa accompanied me to Caesarea, and we all went into the house of Cornelius … And when I began to speak, the Holy Spirit came down on them just as on us at the beginning … It is clear that God gave those Gentiles the same gift that he gave us when we believed in the Lord Jesus Christ; who was I, then, to try to stop God!'

When they heard this, they stopped their criticism and praised God, saying, 'Then God has given to the Gentiles also the opportunity to repent and live.'

Acts 11:4–9, 11–12, 15, 17–18 (GNB)

St Peter affirms that, in receiving the gift of God's Holy Spirit, we are liberated from traditional attitudes in relation to race which divide people from one another.

There are many who believe that those who engage in an enriching, loving, faithful and committed same-sex partnership, which they find to be a blessing to them and to others, are justified by their faith in God, whose kingdom is one of justice, peace and joy, which the Holy Spirit gives.

Month 4 Day 17

Discussion

1. Let vegetarians in the group share their feelings about meat eaters and meat eaters share their feelings about vegetarians.

2. Do members of the one group despise/pass judgement on those of the other?

3. Do members of the one group feel that those of the other have the entire right to make up their own minds for themselves about what they do?

4. Do members of the one group accept that those of the other honour God in their style of eating with thanksgiving to God?

5. Do you feel that you have ever passed judgement on those who share in a same-sex partnership?

6. Do you feel that those who share in a same-sex partnership are entitled to judge for themselves the rightness of the relationship in which they share?

7. Do you feel that those who engage in a same-sex partnership, in which they give thanks to God for their partnership, honour God in what they do?

Graeme Brown

Month 4 Day 17

HEALING

The Healer: A story

In his own way, he was happy. He had been blind and deaf since birth. He had a corner in which to sleep; food which, some days, was sufficient for his needs; and kind people who were prepared to give time to while away the hours with him.

He asked them about the world and how it was getting on. Through a language of touch which they had developed, they built up the picture: There were many fine things in the world but, for good reasons, they were not equally distributed. There were superior types of human beings who had a right of access to a larger share, and inferior types of human beings who naturally got less. It might seem to be all wrong that God should make two different breeds of mankind. But it came right at the end of the day, because, at death, God balanced things up in the life beyond.

The trouble started when the Healer arrived. He examined the man's eyes and said, 'Would you like to see?' Through touch the message was transmitted, and an excited and affirmative answer given. The Healer put ointment on the eyes which had been blind and after two days sight began gradually to return. The Healer went on his way. A few weeks later he found himself in the area once more, and met one of the villagers who had acted as translator. 'How is it with my friend?' he asked. 'Bad,' came the reply. 'Why?' asked the Healer with concern, 'has he lost his sight once more?' 'He has recovered his sight completely – more's the pity!' 'Why do you say that?' 'He is no longer the happy man he was. He has looked on those who live in misery around him and has looked on those who live in abundance. He says there is no essential difference between them, that they are of one humanity – and that life is unjust. It hurts him. He is not at all the contented man he was.'

The Healer continued on his journey, and found that it was as he had been told. He sat down with the man again. Through an interpreter he asked, 'Do you want to have your hearing restored?' The villagers intervened. 'You have done enough damage already,' they said, 'leave the man in peace. We will look after him. We will see that all that he needs is supplied. Only don't cause him more distress by giving him back his faculties.'

'Do you want your hearing restored?' asked the Healer of the man. Less excitedly but still with conviction the man asked for restoration. In spite of the opposition of the villagers, hands were laid on him and healing ointment applied. After two days, the hearing began to come back and the Healer left.

It was a month or two before the Healer returned to the village. When he was seen, a group ran towards him in unconcealed hostility. 'Was it not enough,' they asked, 'to rob a man of his peace, that you had to rob him of his faith as well?' 'What do you mean?' asked the Healer. 'Now that your patient can hear, he has learned of other religions, other understandings of God, other explanations of life's meaning. He no longer has something sure and definite to hold on to that can act as an anchor for his life. He has become restless, he distrusts the understanding of life which his forebears and we ourselves have handed on to him; he searches in every religion and every form of belief to find a sure basis. He is a disturbance to us all.' Just then the man saw the Healer in the distance, ran to him and embraced him. The Healer turned to the group. Looking at the man he said, 'They tell me that I have robbed you of happiness and security by restoring your sight and hearing.'

'They have told you some part of the truth,' said the man. 'I am no longer happy as I was. I am no longer secure as I was. Only now I am alive.'

Ian M. Fraser

I am

I am whatever you need me to be
I am the tranquil peace poured into your turmoil
I am the healer and comforter of your pain and sorrow
I am the listener and adviser for your confusion
I am the stillness you seek in your grief
I am the light in your darkness and fear
I am the caressing hand on your fevered brow
I am the balm for your guilt
I am cool, clear water for your thirst
I am the enthusiasm for your lethargy
I am the friend, the lover, in your loneliness
I am the laughter in your happiness
I am the hope in your despair
I am crucified – I am risen
I am here for you
I am

Christine Green

SOCIAL ACTION

Unimpaired

The nearest I came to getting jailed was in The Philippines in 1977. Ferdinand Marcos had decided on a period of special vigilance. He attempted to seal all exits from the country of information which might be detrimental to his seamy regime. Evidence had been assembled about unjust imprisonments, torture and 'salvagings' (assassinations) – but the channels for getting them to justice and peace organisations in different parts of the world had been blocked. I volunteered to try to get them delivered.

Taking my cue from Edgar Allan Poe's story 'The Letter', I decided that the safest place for the documents might be the most obvious – in my hand luggage. But at the airport I was picked on for a spot check.

The woman who looked through my bag, instead of examining it just for bombs, hand grenades and so on, demanded what the packets were. I replied that they were letters from friends which would reach their destinations quicker if I posted them in Britain. She asked what was in them. I replied, 'I do not read my friends' letters.' She answered, 'You are getting no further until I find out what is in these letters!' We stood facing one another across the table, the bag between us.

At that point a group of Japanese tourists came up behind me, some pushing at the back because they were late for their plane. Those at the front swept me bodily past the point of search. I grabbed the bag with the documents before the woman could. She held up her hands in defeat and gave up any further attempt to challenge me.

At the next stage, another obstacle appeared – the screening chamber in which tapes and films could be scrubbed. During that time in The Philippines I had taken thirty-two interviews, including that of Trining Herrera, the leader of the Tondo Community, speaking about the severe torture she had suffered. What a loss these tapes would be!

When we landed, tape after tape proved to be unimpaired. Trining's voice went out on the 'Sunday' programme of the BBC, telling of her torture and giving direct testimony to what she had endured.

Prayer

Lord God, whose Son had no place to lay his head
except a cross, we pray:

for those who are the victims of human brutality;
for those who languish in jails with no charge made
to justify their imprisonment;
for those who are thrown by torture into a nightmare world.
Draw near to give them courage and hope.

For those who consign others to torture and death;
for torturers, brutalised in order that they may,
in turn, brutalise;
for guards, offered no option but to follow prison routines;
for all who consent to systems of oppression.

We give thanks for countries which welcome strangers;
and for agencies which disclose to the world
atrocities which would otherwise remain hidden.
Amen

Ian M. Fraser

Month 4 Day 19

Church Renewal

Above all, a place of mystery

Last year the Church of Scotland talked a lot about a so-called 'Church Without Walls'. This, in theory anyway, would have been fine. Only the walls which they should have been removing were not touched at all – perhaps they thought that the sky would fall down!

State-of-the-art, high-tech gadgetry may well work for some but without the real issues being addressed then forget it. We're doomed! In an enlightened and post-modern society people, myself included, just will not accept the doctrines that the Church forces us to accept. Many simply will not do it. Who cares whether or not Jesus is God? Who is interested in a long-winded, convoluted and untenable Trinitarian model of God? What is the point of an organisation that's only perceivable raison d'être is to self-propagate? And who in today's world would wish to associate with what is seen to be a homophobic anachronism? These are the walls which need to topple.

The Church must be known for its environment of freedom of thought and diversity of expression. A place of growth, not of certainty. It should be recognised as a house of forgiveness and reconciliation, of creativity and openness, and, above all, as a place of mystery.

For over ten years I have co-led groups of teenagers on pilgrimages to Taizé. It is in this wonderful place that many have found peace and freedom. No one told them what to think. They were encouraged to explore, together with their peers, what it means to love.

Many who have accompanied us to Taizé do not believe in the existence of God. But this was never the point. The point is that they were exposed to an alternative society; something which will stay with them for the rest of their lives. It is a place where one is confronted, confounded even, by the sheer mystery of life. Isn't this such a resplendent vision of what the Church should be?!

When people speak of Taizé they will invariably talk of the music. As beautiful as this is, it is not this which attracts the youth – it is the responsibility that is given to them: the responsibility of freedom and self-expression; and the responsibility that comes when you have found your place within a community – in other words, your responsibility to that community. It is a place to reflect and a place to be challenged.

I will be quiet now, I think I have said way too much.

Michael Black, an Associate of the Iona Community
From the 'Bulletin Board' on the Iona Community's website

The robin in the Abbey

A glimpse, a flicker of red and brown
perching on stone sills,
investigating corners.
A sudden, echoed trill
after the Sanctus.
We turn, point, stare and smile.

Are you happy inside,
you native of hedgerows and fields?
At peace, as the wind
bends shafts of air around
the trembling windows?
Borne up on the waves of our praising,
riding on the currents of our prayers?
Satisfied, pecking at remnants of shared Communion bread?
Gathering up the crumbs under His table?
Enfolded by His presence in the stones?

Or do you want to break the bounds?
Soar unboundaried into uncharted skies,
swept on wind tides to new experiences,
risking the dart of hawk
for joys of wind and sun.

And when you join your song
to ours,
is it praise or anger,
joy or grief you sing?
Are you free, or trapped?
Are we?

Alix Brown

WORSHIP

Holy ground

Think of your road, the bus stop you wait in, or the local shopping precinct where you stand in queues each day. I wonder if you think of them as *holy ground*.

I was fascinated to find out about a project run in Liverpool a year or so ago where someone made a portable altar – a plain green altar designed to be acceptable to people of all faiths – and took it around the streets of the area.

Local people were encouraged to take the altar and put it in specific places – places special to them – and to talk about *why* they were special. The results were recorded in a beautiful photographic book.

Now, shut-down factories and run-down community centres don't look that special. But people chose them because they were important to them.

Pieces of wasteground where schools or shops used to be don't look that special. But to the people who had memories of them, they weren't just special. They were holy ground.

Holy ground doesn't have to be where churches or mosques or synagogues are; it is wherever something has happened which means something special to people.

I like this way of thinking because it means that even if we don't live in beautiful places, we still live in *valuable* places.

You might like to think of *your special place*: the place you went to school, the place where you played as a child, the place where you met your partner, the place where today you meet and chat and feel at home. You might not think of these as holy places. But maybe, in their own way, they are.

John Davies

Shepherd's pie and peas

Was it I?
Or was it the Sunday Eucharist which was sterile?
I don't know.

Either way
I got nothing from the service, and gave nothing to God.
It seemed winter inside as well as out.

Was this what Jesus intended at the Last Supper
when he gave us a shared meal
to celebrate our togetherness?
When he said,
'This is my body'?

That night, I was helping at a night shelter.
The men came into the warmth from the cold and rain.
I joined them as they sat round the table.
Each had his own story,
his own troubles.

Month 4 Day 21

I looked around the table and saw
the face of Christ in each one of them.
He had no form or majesty that we should look at him,
nothing in his appearance that we should desire him.
He was despised and rejected by others;
a man of suffering and acquainted with infirmity;
and as one from whom others hide their faces
he was despised, and we held him of no account. (Isaiah 53:2–3)

I looked and I realised:
This is holy ground.
This is the table of the Lord.

I met Christ that night at his table.
And shared shepherd's pie and peas with him.

Frances Hawkey, an Associate member of the Iona Community

Month 4 Day 21

CALLED TO BE ONE

Wee Danny's last Communion

A lady in the hospice had asked me if I would give her Communion. A Scottish Episcopalian, her priest brought her the Eucharist regularly when she was with us in the hospice. But he was on holiday that week, and so, a good ecumenist, she was happy to receive Communion from a Presbyterian chaplain. As it turned out, there was an Anglican lady who'd been admitted to the same ward the previous day. That made a congregation of two. Word got round. A Church of Scotland elder from two wards away heard about the service. So then there were three. One of the nurses asked if a 'non-practising Methodist' could come as well. Now there were four. Ecumenism in practice. It doesn't get any better.

So we gathered in Ward 1 – two ladies in their beds, the Kirk elder in a wheelchair, and a nurse sitting on a bed – when the door of the conservatory opened and in walked Wee Danny. Daniel Connelly, though very frail, kept himself as active as possible. A committed Roman Catholic, Wee Danny – his choice of name – had taken to calling me 'Faither Tom' – and I never once corrected him.

'What're you up to, Faither Tom?' Danny enquired as he stood in the doorway.

'I'm about to give Communion to these folk,' I replied.

'Great stuff,' Danny responded, 'that'll do for me.' And in he came, plonking himself on the chair by the window.

'Fine,' I offered with a quizzical smile, 'but I should tell you, Danny, that this'll be a Presbyterian Communion and not the Mass you're used to.'

'No problem to me,' Danny affirmed, 'I'll take it from a milk bottle and wi' stale rolls. It's what it means that matters and not how it's done.'

If I could have bottled the moment I would have kept it forever. This was truly an ecumenical event. I was on a high for the rest of the day.

The remainder of the week was particularly stressful. And in the middle of it all, Danny took a sudden downturn, and by the end of the week he had lapsed into a coma: close to the end of his life. By late Friday afternoon I was on my knees with tiredness and I was keen to get home. I was going through the wards but my progress was interrupted by a disembodied female voice: 'Haw, Faither Tom?' This mode of greeting could only mean the voice belonged to a relative of Danny's, and, sure enough, the owner of the voice introduced herself as Danny's niece.

'I wonder if you could give my Uncle Danny Communion again. You see he always gets Communion from his priest on a Friday, but he can't come in today, and he'll miss it if he doesn't get it.'

To be honest, I cursed under my breath, but said OK. Danny's niece declined my invitation to join us for the Eucharist, preferring to slip outside for a smoke. So it was me and Danny, and frankly, I didn't see the point. Danny was unconscious. The Eucharist was only a way of ticking the 'Uncle Danny gets Communion on a Friday afternoon' box for the niece. And I was too tired …

I was just getting things arranged by the bedside when Danny opened his eyes, and in a frail but distinct voice said, 'Hello, Faither Tom. Communion? That's good, 'cause my priest's away …'

I was gobsmacked, and remained so in our brief, shared Communion. We said the Lord's Prayer together, Danny's

weak voice never missing a word. When I concluded the Communion with, 'The Lord be with you,' Danny responded with, 'And also with you, Faither Tom,' and closed his eyes.

I learned on the Monday that Danny had died a few hours later. I heard that his niece was astonished at how peacefully he let go of life. I also heard how surprised the nurses were that Danny had been awake enough to be engaged with a Communion service.

And me? Well, I was surprised as well. Because, after that sacrament with Danny, all my tiredness had gone. I floated home. God had touched me too. Communion had done its job. No labels, no divisions, no differences – and no need for understanding it all either – only mystery, and rightness, and depth, and Danny and me together with the Love of our God.

God of our togetherness,
show me what we have in common,
when I can't see it for myself.

God of our sharing,
offer me what brings us ever closer
even when I thought we were close enough already.

God of our communing,
show me what true communion means
with those who do things differently from me.

God of our connectedness,
show me how to strengthen our bonds,
especially when they threaten to break apart.

God of our understanding,
show me more of the mystery
which takes us beyond our limited knowledge.

God of our tiredness,
re-energise, restore and renew me
with your Spirit's unseen power.

God of our reluctance,
show me more of what is possible
with your way and in your love.

Tom Gordon

MISSION

Chance encounters

China made me see individual people in a new way. It made me see them just as people, as human beings in all the mystery of their humanity, without knowing anything much about them, and certainly not their names.

These encounters were momentary and casual, but, because of this, instantaneous and lasting in their effect. My friends among the Chinese were not made in this way. I got to know my friends at home; through common work and frequent meeting and constant talk. They taught me many things that I might not have learned otherwise. Some of them remain as firmly planted not only in my memory but in my consciousness as any whom I knew from earlier times or know now, despite the fact that I do not know what has happened to them.

It is not of them that I am now thinking. I am thinking of a few individuals with whom chance brought me into momentary contact. It did not matter who they were. It did not matter that I did not see them again. It did not matter that they were Chinese. They were just human beings and I was too and we met.

The examples are supremely trivial. That is why they are important. The point of them was that they revealed to me unexpected truth about people, ordinary people.

The government school across the vacant muddy patch from our house had gone on fire. We had not noticed. But the fire brigade had been called. It consisted of four men pulling a two-wheeled barrow with some hosepipes. But before they went to put out the fire they stopped at our house to let our children know. It would be a shame, they said, if they missed the show. We did not know the men.

They were just ordinary men, doing their job but in the middle of it thinking of children and their pleasure. Of course they deserved the reproof that the disciples loaded on Jesus when he wasted time playing with children. But somehow they seemed to stand where he stood. The second incident is less dramatic. But I remember it with shame. A young Irish woman doctor and I were travelling in a crowded train. It was so crowded that we were jammed tight and could scarcely move. A fellow-passenger opposite me leant forward and flicked my clothes just under my chin. I drew my head up and looked down with the superior look a Britisher is trained to give to impertinence. My friend gently but firmly reproved me. She said that the man was removing a louse that was creeping up to my neck. I ought to have realised that only for such a charitable act would he have been so rude as to touch me. I felt bitterly ashamed and tried to express my thanks to him. I do not like to think what I revealed of human nature to him. He had revealed to me by his consideration something of the mystery of being a human being.

Another incident was a bit different. But it made the same point. It had to do with … our cook. We knew him well for we had daily contact with him. Indeed our daily life depended on him. He did all our buying, baked our bread, cooked our food and with the help of the houseboy did our laundry. When we went on holiday he came with us. He was not a Christian. He was scarcely literate. He came from a very poor home. He had a wife, who lived in a mental world of her own, and no children. It was a disgrace for a Chinese to have no son. It was customary for a man in such

circumstances to send his wife back to her old home and to marry another wife. My wife was naturally hesitant to intrude into his private affairs but she felt that she should say something. So one day she said to him that she hoped that he was not refraining from marrying another wife because he knew that Christians did not approve of this and he was afraid that he would lose his job. She wanted him to know that this was not so: that we quite understood his position. His instant reply was humbling: 'I have seen how the lady has put up with an unprofitable servant for all these years. I can surely put up with an unprofitable wife.' It was a shattering example of common human dignity.

I felt that in meeting people in these casual ways I was getting to know Jesus. It never occurred to me that I had a duty to tell such people about Jesus as if they did not know him, even though they did not know his name. He was no stranger to them, or so I thought. Indeed I was seeing him for the first time in human life and not in a book. The Church seemed to be concerned with names and the right to use names. The very anonymity of the chance encounter seemed to reveal Jesus far more vividly that the accredited Christian witness …

These chance encounters showed me the wonder of what was common to humanity and therefore recognisable in Jesus. We all have experience of chance encounters with people that reveal other facets of human nature – disdain, pride, fear, cruelty. But these are all distortions of human nature. And we know them as such. We are ashamed of them, or, more often, we try to justify them. The unexpected revelations of dignity, consideration and even humour are of a different and eternal order. They are not distortions of our natures. They are rather the momentary breaking forth of what people really are. I suppose this is what people in Galilee so long ago saw in Jesus and why they responded to him and believed in him or feared him. They saw this in a man who to them was only the carpenter's son. We have to see him in nameless people if we are to see him for ourselves. I had to see people right outside the Church, to see them in themselves in their simplicity, to learn this fundamental truth. It was a lesson worth going to China to learn.

T. Ralph Morton, Former Deputy Leader of the Iona Community, 1976

Month 4 Day 23

WORK

A lesson from Old Mrs Renton

On the south wall of Iona Abbey, above the Communion table, there are two discreet medieval carvings – a monkey and a cat. Strange carvings to find in an old abbey, you might think! Yet they're there to symbolise the two sides of the monastic life: the active, relentless busyness of the monkey – the world of work and service; and the contemplative, restful life of the cat – the world of prayer and renewal. Today, they offer the two contrasting sides of every Christian life: the busy, giving, serving side; and the quiet, prayerful, absorbing side. One balances the other, to make the complete and rounded life of a servant of Christ. Be busy, with no time to pray and reflect, you get burn-out. Too much reflection and otherworldly holiness, and you're too heavenly minded to be of any earthly use. The monks of old knew that.

Old Mrs Renton knew that too. Mrs Renton was one of those people – and every church has one – who comes to worship ages before everyone else. Maybe it was the time of the buses, or that she was always up early, or she wanted the best seat in the church. I never knew and I never asked. But Mrs Renton was in her place every Sunday, 45 minutes before worship began, in glorious isolation, sucking pan drops, idly thumbing through her hymnal – while around her flowers were put in place; colours were changed for the appropriate Christian season; the music group rehearsed the praise; and yours truly rushed around, full of frenetic activity as the start of worship rapidly approached. Of course I would say 'hello' to Mrs Renton as I went by; 'good morning' on route to the vestry; 'hello again' as I returned; 'nice day' as I went up to the chancel, an embarrassed smile as I returned. It was the same every Sunday.

One morning, Mrs Renton stopped me in my tracks.

'Excuse me,' she said, 'have you got a moment?' I skidded to a halt – like Charlie Chaplin in a silent movie – and enquired what she wanted.

'Sit down here,' she replied, patting the seat beside her. Impatiently, I did as I was bidden.

'Well? …' I asked, with barely concealed irritation. There was a long silence. 'Well?…' I offered again, as an encouragement to my companion to get on with things. 'You wanted a word, Mrs Renton?'

The old lady turned to me, and smiled. 'No,' she replied. 'Actually, I just wanted to see if you could sit down.'

Mrs Renton was a wise woman. She would have done well as an ancient monk.

Tom Gordon

Playing for God

The beginning of the Bible tells us that God created the universe, saw that it was good and rested. This tells us something about the nature of God, a creator, a craftsperson, one who seeks human company but does not force it on us, and one who takes time to enjoy the fruits of labour. So, if we are created in the image of God, such attributes must be part of our very being.

It also tells us something very important about creation. We human beings are not at the pinnacle. On the seventh day, God created rest. God created the time to reflect on what had been achieved, to delight in it. And God created us to be companions in work, in rest, and in the enjoyment of creation.

We know that we all need to work, and that loss of work can be very damaging to our sense of self. Those of us who are employed contribute to society through our paid work. For some of us, study is our current work, while many of us engage in unpaid activities.

We know that we also need rest, time to be with other people, time to explore our hobbies and interests, and especially, time to be with God. Without these times of companionship, change and refreshment, life can become drab and bitter.

Our lives are now so busy that work doesn't always seem fruitful. Space for growth and refreshment often seems crowded out. Meals may be bolted down alone, in front of the television rather than shared with other people. Even family life can be hard to find time for. And Christians, especially those in ministry, may be the worst at working themselves to death. We may even make ourselves believe that long hours are a virtue, rather than a temptation drawing us away from the goodness of life God intended for us. Or it may just seem that we are trapped on a treadmill, that somehow all the paperwork, phone calls, e-mails, administration, to say nothing of the meetings, just have to be got through.

All the same, people who take prayer seriously and give time to it, still seem to get through as much as the rest of us. Prayer may need lots of attention while we are doing it, but we certainly feel rested and energised as a result. We get a taste of what life was meant to be like.

The Book of Proverbs describes ancient Wisdom, who was there from the beginning of time, working with God in creation, like a master craftsperson:

and I was daily God's delight,
rejoicing before God always,
rejoicing in the inhabited world
and delighting in the children of Man. (Proverbs 8:30–31)

One of God's great gifts to us is play. We are meant to work, but also to spend time doing something else, being absorbed, probably with other people, being curious and learning new skills.

Play is not just for children. Even parents who play with their children also need time alone for their own growth. Perhaps we should make sure that we set aside time each week for our own Sabbath, a time to come aside, to rest, relax and play, to delight in God's gifts of creation and creativity, with others and in the company of

---

Month 4 Day 24

God.

Jesus, our model for how to live, knew the songs of the children, and told jokes and funny stories to illustrate God's desire for us. Jesus enjoyed work, but also enjoyed rest, meals with friends, time alone praying, and time to be together with his closest friends.

Time for work, time for relaxing, time for life with our families if we have them, time for prayer and time for play. We need them all.

There is a Jewish story that when we meet God at death, the first question will be: 'Well, did you enjoy yourself?'

Rosemary Power

THE POOR AND DISADVANTAGED

Poverty – why bother?

What about poverty anyway? Who are the poor? They are people who are crushed under the burden of simply maintaining life from day to day when every act of survival seems only to serve to tighten the merciless bonds of poverty and debt and hopelessness. They are people who are despised and outcast from society because they are strangers, disabled, refugees, slaves, homosexuals, gypsies, Jews, women. Society's capacity for selecting categories to humiliate and demonise seems never-ending. People are made poor because of injustice and prejudice. People are poor because other people are rich.

'If God is not involved in human history, then all theology is useless and Christianity itself is a mockery, a hollow meaningless diversion' is the passionate assertion of the American theologian James Cone. And biblical evidence is pretty unambiguous that that involvement is on the side of the poor and the oppressed.

In the Old Testament, the choosing of Israel as the people of God is inseparable from their slave status in Egypt and God's covenant with them is founded in their liberation from oppression. 'You have seen what I did to the Egyptians, and how I bore you on eagles' wings and brought you to myself. Now therefore, if you will obey my voice and keep my covenant, you shall be my possession among all peoples' (Exodus 19:4–5a).

The Lord spoke to Moses on Mount Sinai about the rhythm of life (Leviticus 25), about the seventh year being a year of rest for the land: the immutable nature of human life is that, without social mechanisms of restraint, the rich become out-of-sight rich and the poor are trapped in unremitting poverty. He gives Moses the instruction that there should be a Jubilee year: a year of restoration, a mechanism to re-establish social cohesion.

It is in the life of Jesus that the involvement of God in human history sheds all ambiguity. 'The Spirit of the Lord is upon me, because He has anointed me to preach good news to the poor. He has sent me to proclaim release to the captives and recovering of sight to the blind, to set at liberty those who are oppressed, to proclaim the acceptable year of the Lord' (Luke 4:18–19).

Jesus's pronouncements seek to transform social reality. They seek the radical subversion of society – it is the wealthy, the Pharisees, doctors of the Law, priests and civil rulers who are denounced. In the proclamation of Jesus the love of God is made concrete in terms of strength for the weak, the embracing of the outcast, and the defeat of poverty. Jesus was a menace to 'orderly' society and had to die. St Paul continues the insane challenge by arguing that the Cross is the wisdom of God.

In our world of increasing globalisation the sinful power of economic structures magnifies and multiplies the power of sin. The destruction or impoverishment of human life is a theological problem – the problem of sin in action and the problem of life denied in human existence.

Aneurin Bevan challenged an earlier generation of clerics: 'As for you, I tell you what the epitaph on you Scottish dissenters will be – pure but impotent. Yes, you will be pure all right. But remember at the price of impotency. You will not influence the course of British politics by as much as a hair's breadth. Why don't you get into a nunnery and be done with it?'

Poverty? Why bother? Simply because as followers of Christ we can do no other.

Erik Cramb

This year I'm not coming

While visiting basic Christian communities in Italy, Ian Fraser collected the following poem-prayer. It was written by thirteen-year-old Massimiliano Tortis for Christmas Eve mass held in the public square. The mass was attended by almost the whole town, notwithstanding the freezing cold; no one went to the parish church mass. The following is a translation of the poem-prayer:

This year I'm not coming.
I'm not coming because I'm fed up with coming every year.
On your earth no one listens to me.
I speak of friendship and you kill each other.
I told you to help each other and instead you think of yourselves.
I told you to become poor and instead you always strive to become rich.
I told you to break bread with the hungry and you exploit them.
I told you not to rob and you instead make away with the money of the poor.
How can I come on your earth – which I gave you?!
How can I come on an earth divided into two categories: 'haves' and 'have-nots'?
How can I come on an earth which calls itself civil and then kills its brother?
Listen to me closely. I have but one thing to say:
Repent, because the kingdom of heaven is near.
And you rich ones, Pharisees and exploiters, will not enter my kingdom.
No!

It will be those whom you have treated as beggars,
as *Cafoni**, as ignorant, who will enjoy eternal life.
I gave you the Word in order to place it at the disposition of the weak,
but you have made it private property to exploit the humble.
I told you to preach my words,
but you have closed yourselves in large buildings.
Many babies are born in your world just as I was in a stall:

a bare and dark stall
in which mothers fear that the baby will awake
because they have nothing to give it;
but you don't even look at them.

You beat people because of the colour of their skin.
On Christmas, instead of thinking about the poor,
you enjoy yourselves eating and drinking.
You treat the poor like you treated me.
But I say to you:
Blessed are those who cry, for they will be consoled.
Blessed are those who are hungry, for they will be satisfied.
Blessed are those who are naked, for they will be clothed.
My kingdom will be composed precisely of these.

*Could be translated as 'human trash'

Basic Christian Communities

Ian Fraser has spent much of his life visiting small Christian communities throughout the world. From America to The Philippines, from Nicaragua to Rome:

The whole fabric of created life

In his time, Cardinal Ovando y Bravo in Nicaragua, with his declaration that good Christians do not engage in politics, was countered not only by the small Christian communities in Managua and Masaya but by Baptists in Rome. Nicaraguan small Christian communities who had taken part in the Nicaraguan revolution to an unprecedented extent saw the gains of that revolution being eroded – especially regarding education and healthcare for all – and set their faces against what they considered to be a threat to what were the signs of God's Kingdom and righteousness. The Baptist pastor in Rome, whose flock had teamed up with Roman Catholics to form ecumenical small Christian communities, discovered that the revelation of God's will and purpose had to be related to situations which called for remedy if it were to be truly gospel. Reflecting on those who opted for either revelation or situation, not both, he produced the stunning saying: 'We must never retreat into the Bible or retreat into politics.'

Jesus did not come announcing church but Kingdom – the whole fabric of created life being transformed so that it evidences God's mind and purpose in every part. This is to be sought actively in every age and is to be fulfilled in the city of God, where no church building exists because the church by then shall have fulfilled its assignment. How can the affairs of the world be neglected by believers who know that God so loved the world that he sent his Son? …

Ian M. Fraser

Prayer

God of compassion and justice,
we pray for the suffering people of your world.

We stand with them
in their struggle
and we pray they will find the strength
to stand firm in hard times.

We make our prayer in the strong name of Jesus,
who stands with his struggling ones,
sits with his suffering ones,
and dances with his hopeful ones. Amen

Alison Adam

NON-VIOLENCE AND PEACEKEEPING

Based on personal experience

I was born and grew up in Las Vegas, a city famous worldwide for gambling – and for atomic testing. As a child, I had first-hand experience of nuclear tests, which were conducted just 90 miles away at the Atomic Test Site. In primary school I was taught to duck under my desk, shut my eyes, and wait until the teacher released us from the classroom. I have a vivid memory of sitting outside my house, my back to the Site, hugging my knees to my chest, with my hands covering my closed eyes. First came the flash – the light so bright that it could be detected through my hands and closed eyelids. It was brighter than the noon day sun. After the flash, we waited ...... until we could feel the shock wave travel through the earth. Then came the sound of the wave. It was loud.

Following one of the tests, manikins were displayed in stores along Fremont Street, the main street of the city. They had been placed in the mock village that was only a few miles from the ground zero of the atomic test. Some of the manikins were charred, some had their clothing burned off, some had their clothing ripped off, and some looked as though nothing had happened to them. The display was part of the Atomic Energy Commission's efforts to do good public relations. There were pictures of the structures in which the manikins had been placed. Some were blown away. Some had only a wall knocked out. Some looked untouched. Of course the Atomic Energy Commission told us that we had nothing to fear, that we would not be exposed to any radiation.

During one of the tests, military personnel were ordered into bunkers and trenches just a short distance from ground zero so that the military command and the scientists could determine if any of the soldiers would have complications due to radiation exposure. As time passed, many of those soldiers died of cancers and from other atomic-exposure-related illnesses.

As a Boy Scout, I was taken in a bus to that same ground zero village some years after that atomic test. As part of the mock city, a highway bridge had been built over a roadway prior to the atomic test. The first sight I had of that village were the steel girders of the bridge. They had been broken and twisted like toothpicks by the force of the atomic blast. The sand of the desert floor had been melted into glass.

I had two uncles who were lorry drivers at the Atomic Test Site. Both of them died of lung cancer. They were among a number of civilian employees who had exposure to radiation in the course of their work for the Atomic Energy Commission.

My opposition to nuclear weapons and nuclear power is based on personal experience few others have had.

The atomic genie is out of the bottle. A heavy price is being paid. Chernobyl and the melting glaciers here in Alaska are grim warnings: we are not God. It is time for the human family to rediscover the virtue of humility.

Dr Israel Nelson, an Associate of the Iona Community who lives in Alaska

Month 4 Day 27

A peaceful land

*What is being a nation? A talent springing in the
heart. And love of country? Keeping house among
a cloud of witnesses.*

Waldo Williams

When one hundred thousand people
met to march from Glasgow Green,
there were millions more walked with them,
a cloud of witnesses unseen,
from the past and from the future,
and the cry on every hand:
'Not in our name do you go to war,
this must be a peaceful land.'

And how shall we teach our children
love of country, pride of place?
Shall we say, we once were heroes,
of a fiery, fighting race;
and forget the stains of violence –
people beaten, enslaved and banned?
Or shall we now be peacemakers
in a hospitable land?

From the Pentland to the Solway,
from the Forth down to the Clyde,
city streets and quiet places
and the turning of the tide;

shall we rise on wings of eagles
soaring over wave and sand,
never seeing beneath the surface
to the scars upon the land?

We are armoured and defended
like an empire dressed for war.
But we face no threat or peril
and we don't know what it's for.
Take the missiles from the waters,
it's our dream and our demand.
Turn the weapons into ploughshares,
give us back a peaceful land.

There's a choice that lies before us.
How shall Scotland best be known?
For the glories of its history
and its loveliness alone?
Or shall care for all earth's people
be the song for which we stand,
and the flowering of our nation
as a just and peaceful land?

Kathy Galloway

INTERFAITH

The interior life (On a trip to India)

… Most of my time was spent in the ashram, or religious community, of Bede Griffiths in Tamil Nadu, along the sacred River Cauvery in South India. There Bede and his fellow Benedictine brothers have committed themselves to a contemplative life of prayer, following the Rule of St Benedict, as well as studying Hindu doctrine and making use of Hindu methods of prayer and meditation.

Like so many reared in the Western traditions of the Church, I have a strong sense of the external, material realm. And with that has come a looking out to the exterior world of Christ: a listening for the Word of God in the scriptures and in creation; a looking for Christ in the sacrament of bread and wine and in the corporate life of the community of faith; and a searching for Christ in the poor and the betrayed of the world. The concentration on these outward signs and embodiments of Christ in the exterior realm is part of the rich inheritance of Western Christianity, but I received a particular blessing from the East's emphasis on the interior life.

An ashram seeks to enable people to discover the hidden mystery within and beyond this world. The mystery beyond the external and the sacramental; the mystery that we all face in death, the collapse of the external. Life in the ashram called me to the interior realm, and encouraged me towards a greater delight in being. Being in the presence of God is the context of action, and thus a true acting in love flows from a confident being in love. On Iona, the Celtic prayers of the past provide us with a rhythm of prayer to Christ above us, Christ beside us, Christ beneath us, Christ within us. The ashram provided me with a focus on the latter:

Christ within me. Through a very simple technique of contemplation, which even I as a distracted Westerner could follow, each day we meditated at the rising and setting of the sun alongside the River Cauvery. The emphasis was on bringing the mind into stillness, and sinking deep within to the Word that was in the beginning, the Word that calls us all into life, who is deep within us and within all creation. Sitting at the edge of the vast river-bed, as the Indian sun rose or set over the Cauvery, were times of calm and of awareness that the God within is closer to us than our very breath and profoundly connects us with one another and with the whole of creation around us.

That sense of calm not only pervaded the times of meditation and ashram life generally, but characterised many aspects of village and agricultural life around the ashram, even in the midst of an almost continual honking of vehicle horns along the main dirt road nearby. One afternoon I saw a group of men loading coconuts into a lorry in perfectly coordinated rhythm. Each man reached for a coconut and threw it into the container at the same time, so that instead of clashing movements and sounds there was a rhythmic thud of coconuts simultaneously landing. A sense of inner connectedness of life often so expressed itself in the detail of the external.

Similarly the slow pace of men and women walking along the roads – which it may well be said is necessitated by the sheer heat of the country – nevertheless suggested the same calm and sense of reverence in the ordinary routines of life. And the taking off of our shoes and sandals before worship in the temple, and meditating along the river, and again at mealtimes, spoke of a sensitivity to the presence of the mystery in the earth and in one another …

J. Philip Newell, 1990

COMMITMENT

We did not want to go

This is the testimony of four followers of Christ who can be found in the Gospels and in the churches today.

It should be read by four people, scattered throughout the worship area, each of whom has a symbol that represents what they are asked to give up.

The symbols should eventually be placed in a visible central location, perhaps on the altar or Communion table or on four pedestals. They are put there one by one after each character has spoken and while the congregation sings a response. Alternatively, all can wait until VOICE A says, 'Yet we went.' Then all four can walk to the centre together, place their symbols appropriately and, after the words 'We gave up everything and lost more', say together the last line, 'And we gained the Kingdom of Heaven.'

Prayers may follow, or silence, focused on what we are individually asked to forego for the sake of the Kingdom of Heaven.

Suitable sung response: Your Kingdom Come, O Lord (Russian Orthodox, Many and Great, *John L. Bell and Graham Maule, Wild Goose Publications)*

Voice A: He called me
           but I did not want to go.
           I had some business to attend to – private business.

           I was a self-made man,
           fired by the spirit of free enterprise.

           It took a lot of my time, most of my time …
           that's the way it is with private business.

           And he expected me to give it up when he called:
           give up my independence and go public,
            give up competition and go cooperative.

           I did not want to go.

(Sung response)

Voice B: He called me
           but I did not want to go.
           I had a relationship to attend to –
           a private relationship.

           I was involved with one person
           whom I coveted, adored
           and who kept me infatuated …

           that's the way it is with some private relationships.
           And he expected me to give it up when he called:
           give up my obsession for one person

           _____

           Month 4 Day 29

and love everybody;
give up caring only for one individual
and start caring for the world.

I did not want to go.

(Sung response)

Voice C: He called me
but I did not want to go.
I had some money to attend to – private money.
I had inherited a small fortune from my parents;

I had made some fast money on the stock market,
and I was making inroads into the black market …
that's the way it is with private money.

And he expected me to give it up when he called:
give up my private wealth and share it around;
live on less so that others could live on more.

I did not want to go.

(Sung response)

Voice D: He called me
but I did not want to go.
I had my faith to attend to – my own private faith.

I was devoted to a god
whom I imagined was like me.

Month 4 Day 29

I worshipped that god
my own personal way …

that's the way it is with private faith.
And he expected me to give it up when he called:
give up my private faith and make it public;
serve God in society and not just in my soul.

I did not want to go.

(Sung response)

Voice A: He called us,
           but we did not want to go.

           We did not want our business, our love,
           our fortune, our faith
           to be infected and affected by his touch.

           Yet we went.

           We gave up everything and lost more.
           And we gained the Kingdom of Heaven.

           (Sung response)

John L. Bell

Month 4 Day 29

THE REDISCOVERY OF SPIRITUALITY

Clearing out the attic

One day, quite out of the blue, William appeared at our Centre and asked 'to see the boss'. Having identified him as the patient who had been referred to us some weeks before, our Medical Director sat down with him to talk, and William expressed his purpose in seeking out the boss. 'I need some help,' he said, 'to clear out my mental attic before I die.' In the discussion which ensued, William was offered a number of resources – social worker, doctor, home care sister, chaplain – to help him clear out his attic. William chose the chaplain. Why he did so, I do not know. I can only surmise. But the next day, following a telephone contact to arrange a convenient time, he and I met for the first time.

Once we had gone through the niceties of tea and biscuits, I was quite unprepared for his opening gambit. 'When I was told that I had cancer,' he began, 'I set aside an evening for myself to work out the answers to two questions: Firstly – am I religious? And secondly – do I believe in God? After much heart-searching, I decided that my answer to both questions was no. Now, chaplain, is that a problem for you?' 'No,' I replied. 'It's not a problem at all. And now that we've got that out of the way, what help do you need to clear out your mental attic?'

Over four afternoons, a week apart and an hour-and-a-half each time, William laid bare the dark corners of his attic – and it was extensive and very messy. Issues of guilt, broken relationships, his struggle with being gay, childhood rejections, his lack of self-worth, what his will might contain, his fears for his alcoholic friend, and much more, were carefully explored. We even talked about his funeral. (He wanted a huge firework display, I recall, 'the kind they have at the end of the Edinburgh

Festival'. But he had discovered that to have such a display required clearance from Air Traffic Control at Edinburgh Airport because it could disrupt the aircraft flight-paths. So they needed to know the date and the time of the firework display. And it wasn't possible to predict that! So he'd had to adjust his plans.)

There was much in William's attic which needed clearing. And though time was short, William was not to be rushed, and sought to deal with each issue, each tidying process, carefully and thoroughly. Eventually, to his satisfaction, the job was completed. At the end of our final session together, he thanked me for my time. The attic was in order. I wouldn't see him again. And he and I wished each other well. To this day, I do not know what happened to William. He will have died a long time since. But I do know that the task William had set himself was completed, and because of that he was at peace.

This image of clearing the untidy attic is a powerful one, and I don't think I have ever come across someone who has been so focused on the task of clearing it out. William was, I believe, a spiritual being clearly engaged in a spiritual search – despite his protestations about being non-religious. As he struggled to find meaning for his complicated life – to tidy his attic before he died – he was going to the core of his being, seeking meaning, purpose and fulfilment. That is fundamental to the human condition. And it is spiritual!

Meister Eckhart wrote: *A man has many skins in himself, covering the depths of his heart. Man knows so many things; he does not know himself. Why, thirty or forty skins or hides, just like an ox's or a bear's, so thick and hard, cover the soul. Go into your own ground and learn to know yourself there.*

I have no doubt that before he died, having stripped away layers of covering in this spiritual search, William somehow succeeded in finding his soul, and went into his own ground and learned to know himself – perhaps for the very first time.

We are all spiritual beings. Spirituality is so hard to define that it is often labelled as esoteric, dismissed as peripheral, or seen as the pursuit only of the high-minded. And yet, if holistic care includes the spiritual dimension, to dismiss it or avoid it is to do an injustice to the person for whom we care. William knew that, and therefore in seeking purpose and fulfilment for his life before he died he was on a spiritual journey, moving towards being a whole person.

In his case, he needed help. His attic was too scary a place to venture into alone after all those years, and too messy by far. Many who seek to make sense of life in the face of death have few, if any, resources within themselves, of language, symbols or beliefs, upon which they can draw. It is our task as carers to help them find these resources to finish their task.

The job William needed to do could not and should not be confined to a religious framework. He had no belief in a divine being and he was not a religious man. And yet he still had a spiritual search. And this, for some, is a problem. From the 'religious' side there is the misconception that religion alone defines spirituality and only the religious are spiritual people; and from the 'secular' side there is the naive assumption that religion and spirituality are synonymous. William had ditched concepts of God and religion. He also knew I was a religious man. But to begin his search, it was necessary for William to be affirmed where he was – and that was in his attic and not mine.

If we are to be genuine with people in their spiritual search, then sometimes concepts of God have to be left to one side. Religion does not work for everyone, and God does not have to be imposed on every facet of spiritual care. You can ask people like William! …

The advantage of the 'search for meaning' approach to spiritual care is that it takes people seriously, for it contains an understanding that all people have spiritual needs, and in dealing with them the focus is on helping people find their own meaning rather than the carers sharing their faith.

Until we fully grasp this approach, is it any wonder that the caring professions remain suspicious of spiritual care if they have a false concept of it? And is it any wonder that spiritual care is neglected in professional training if it is assumed that you have to be religious to give and receive a grounding in spiritual issues?

Tom Gordon

THE THIRTY-FIRST DAY

A good day to die
(A sermon preached in Iona Abbey on Low Sunday, 2003)

When it is a fine day the Lakota people do not say, 'What a good day to be alive.' They say, 'Today is a good day to die.' They see death as a necessary part of life that can be embraced and even planned for. A good death is to be desired. Because of this acceptance of death, life itself is given fresh meaning.

It is about living in balance, in wholeness, with integrity. Life is about dying at peace. The American artist Barbara Bloom said, 'You have to choose where you look and in making that choice you eliminate entire worlds.' In our unbalanced, compartmentalised, totally individualised society we constantly eliminate entire worlds. This is what Christ came to address.

Jesus came to show us what God is like, to offer us the opportunity, even the choice, to discover the balanced world that is God's love – Jesus came to tell us that God loves us and that we belong. Our mark of belonging is our living in alignment with God, in the knowledge and joy that God loves us so much that God was prepared to die. And because of this, God brings us all to new life, to be healed and reconciled, to live authentically and with integrity in a new world. Do you live in that knowledge and joy?

In a Radio 4 series on the early Church, the India-based journalist Mark Tully investigated the evidence for the Resurrection. He came to the conclusion that it actually happened. This conclusion was based on the changed behaviour of the disciples. The disciples were very much like us: full of fear, ignorance and prejudice. But after the Resurrection they dramatically changed from being terrified individuals with their world torn apart to being dynamic, incredibly brave, motivated people building new communities of love and hope despite facing persecution, torture and death.

Mark Tully concluded that only something huge, something overwhelming could have happened which totally overturned their world and demanded that they completely re-evaluate their lives. They were forced to look somewhere different and they discovered new worlds. They met the risen Lord and were never the same.

The risen Lord they met was obviously not the same in the flesh as the Jesus they had known in life for they did not recognise him until he had spoken (or demonstrated who he was by familiar actions such as the breaking of the bread). Once he had greeted them they knew him and accepted him. He integrated their worlds. We have the Spirit to integrate our world, to give us new vision and to build community, to bring us to new life and hope.

An understanding I have gradually come to is that throughout scripture and history God never restores to what has been, but always makes new. Jesus is alive but he bears the scars. He is not as he was. This is the heart of the Easter story. Resurrection is about making radically new.

We all have experience of resurrection. Of dying to what has been and rising to new life. Some will be small everyday incidents which suddenly bring a fresh insight and hope. Others will be cataclysmic and will precipitate a massive change of direction.

I have had several resurrection experiences, including surviving abuse, both child sexual abuse and domestic abuse, which have led me to a new relationship with God

and a new understanding of the gospel. God does not stop us from experiencing dark times, but is with us as the light in our tunnel, holding us when we are in pain. As the translation of the Prayer of Jesus in the *Iona Abbey Worship Book* says: 'Save us in the time of trial', instead of 'Lead us not into temptation'. My latest time of trial and subsequent resurrection has been one of the most challenging:

Last December I found two lumps, one in my armpit and one in my breast. I was diagnosed with breast cancer, was whipped into hospital the next day and had about one-and-a-half days to decide between a lumpectomy and a mastectomy. I was still breast-feeding my baby Millie until the biopsy. As you can imagine, I changed my mind at least ten times but, in the end, after much prayer and discussion, opted for the bigger operation, which has turned out to be a wise decision. I am now over halfway through a course of chemotherapy and find the idea of being poisoned for the good of my health an interesting one! One Bible verse that speaks strongly to my condition is Romans 8:28: 'All things work together for good for those who love God'. Therefore I believe I must put my trust in God and in those through whom God works, and not worry. I am trying to be as positive as I can with God's help, the support of my family and the communion of saints. And I thank God daily for the greatest of gifts – a sense of humour, which puts things truly in perspective!

I have come to the realisation that cancer is not really about death. Cancer is about too much life. Cancer cells do not die, but live growing at the expense of healthy cells. Maybe that is why we have so much cancer in the so-called

Month 4 Day 31

civilised world, because our lives are out of balance, spiritually and physically, locally and globally.

In having cancer I have been given a great gift. That may sound strange, but how often are we given the chance to put life in perspective? How often do we truly start again, even though this is a key part of our faith?

In our culture we shy away from addressing our mortality. We think that we will go on for ever.

Whilst waiting for my chemo session last week we had an interesting discussion about folk who want to be frozen when they die so that they can be 'reborn' and therefore live for ever, but in exactly the same state as before. (One of my fellow patients said she would expect *Coronation Street* to still be on the telly!) But this is a false dream, a temptation. Life can't be pickled. Each moment is unique and part of the ongoing journey.

As Christians we are called to be born again, but we should be being reborn every day! It's not a one-off event. And as repentance is at the heart of the gospel then we should always be prepared to turn around, to change direction. Jesus said, 'Follow me' and that implies movement.

I have been given the gift of a wake-up call – the realisation that one day I will die. And I have been given the wonderful gift of life by the Holy One who has created all life – humans, animals, the earth, sea and sky. I should treasure this gift and value each precious moment, for to waste a minute by longing for the past or rushing towards the future is to throw this gift in the face of the Creator.

Like each one of us, I am unique and loved and have a special place which is here and now. I have been given the chance to be healed, to seek reconciliation, to be at peace with God, with all creation and with myself, to live whatever is my allotted span with integrity, and to die a good death. Like Jesus I have my scar, but it is a sign of my new body – my new life. When my husband saw my scar for the first time he said, 'Wow! You look like you've been chomped by a dinosaur!' I've wrestled a monster and I've survived – with new life.

This new life is not just for me. As a member of the Iona Community I have made a commitment (part of the community's five-fold Rule) to work for justice and peace – new life for all. My wake-up call has opened me to the necessity of working for justice and peace with renewed vigour. This is not an optional extra but an intrinsic part of the gospel. I have been opened to the wonder that lies in God's creation and the joy that is at the heart of the gospel: that God accepts us and loves us and wants us to live in justice, peace and love. That each person, everywhere in the world, is made in the image of God, whether we like it or not.

The main lesson from my experience is that through the gift of free will we can choose how we react to whatever life throws at us. We can choose to ask for help or to be alone. We can choose to accept God's grace or not.

After the bleakness and pain and despair of the crucifixion there was the new life, joy and hope of the Resurrection. As Christians that joy and hope must undergird how we live, together with the knowledge that the whole world is our kin, that we must live the 'Kindom'* by working for justice and peace, and that to destroy another part of creation is to harm God. Throughout the gospels Jesus emphasises that it is our motivation, our attitude and, most importantly, our actions that show our faith – not our words.

I am passing on this resurrection wake-up call to you. Are you choosing to be liberated and healed? Are you working for the Kindom to ensure God's justice and peace is a current reality? Are you fully living each precious moment now with joy? If not, why not? What is stopping you?

Living with cancer

Thank you for giving me a wake-up call:
to look at the world with new eyes,
to live NOW –
not stuck in the past,
not fretting away for an unknown and unknowable future.
Thank you for giving me the chance to look at life afresh.

Month 4 Day 31

I know to trust you and not to worry:
to live fully and value each precious moment,
to cherish each part of your creation,
to seek you in each person I meet,
to live with joy,
which I have too often denied.

Thank you for blessing me.

Zam Walker

Kindom – 'a word issuing from Mujerista theology [which] means that we are all kith and kin, brothers and sisters in the new creation.' Mary Grey, Introducing Feminist Images of God, *Sheffield Academic Press, 2001, p. 117.*

End Piece

The important part is the doing, the stepping out in faith. Doing our utmost, to the very limit of our being, and then being free to let go of the result; not to be bound by success, but to hold on to the confidence that the outcome will be taken up by others and the flame continue to burn …

Perhaps a reminder here about the meaning of heroics is in order. We have all looked at the deeds of others and said, 'I could never do that.' That is not the point. Heroism is not necessarily about great dramatic deeds of daring. We are not called to imitate each other's actions nor to feel disappointed by our failure to be what we are not. We are called to be faithful, to follow our own inner leadings, in our own time, using the particular and special gifts that are unique to each one of us.

But the importance remains in the doing. It involves taking risks, daring to be different from the crowd, keeping in touch constantly with our inner Light, knowing that countless others are doing the same, all making a difference.

Undoubtedly one of the lowest moments of my life was when HMS *Vanguard*, first of Britain's Trident submarines, arrived on the Clyde. Although we had known it was coming for years and had been campaigning vigorously and creatively for just as many years, I don't think anything could have prepared us psychologically for the shock of its reality. Just seeing the huge grey-black bulk being manoeuvred into position at the end of the loch, and realising the full significance of its deadly potential for total annihilation of all that we valued and held dear, was a desperate, heart-stopping moment.

… We all launched our little boats as a protest against its progress up the loch. My canoe had been stopped by a boatload of marines, who, having informed me that they were saving my life, held firmly on to my craft. I could only sit there in tears watching the inexorable progress of *Vanguard* as it thrust its way up the Gareloch. I had never felt so helpless and powerless in my life. When we came on shore, people gathered round and began singing 'We Shall Overcome'. I simply couldn't join them.

Unexpected as it may seem, this for me is the point of resurrection. The point where we have done all we can to the best of our ability, however feeble or seemingly useless, and then we have to hand it over, to let go. Let go of the outcome of one's actions in trust and confidence that they are not in vain, that somewhere in the secret workings of God, a change is taking place.

Because the evidence of history is that change *does* happen – indeed, that is what history is.

Helen Steven

PRAYERS FOR THE DAYS

DAY 1 – 'New ways to touch the hearts of all'

Pray for 'new ways to touch the hearts of all'.

For writers, musicians, artists, dancers, liturgists …
For all those working creatively in the fields of politics,
community development, human relations …

For risk takers,
for enablers …

God, you are always calling your people
to follow you into the future,
inviting them to new ventures, new challenges,
new ways to care,
new ways to touch the hearts of all.
When they become fearful of the unknown, give them courage.
When they worry that they are not up to the task,
remind them that you would not call them
if you did not believe in them.

When they get tired,
or feel disappointed with the way things are going,
remind them that you can bring change and hope
out of the most difficult situations.

Day 2 – Economic witness

Pray for organisations working to bring about a more just economic order;
people and countries held captive in the chains of debt.

Jesus Christ, Lord of all,
help me to live more simply
and with greater faith in you.

Day 3 – Youth concern

Pray for children
and for youth.

May children be protected, nurtured and encouraged.
May they have the chance to learn,
the space to dance,
the room to grow.

May youth be valued and heard,
supported and challenged,
and be given real opportunities
to help in the reshaping of the Church and the world.

Day 4 – The Word

For the word of God in scripture,
for the word of God among us,
for the word of God within us,
thanks be to God.

Day 5 – Hospitality and welcome

Pray for houses and centres of hospitality and welcome.

For those who are not welcomed:
refugees and asylum-seekers;
all who are homeless.

As the poor widow welcomed Elijah,
let me be open
to the richness and miracle in meeting.
As Abraham and Sarah welcomed passing strangers,
let me entertain the possibility of
angels in disguise.
Let my eyes be opened
that I may recognise in my neighbour
the divine presence of Christ.

Day 6 – This is the day

God, your kindness has brought the gift of a new day.
Help me to leave yesterday,
and not to covet tomorrow,
but to accept the uniqueness of today.
Amen

Day 7 – Iona

You are an island in the sea, O God,
you are a hill on the shore,

you are a star in the darkness,
you are a staff to the weak.
O, my soul's healer,
when I am lost and tired and stumbling
you shield and support me.
God, help me to give light, love and support to others.

Day 8– Life in community

Pray for all those living and working in intentional communities,
giving thanks for their counter-cultural witness.

For volunteers everywhere.

May people find meaningful ways to contribute to their communities.
May their gifts and talents be recognised and encouraged.

Day 9 – Women

Pray for women who are discriminated against,
who are marginalised,
who suffer violence and abuse.

For women bearing heavy responsibilities and pressures:

women on the way to the well
women supporting whole families by themselves …

For equal opportunities
and women's issues.

Jesus, women were always close to you,
did not run away –

from pain
from commitment
from grief and emptiness.

May the contributions, wisdom and strength of women
be recognised in wider society.

Day 10 – Prayer

Lord, give me a moment to be still:
to listen for your voice within my heart.

Day 11 – Justice and peace

The Spirit of the Lord is upon me.
He has chosen me to bring good news to the poor.
He has sent me to proclaim liberty to the captives
and recovery of sight to the blind;
to free the oppressed
and announce that the time has come
when the Lord will save his people.

Luke 4:18–19

Day 12 – The integrity of creation

Pray that nations may have the political will
to protect this fragile planet,
and that people everywhere
may think globally and act locally.

Pray for fair trading organisations
as they seek to guard the rights and incomes
of work forces in developing countries.
Pray for the indigenous peoples of the world.

Almighty God, Creator,
the morning is Yours, rising into fullness.
The summer is Yours, dipping into autumn.
Eternity is Yours, dipping into time.
The vibrant grasses, the scent of flowers, the lichen on the rocks,
the tang of seaweed,
all are Yours.
Gladly we live in this garden of Your creating …

George MacLeod

Day 13 – Columban Christianity and the Celtic tradition

O God, be a bright flame before me,
a guiding star above me,
a smooth path beneath me,
a kindly shepherd behind me.

Attributed to St Columba

Day 14 – Racism

Pray for racial justice,
for those working to overcome racism in our society,
and pressing for changes in nationality law and immigration policy.

Peace between nations,
peace between neighbours,
peace between lovers,
in love of the God of life.

Day 15 – Community

Pray for the local community, community development and community relations;
the community of the world.

May diversity be valued, barriers crossed,
and ordinary people empowered.
May neighbourhoods be places
where all have a part to play.

Day 16 – Pilgrimage

Pray for all pilgrims and seekers
and companions on the way;
for all travellers.

May our journey ahead
be blessed with
God's laughter,
silences,

risks,
challenges,
healings,
questions,
promises,
protests,
answers,
tears,
solidarity,
often uncomfortable peace and
compassion-filled surprises –
perhaps all in one day.

DAY 17 – Sexuality

Pray for lesbian, gay and transgender rights.

God of compassion,
you made us
in your own image
and our prayer is
that each day you will
illumine our minds,
enlarge our awareness
and
free us from prejudice,
so that we cease to
marginalise,
judge
and condemn others

because of their
sexual orientation.
And, along the way,
help us to
examine with honesty
our own
inner contradictions
sexual fears
and emotional longings.

Day 18 – Healing

Pray for health, wholeness and the ministry of healing.
For victims of violence and injustice.

Watch now, dear Lord,
with those who wake or watch or weep tonight,
and give your angels charge over those who sleep.
Tend your sick ones, O Lord Christ,
rest your weary ones,
bless your dying ones, soothe your suffering ones,
pity your afflicted ones, shield your joyous ones,
all for your love's sake.
Amen

St Augustine

DAY 19 – Social action

Pray for prisoners of conscience;
for political prisoners;
for those who are tortured
and detained without trial.

Living God,
you have taught that faith without works is dead,
so temper our faith with love and hope
that we follow Christ and give ourselves freely to people in their need:
then the lives we live may honour you for ever.
Amen

DAY 20 – Church renewal

Pray for local church renewal;
local church community.

Lord God,
whose Son was content to die
to bring new life,
have mercy on your church
which will do anything you ask,
anything at all,
except die
and be reborn.

Lord Christ,
forbid us unity
which leaves us where we are

and as we are:
welded into one company
but extracted from the battle;
engaged to be yours
but not found at your side.

Holy Spirit of God –
reach deeper than our inertia and fears:
release us into the freedom of the children of God.

DAY 21 – Worship

Pray that the worship of the Church may be renewed
through scripture, song and honest prayer.

Lord Christ, let Your Resurrection light radiate all our worship:
by the power of the Holy Spirit.

DAY 22 – Called to be One

Pray for relations between denominations in Britain
and the world.

May differences be celebrated.

May Christians be made one in Jesus,
who died to bring peace and reconciliation.

DAY 23 – Mission

Pray for church centres
and church organisations.

For an approach which is open, inclusive and sensitive;
imaginative and risk-taking.

God, write a message upon my heart,
bless and direct me,
then send me out –
a living letter of the Word.

DAY 24 – Work

Pray for the unemployed,
for industrial mission,
for those whose work is exploited.

For those who have no work, and those who have too much;
for work that is meaningful and shared;
for a society where people are valued for themselves.

O Christ, the Master Carpenter,
who at the last, through wood and nails,
purchased our whole salvation,
wield well your tools in the workshop of your world,
so that we who come rough-hewn to your bench
may here be fashioned to a truer beauty of your hand.
We ask it for your own name's sake.
Amen

Day 25 – The poor and disadvantaged

Pray for the poor and disadvantaged.

For those who choose to live and work
in areas of multiple deprivation;
for all involved in homeless projects and credit unions.

Christ of the poor,
forgive us for keeping silence in the face of injustice
and for burying our dreams;
for not sharing bread and wine,
love and land,
among us, now.

A prayer from Central America

Day 26 – Basic Christian communities

Pray for basic Christian communities throughout the world,
giving thanks that, amid poverty and oppression,
people are finding a biblical faith that empowers and liberates,
as they work together for grassroots change.

Day 27 – Non-violence and peacekeeping

Pray for organisations involved in international aid and peacekeeping;
for individuals working in the peace movement
and engaged in non-violent resistance.

For victims of war and violence;
for the abolition of nuclear weapons.

Lord, make me an instrument of your peace.
Where there is hatred, let me sow love,
where there is injury, pardon
where there is doubt, faith
where there is despair, hope
where there is sadness, joy.
O Divine Master,
grant that I may not so much seek
to be consoled as to console,
to be understood as to understand,
to be loved as to love.
For it is in giving that we receive,
it is in pardoning that we are pardoned,
it is in dying that we are born again
to everlasting life.
Amen

St Francis

Day 28 – Interfaith

Pray for interfaith dialogue;
for people of other faiths and ideologies;
for situations and places in the world
where there is war and conflict.

May people of different faiths and beliefs find understanding
in their common search for meaning.

Day 29 – Commitment

O most merciful Redeemer, friend and brother,
may I know thee more clearly,
love thee more dearly,
follow thee more nearly:
for ever and ever.

St Richard of Chichester

Day 30 – The rediscovery of spirituality

Pray for the growth and deepening of the spiritual life.

God help me to maintain a spirituality that is both tough and tender,
and to seek you not only in the sacred places
but in the midst and the margins of daily life.

Day 31 – The thirty-first day

Pray for those who have died
and for those who grieve.

As you were before us at our life's beginning
be you so again at our journey's end.
As you were beside us at our soul's shaping,
God be also at our journey's close.

Prayer sources

Prayer for Day 1, Kathy Galloway, adapted from *The Pattern of Our Days*, Wild Goose Publications

Prayer for Day 3, Brian Woodcock (youth prayer)

Prayer for Day 4, *Iona Abbey Worship Book*, Wild Goose Publications

Prayer for Day 5, Neil Paynter, *Iona Abbey Worship Book*, Wild Goose Publications

Prayer for Day 6, *Iona Abbey Worship Book*, traditional (adapted)

Prayer for Day 7, Gaelic traditional, adapted from *Each Day & Each Night*, J. Philip Newell, Wild Goose Publications

Prayer for Day 10, Peter Millar

Prayer for Day 12, George MacLeod, *The Whole Earth Shall Cry Glory*, Wild Goose Publications

Prayer for Day 14, Traditional (adapted), *Iona Abbey Worship Book*

Prayer for Day 15, Brian Woodcock

Prayer for Day 16, Peter Millar, from *Our Hearts Still Sing*, Wild Goose Publications

Prayer for Day 17, Peter Millar, *Waymarks: Signposts to Discovering God's Presence in the World*, SCM-Canterbury Press

Prayer for Day 19, Iona Community, *Iona Community Worship Book*, 1988 edition

Prayer for Day 20, Ian M. Fraser

Prayer for Day 21, George MacLeod, from *The Whole Earth Shall Cry Glory*, Wild Goose Publications

Prayer for Day 23, Neil Paynter, *Iona Abbey Worship Book*

Prayer for Day 24, *Iona Abbey Worship Book*, Wild Goose Publications

Prayer for Day 26, Brian Woodcock

Prayer for Day 30, Brian Woodcock

Prayer for Day 31, Traditional, *Iona Community Worship Book*, 1988 edition

Prayer concerns for the days, Brian Woodcock or Neil Paynter;

other prayers for the days, Neil Paynter

BIBLE READINGS

New ways to touch the hearts of all
Psalm 33:3; Psalm 40:3; Psalm 98:1; Isaiah 43:19; Ezekiel 11:19; Matthew 9:17; Luke 5:36; Luke 24:28–35; John 13:34; Romans 6:4; Romans 7:6; 1 Corinthians 11:25; 2 Corinthians 5:17; Colossians 3:10

Economic witness
Leviticus 25:10–14; Jeremiah 6:13–16; Matthew 6:19–24; Luke 12:13–27; Luke 12:32–34; Luke 21:1–4

Youth
Ru 1: 16–17; I Sa 17:33; Matthew 9:18–26; Matthew 11:25–26; Matthew 18:1–6; Matthew 19:13–14; Luke 2:41–52; Luke 7:11–15; Luke 10:21–24; Luke 18:15–17; 1 Timothy 4:11–16

The Word
Psalm 56:10–11; Psalm 119:105; Isaiah 40:8; Amos 8:11; Matthew 4:4; Luke 8:11; Luke 11:1–4; John 1:1–14; Acts 4: 31; Hebrews 4:12

Hospitality and welcome
Genesis 18:1–15; Exodus 22:21; Leviticus 19:33–34; Deuteronomy 24:17; 1 Kings 17:8–24; Matthew 2:13–15; Matthew 10:40–42; Matthew 26:6–13; Luke 10:38–42; Luke 15:11–32; Luke 19:1–10; John 2:1–11; Acts 28:1–10; Hebrews 13:1–2

This is the Day
Genesis 1:5; Psalm 118; Matthew 5:14; Matthew 26:6–13; Mark 1:16–17; Mark 4:21; Mark 9:2–8; Mark10:13; Luke 2:1–7; Luke 16:19–31; John 1:14–18; John 14:27; John 20: 1–18; Rom 13:11–14; 2 Corinthians 6:1–3; Ephesians 3:18–19; I Thessalonians 5:15–22

Women
Genesis 18:11–15; Exodus 2:1–10; Joshua 2:1–7; 1 Samuel 2:1–11; Matthew 26:1–13; Matthew 27:55–56; Matthew 28:1–20; Luke 1:26–45; Luke 1:46–55; Luke 8:1–3; Luke 24:1–12; John 4:27–30; John 19:25–27; Acts 9:36–43; Acts 16:13–15; Acts 18:24–28; Romans 16:1–2; Philippians 4:1–3

Prayer

1 Chronicles 29:10–20; Psalms 4:1–3; 19:14; 39:12; 46:10; 55:1–2; 61; 62:1–2; 66:20; 69:13–18; 86:1–7; 88; Isaiah 37:14–20; Matthew 6:5–24; Matthew 7:7–13; Matthew 26:38–46; Luke 18:1–14; John 17:1–26; Acts 1:12–14; Acts 4:23–31; Acts 16:25–26; Romans 8:26–27; Ephesians 3:14–21; Philippians 4:4–7; James 5:13–20

Justice and peace

Old Testament: Genesis 9:8–17; Deuteronomy 30:9–14; 1 Samuel 2:1–10; Psalms 9; 10; 22; 51; 72; 85:10; 96; 97; 98; 113; 140; Proverbs 8:20; Isaiah 2:1–5; 42:1–4; 58:1–12; 61:1–4; Jeremiah 31:31–34; Amos 5:10–24; Micah 4:1–4; 6:1–8; Malachi 3:1–5

New Testament: Matthew 5:1–20; 16:24–26; 23:1–4, 23–24, 37; 28:1–10; Luke 1:46–55; 4:16–30; 6:20–38; 12:13–21, 32–34; 18:18–30; John 20:19–29; Acts 4:32–36; 2 Corinthians 8:1–9; Ephesians 2:13–22; James 2:1–5; 5:1–6; 1 Peter 3:8–17

The integrity of creation

Genesis 1:26–31; Genesis 6–9; Exodus 17:1–6; Job 12:7–10; Job:38; 39; Isaiah 24:4–6; Psalms 8; 29; 46; 65:5–13; 67; 72; 80; 84; 96; 104; 147; 148; Isaiah 24:4–6; Ezekiel 34:18–19; Matthew 6:25–31; John 4:7–14; Romans 8:18–25; Colossians 1:15–20

Racism

Genesis 11:1–9; Luke 10:29–37; Acts 2:1–13; Acts 10:34; Acts 17:22–34; Romans 2:11; Colossians 3:9–15

Community

Ex 16:1; Psalm 133; Matthew 5:43–48; Matthew 7:1–5; Luke 19:35–40; Luke 22:7–38; John 13:6–20; Acts 2:1–21; Romans 12:9–21; 1 Corinthians 11:17–34; 1 Corinthians 12:1–31; 1 Corinthians 13:1–13; Galatians 5:22–26; Ephesians 4:1–16; Ephesians 4:25–32; Colossians 3:12–17; 1 Thessalonians 5:11–28; 1 Timothy 6:11–16; James 4:11–12; 1 Peter 3:8–12; 1 John:3:18; 1 John 4:7–12

Pilgrimage

Genesis 12:1; Exodus 15:22–27; Exodus 16:1–36; Numbers 20:2–13; Numbers 21:4–5; 1 Chronicles 29:15; Psalm 23; Jeremiah 31:21; Luke 24:13–29; Ephesians 5:8–10; Hebrews 12:1–2

Relationships
Genesis 2: 15–25; Ruth 1–4; 1 Samuel 18:1–5; Song of Solomon 1–8; John 15:1–17

Healing
Psalms 6; 13; 16; 27:13–14; 28:6–9; 30; 34; 36:7–9; 40:1–3; 42; 51:15–17; 139:1–18; Isaiah 43:1–4; Matthew 5:1–12; Matthew 8:1–17; Matthew 8:28–34; Mark 1:29–45; Mark 5:1–20; Mark 8:22–26; Luke 5:12–26; Luke 13:10–17; John 5:1–18; John 10:10; John 11:1–44; Acts 3:1–10; Acts 8:14–25

Action
Exodus 4:10–16; Matthew 7:21–23; Matthew 11:2–6; Matthew 21:28–32; Matthew 25:34–36, 40; Luke 4:16–21; Luke 11:37–54; Luke 12:32–35; Luke 19:1–10; John 4:1–15; Ephesians 6:13–16; James 1:22–25; James 2:14–26

The Church
Acts 9:31; Acts 11:19–26; 1 Corinthians 1:10–31; Revelation 2:1–22

Worship
Exodus 32:1–6; Psalms 95:1–7; 98:1–6; 100; 134; 149; 150; Amos 5:21–24; Acts 13:13–52; Acts 14:1–7; Acts 18:12–14; 1 Corinthians 14:26

Called to be One
John 17:18–23; Acts 2:1–21; Acts 17:22–34; 1 Corinthians 12:12–16, 26–27; Galatians 3:28–29; Ephesians 4:1–16; Colossians 3:1–17

Mission
Psalm 37:31; Matthew 5:13–16; Matthew 10:5–42; Luke 5:1–11; Luke 10:1–20; Luke 21:5–19; Luke 24:44–49; Acts 27:13–26; 2 Corinthians 3:1–3; 2 Corinthians 5:20–21; 2 Corinthians 6:1–13; 2 Corinthians 11:16–33; 2 Timothy 2:1–7

Work
Psalms 118:22; 127:1; 135:15–18; Amos 8:4–6; Matthew 4:18–22; Matthew 11:28–30; Matthew 20:1–16; Matthew 25:37–40; Luke 16:1–18; John 2:13–16; John 6:27–34; Ephesians 2:19–22; 1 Thessalonians 5:12–22; 2 Timothy 2:15; Philemon 23–25; James 5:1–6

The poor and disadvantaged
Job 24:1–8; Psalms 9:18; 113:2–8; Isaiah 58:6–9; Jeremiah 22:13–16; Matthew 19:16–30; Matthew 25:37–40; Luke 2:1–7; Luke 14:15–24; Luke 16:19–31; Luke 21:1–4; James 2:1–7

Basic Christian communities
Jeremiah 18:4–5; Mark 1:16–20; Luke 1:46–53; John 3:8; Acts 1:12–14; 1 Corinthians 14:20; 1 Corinthians 14:26–33; Galatians 5:1; Ephesians 4:1–16

Non-violence and peacekeeping
Isaiah 2:1–4; Isaiah 53:4–7; Matthew 5:9; Matthew 5:38–45; John 18:3–12; Romans 12:14–21; Philippians 4:4–7; Revelation 22:1–2

Interfaith
Read from a book from another faith or belief – *The Upanishads*, *The Bhagavad Gita*, *The Dhammapada*, *The Koran,* the *Tao Te Ching* …

Commitment
Matthew 3:13–17; Matthew 4:18–22; Matthew 10:5–42; Matthew 14:28–30; Matthew 16:21–28; Matthew 19:16–30; Mark 2:13–17; Mark 10:46–52; Luke 9:57–62; John 15:1–27; Hebrews 13:12–16

The thirty-first day
Psalm 23; Matthew 5:4; Matthew 28:5–6; John 14; 2 Corinthians 4:16–18; Hebrews 12:1–2; Revelation 21:1–4

THE RULE OF THE IONA COMMUNITY

The five-fold Rule calls members to:

1. Daily prayer and Bible reading

2. Sharing and accounting for the use of our money

3. Planning and accounting for the use of our time

4. Action for justice and peace in society

5. Meeting with and accounting to each other

THE JUSTICE AND PEACE COMMITMENT OF THE IONA COMMUNITY

We believe:

1. that the gospel commands us to seek peace founded on justice and that costly reconciliation is at the heart of the gospel;

2. that work for justice, peace and an equitable society is a matter of extreme urgency;

3. that God has given us partnership as stewards of creation and that we have a responsibility to live in a right relationship with the whole of God's creation;

4. that, handled with integrity, creation can provide for the needs of all, but not for the greed which leads to injustice and inequality, and endangers life on earth;

5. that everyone should have the quality and dignity of a full life that requires adequate physical, social and political opportunity, without the oppression of poverty, injustice and fear;

6. that social and political action leading to justice for all people and encouraged by prayer and discussion is a vital work of the Church at all levels;

7. that the use or threatened use of nuclear and other weapons of mass destruction is theologically and morally indefensible and that opposition to their existence is an imperative of the Christian faith.

As members and family groups we will:

8. engage in forms of political witness and action, prayerfully and thoughtfully, to promote just and peaceful social, political and economic structures;

9. work for a policy of renunciation by our own nations of all weapons of mass destruction and for the encouragement of other nations, individually or collectively, to do the same;

10. celebrate human diversity and actively work to combat discrimination on grounds of age, disability, mental well-being, differing ability, gender, colour, race, ethnic and cultural background, sexual orientation or religion;

11. work for the establishment of the United Nations Organisation as the principal organ of international reconciliation and security, in place of military alliances;

12. support and promote research and education into non-violent ways of achieving justice, peace and a sustainable global society;

13. work for reconciliation within and among nations by international sharing and exchange of experience and people, with particular concern for politically and economically oppressed nations.

Notes

1. Speech at the 2002 AGM of the South African New Economics Network (SANE).

2. From 'The Cross stands empty', Yvonne Morland, *Iona Dawn: Through Holy Week with Iona Community*, Neil Paynter (ed), Wild Goose Publications, 2006.

3. 'When I needed a neighbour' – words and music by Sydney Bertram Carter. Reproduced by permission of Stainer & Bell Ltd.

4. Dietrich Bonhoeffer, *Letters and Papers from Prison*, edited by Eberhard Bethge, translated by Reginald H. Fuller, Fontana, London, 1959.

5. *The Sufis*, Idries Shah, Anchor, p. 24.

6. *Open Christianity: Home by Another Road*, Rev. Jim Burklo, Rising Star Press, p. 200. Used by permission of Jim Burklo.

7. Information from the report *Avoiding Dangerous Climate Change*, Editor in Chief: Hans Joachim Schellnhuber; Co-editors: Wolfgang Cramer, Nebojsa Nakicenovic, Tom Wigley, Gary Yohe. Published by the Hadley Centre.

8. *The Prophetic Imagination*, Walter Brueggemann, Fortress Press, 2001, p. 5-6.

9. *The Prophetic Imagination*, Walter Brueggemann, Fortress Press, 2001, p. 39.

10. *God's Politics: Why the Right gets it wrong and why the Left doesn't get it*, Jim Wallis, HarperSanFransisco 2005, p. 228 and p. 237.

11. 'Dr Atiq Rahman … stranded' – taken from the article 'A country under water' by Anjali Kwatra, *Christian Aid News*, Issue 32, Summer 2006. Used by permission of Christian Aid.

SOURCES AND ACKNOWLEDGEMENTS

Some of the pieces in Gathered and Scattered *first appeared in* Coracle: the magazine of the Iona Community *www.iona.org.uk* Editors: Kathy Galloway; Ruth Harvey.

Month 1

'Glory to God in the high street' – by George MacLeod, from *Only One Way Left*, George MacLeod, 1954. Republished by Wild Goose Publications, 2006. Also published in *Daily Readings with George MacLeod,* Ron Ferguson, Wild Goose Publications, 2001.

'The spirituality of economics' – by Kathy Galloway, from *Spirituality and Economics: Envisioning a World Where People Matter*, Kathy Galloway and Bernadino Mandlate, Christian Socialist Movement, CSM Lectures 2003. Used by permission of the Christian Socialists Movement and Kathy Galloway. To order this pamphlet please contact: CSM, Westminster Central Hall, London SW1H 9NH Tel: 020 7233 3736; email: info@thecsm.org.uk/www.thecsm.org.uk

'God's authority' – used by permission of Ian M. Fraser.

'Interwoven with the wire' – by Ruth Burgess, from *At Ground Level*, Ruth Burgess, Wild Goose Publications. Out of print.

'There is a line of women' – by John L. Bell, from *One Is the Body: Songs of Unity & Diversity*. Used by permission of the Wild Goose Resource Group. © Wild Goose Resource Group, 2002.

'Be still, my children' – by Ruth Burgess, from *At Ground Level*, Ruth Burgess, Wild Goose Publications. Out of print.

'A way of interceding' – by Lynda Wright, from *Bread for the Journey*, Tabor Retreat Centre, Key House.

Tabor Retreat Centre, Key House, Falkland, Fife, Scotland:

Key House is a small informal space, offering residential accommodation for individuals or groups in four twin rooms, which can be booked singly for individual breaks.

We meet together socially in the large cosy kitchen for meals. At other times, unless coming with a group or to a programmed event, we encourage guests to make the best use of the quiet of

the house and its setting – resting, reading, walking or reflecting.

We have a peaceful garden which opens at the back of the house into the Palace orchard. The house sits beside the Palace in the High Street of this small conservation village. There are country walks from the back door, with views to the Lomond hills.

For individuals we offer spiritual direction both for residents and non-residents, and space for day retreats.

For groups of up to twelve we offer a day's programme of guided prayer and reflection, or the opportunity to follow their own programme.

The simple chapel in the converted stable at the back of the house is also available for individual use or group prayer.

There is a meditation each evening for those staying with us.

The house is ecumenical and welcomes both men and women of all traditions or none.

From the Tabor Retreat Centre website www.keyhouse.org
Tabor Retreat Centre – Key House, High Street, Falkland, Fife, KY15 7BU

'Let's pretend we're Christians' – Peter Millar, from *Letters from Madras*, Peter and Dorothy Millar, 1988.

'We confess, O Lord, that we live with the demonic powers of violence ...' – © The Iona Community, from *The Iona Community Worship Book* ('The Black Book'), Wild Goose Publications, 1988.

'Moved to action' – by Helen Steven, from *No Extraordinary Power: Prayer, Stillness and Activism*, Helen Steven, Quaker Books, Swarthmore Lecture, 2005. ISBN 0852453795 www.quaker.org.uk Used by permission of Helen Steven and Quaker Books.

'Something almost counter-cultural' – by Norman Shanks, from *Thought for the Day*, BBC Radio. Used by permission of Norman Shanks.

'The love of God comes close' – by John L. Bell and Graham Maule, from *Enemy of Apathy: Songs of the Passion and Resurrection of Jesus, and the Coming of the Holy Spirit*, John L. Bell and Graham Maule, Wild Goose Publications, 1988. Used by permission of the Wild Goose Resource Group. © Wild Goose Resource Group, 1988.

'Pilgrimage prayers' – by Pat Bennett, from the booklet *Traidcraft at Iona: Justice & Peace Prayers*, published by Traidcraft. Out of print.

'All are one in Jesus Christ' – by Simon de Voil, originally published in *Juicy Bits*: the magazine of the Iona Community Youth Department www.iona.org.uk

'Holding someone in the Light' – by Helen Steven, from *No Extraordinary Power: Prayer, Stillness and Activism*, Helen Steven, Quaker Books, Swarthmore Lecture, 2005. ISBN 0852453795 www.quaker.org.uk Used by permission of Helen Steven and Quaker Books.

'Life beyond death row' – by Rosemary Power, originally published in the *Swindon Evening Advertiser*. Used by the permission of Rosemary Power.

'Behind the scenes' – by Ian M. Fraser, from *Holy Ground: Liturgies and Worship Resources for an Engaged Spirituality*, Neil Paynter and Helen Boothroyd, Wild Goose Publications, 2006.

'A new heaven and a new earth' – by John L. Bell, from *Hard Words for Interesting Times: Biblical Texts in Contemporary Contexts*, John L. Bell, Wild Goose Publications, 2003. Used by permission of the Wild Goose Resource Group. © Wild Goose Resource Group, 2003.

'On our doorsteps – used by permission of Ian M. Fraser.

'Time to rest and recuperate' – by Ghillean Prance, *from The Earth Under Threat: A Christian Perspective*, Ghillean Prance, Wild Goose Publications. Used by permission of Ghillean Prance.

'Jesus said' – by Ron Ferguson, from *The Pattern of Our Days: Liturgies and Resources for Worship*, Kathy Galloway, Wild Goose Publications, 1996.

'God in the other' – by Helen Steven, from *No Extraordinary Power: Prayer, Stillness and Activism*, Helen Steven, Quaker Books, Swarthmore Lecture, 2005. ISBN 0852453795. www.quaker.org.uk

'When I needed a neighbour' – by Sydney Bertram Carter. Extract from 'When I needed a neighbour' used by permission of Stainer & Bell Ltd, PO Box 110, Victoria House, 23 Gruneisen Road, London, England N3 1DZ www.stainer.co.uk © 1965, Stainer & Bell Ltd.

'Political meetings, law courts, pubs' – by Ian M. Fraser, from *Strange Fire: Life Stories and Prayers*, Ian M. Fraser, Wild Goose Publications, 1994.

'Death' – by Kate McIlhagga, from *The Green Heart of the Snowdrop*, Wild Goose Publications, 2004 © Donald McIlhagga.

Month 2

'Lectio divina – The Word as the Bread of Life' – by Lynda Wright, from *Bread for the Journey*, Tabor Retreat Centre, Key House.

'The Maker's blessing …' – by Ruth Burgess, from *The Pattern of Our Days: Liturgies and Resources for Worship*, Kathy Galloway, Wild Goose Publications, 1996.

'Make yourself at home' – by Gerard Hughes, from *For God's Sake … Unity: An Ecumenical Voyage with the Iona Community*, Wild Goose Publications, 1998.

'Over a pot of boiling soup' – by Sarah Turner, from the Macalester College website. Used by permission of Sarah Turner.

'The wound of the daughter of my people' – by Kathy Galloway, from *Movement* (Magazine of the Student Christian Movement, SCM, Issue 110) www.movement.org.uk Used by permission of Kathy Galloway.

'An act of solidarity' – by Norman Shanks, from *Thought for the Day*, BBC Radio, September 22, 2004. Used by permission of Norman Shanks.

'Send us out' – by Neil Paynter, from *Holy Ground: Liturgies and Worship Resources for an Engaged Spirituality*, Wild Goose Publications, 2006.

'Ninth-century Irish prayer' – translated by Frank O'Connor, from *A Book of Ireland*, Frank O'Connor, Glasgow, Fontana/Collins, 1959, p. 363–4. Reprinted by permission of Harper-Collins publishers Ltd © Frank O'Connor, 1959.

'Engaging in conversation' – excerpt from a reflection by Peter Millar in the chapter 'Facing up to racism' in *Waymarks: Discovering God's Presence in the World*, Peter Millar, Canterbury Press, 2000, ISBN 1853113360. Used by permission of Peter Millar and Canterbury Press.

'I will sing a song of love' – by John L. Bell, from *I Will Not Sing Alone: Songs for the Seasons of Love*, John L. Bell, Wild Goose Publications, 2004. Used by permission of the Wild Goose Resource Group. © Wild Goose Resource Group, 2004.

'Iona pilgrimage: Thick and thin (A sermon from Iona Abbey)' – by Murphy Davis, from *Hospitality: the newspaper of the Open Door Community* www.opendoorcommunity.org

'Bill's story' – from *Lesbian and Gay Christians*, Issue 57, March 2000. Used by permission of The Lesbian and Gay Christian Movement.

'Jeremiah 20:7–9; 14–18' – from the Holy Bible, New International Version®. Copyright © 1973, 1978, 1984 by International Bible Society.

'Damascus Gate' – by John Rackley, from *Thin Places,* John Rackley, Open House Publications, 1988.

'Less concerned about self' – by David Orr, from *The House Church – An Experiment in Church Life,* Iona Community Publishing Department, 1962.

'A favourable time' – by Ian M. Fraser, from *The Way Ahead: Grown-up Christians,* Wild Goose Publications, 2006.

'The whole' – by Alison Adam, originally published in *GOOSEgander: the newsletter of the Wild Goose Resource Group.* www.iona.org.uk/wgrg.html

'Remember me' – by Kathy Galloway, from *The Dream of Learning Our True Name,* Wild Goose Publications, 2004.

'God in the thick of things and beyond' – by Ian M. Fraser, from *The Fire Runs: God's People Participating in Change.* Used by permission of Ian M. Fraser.

'Power of Love: What Can Non-violence Say to Violence?' – by Alastair McIntosh, from *Resurgence* magazine, Resurgence no. 219 July/August 2003. Used by permission of Alastair McIntosh and *Resurgence* www.resurgence.org

'Invitation to the great adventure: a meditation' – by Lynda Wright, from *Bread for the Journey,* Tabor Retreat Centre, Key House.

'Life in all its fullness' – by Norman Shanks, from *Thought for the Day*, BBC Radio, March 1, 2005. Used by permission of Norman Shanks.

'The desert of that single room' – by Tom Gordon, from *Need for Living*: *Signposts on the Journey of Life and Beyond,* Wild Goose Publications, 2001.

Month 3

'The Human One' – by Helen Steven, from *No Extraordinary Power: Prayer, Stillness and Activism*, Helen Steven, Quaker Books, Swarthmore Lecture, 2005. ISBN 0852453795 www.quaker.org.uk Used by permission of Helen Steven and Quaker Books.

'How will I find you?' – by Pat Bennett, from the booklet *Traidcraft at Iona: Justice & Peace Prayers,* published by Traidcraft. Out of print.

'Grown into fullness' – by Ian M. Fraser, *Strange Fire: Life Stories and Prayers*, Ian M. Fraser, Wild Goose Publications, 1994.

'Prayer becomes the very mainspring of action' – by Helen Steven, from *No Extraordinary Power: Prayer, Stillness and Activism*, Helen Steven, Quaker Books, Swarthmore Lecture, 2005. ISBN 0852453795 www.quaker.org.uk   Used by permission of Helen Steven and Quaker Books.

Month 4

'Fair play' – by Rosemary Power, originally published in the *Swindon Evening Advertiser*. Used by the permission of Rosemary Power.

'The beauty in the fearsome' – by Rosemary Power, originally published in the *Swindon Evening Advertiser*. Used by the permission of Rosemary Power.

'St Columba's Day reflection – by Norman Shanks, from *Thought for the Day*, BBC Radio. Used by permission of Norman Shanks.

'From Erin's shores' – by John L. Bell and Graham Maule, from *Love From Below: Sixty-two songs of discipleship and the Church's sacraments and seasons,* Wild Goose Publications, 1989. Used by permission of the Wild Goose Resource Group. © Wild Goose Resource Group, 1989.

'Galatians 3:27–28; Acts 11:4–9, 11–12, 15, 17–18' – Scriptures quoted from *The Good News Bible* published by The Bible Societies/HarperCollins Publishers Ltd, UK, © American Bible Society, 1966, 1971, 1976, 1992.

'The healer: a story' – by Ian M. Fraser, from *The Fire Runs: God's people participating in change*. Used by permission of Ian M. Fraser.

'Unimpaired' – by Ian M. Fraser, from *Strange Fire: Life Stories and Prayers*, Ian M. Fraser, Wild Goose Publications, 1994.

'Chance encounters' – by T. Ralph Morton, from *China: The Teacher*. To order the book *China: The Teacher*, please write to: 313 Lanark Road West, Currie, Edinburgh EH14 5RS: £5.00, including postage.

'Playing for God' – by Rosemary Power, originally published in the *Swindon Evening Advertiser*. Used by the permission of Rosemary Power.

SOME BOOKS BY AUTHORS IN *GATHERED AND SCATTERED*

Warren Bardsley:
Against the Tide: The Story of Adomnán of Iona, Wild Goose Publications

John L. Bell and Graham Maule, the Wild Goose Resource Group, the Wild Goose Worship Group:
Cloth for the Cradle: Worship Resources and Readings for Advent, Christmas and Epiphany, Wild Goose Publications
Come All You People: Shorter Songs for Worship, Wild Goose Publications
Courage to Say No: Songs for Lent and Easter, Wild Goose Publications
Enemy of Apathy: Songs and Chants for Lent, Eastertide and Pentecost, Wild Goose Publications
God Comes Tomorrow: Music for Advent and Christmas, GIA Publications
God Never Sleeps: Songs from the Iona Community (Octavos, CD), Wild Goose Publications
Hard Words for Interesting Times: Biblical Texts in Contemporary Contexts, Wild Goose Publications
He Was in the World: Meditations for Public Worship, Wild Goose Publications
Heaven Shall Not Wait: Songs of Creation, the Incarnation and the life of Jesus, Wild Goose Publications
I Will Not Sing Alone (Songbook, CD), Wild Goose Publications
Innkeepers and Lightsleepers: Seventeen Songs for Christmas (Songbook, CD)
Jesus & Peter: Off-the-record Conversations, Wild Goose Publications
Last Journey: Seventeen Songs for Times of Grieving (Octavos; Book; CD; Book and CD), Wild Goose Publications
Love and Anger: Songs of Lively Faith and Social Justice (Songbook, CD), Wild Goose Publications
Love From Below: Sixty-two Songs of Discipleship and the Church's Sacraments and Seasons (Songbook, CD), Wild Goose Publications
Many and Great: Songs from the World Church (Songbook, CD), Wild Goose Publications
One is the Body: Songs of Unity & Diversity (Songbook, CD), Wild Goose Publications
Present on Earth: Worship Resources on the Life of Jesus, Wild Goose Publications
Psalms of Patience, Protest and Praise (Songbook, CD), Wild Goose Publications

Sent by the Lord: World Church Songs (Songbook, CD), Wild Goose Publications
Seven Psalms of David (Octavos), Wild Goose Publications
Seven Songs of Mary/Seven Psalms of David (CD), Wild Goose Publications
Stages on the Way: Worship Resources for Lent, Holy Week and Easter, Wild Goose Publications
States of Bliss and Yearning: The Marks and Means of Authentic Christian Spirituality, Wild Goose Publications
Take This Moment (Octavos, CD), Wild Goose Publications
There is One Among Us: Shorter Songs for Worship (Songbook, CD), Wild Goose Publications
The Singing Thing: A Case for Congregational Song, Wild Goose Publications
The Singing Thing Too: Enabling Congregations to Sing, Wild Goose Publications
When Grief is Raw (Songbook), Wild Goose Publications
Wrestle and Fight and Pray: Christianity and Conflict, St Andrew Press

Helen Boothroyd:
Holy Ground: Liturgies and Worship Resources for an Engaged Spirituality (with Neil Paynter), Wild Goose Publications

Ruth Burgess:
A Book of Blessings, Wild Goose Publications
Candles and Conifers: Resources for All Saints' and Advent, Wild Goose Publications
Eggs & Ashes: Liturgical & Practical Resources for Lent and Holy Week (with Chris Polhill), Wild Goose Publications
Fire & Bread: Resources from Easter Day to Trinity Sunday, Wild Goose Publications
Friends and Enemies: A Book of Short Prayers and Some Ways to Write Your Own, Wild Goose Publications
Hay and Stardust: Resources for Christmas to Candlemas, Wild Goose Publications
Hear My Cry: A Daily Prayer Book for Advent, Wild Goose Publications
Praying for the Dawn: A Resource Book for the Ministry of Healing (with Kathy Galloway), Wild Goose Publications

Nancy Cocks:
Growing Up with God: Using Stories to Explore a Child's Faith and Life, Wild Goose Publications
Invisible We See You: Tracing Celtic Threads through Christian Community, Wild Goose Publications, Novalis

Ian Cowie:
Jesus' Healing Works and Ours, Wild Goose Publications
Prayers and Ideas for Healing Services, Wild Goose Publications

Maxwell Craig:
For God's Sake ... Unity: An Ecumenical Journey with the Iona Community, Wild Goose Publications

Ian M. Fraser:
Many Cells – One Body: Stories from Small Christian Communities, World Council of Churches
Salted with Fire, St Andrew Press
Signs of Fire: Stories of Hope, Struggle and Faith (cassette), Wild Goose Publications
Strange Fire: Life Stories and Prayers, Wild Goose Publications
The Way Ahead: Grown-up Christians, Wild Goose Publications

Ron Ferguson:
Donald Dewar Ate My Hamster and Other Tales, Northern Books (Famedram)
Hitler Was a Vegetarian and Other Tales, Northern Books (Famedram)
Love Your Crooked Neighbour: Thoughts on Breath, Bread, Breasts and Brokenness, St Andrew Press
Mole Under the Fence: Conversations with Roland Walls, St Andrew Press

Kathy Galloway:
Dreaming of Eden: Reflections on Christianity and Sexuality, Wild Goose Publications
Getting Personal: Sermons and Meditations, SPCK
Praying for the Dawn: A Resource Book for the Ministry of Healing (with Ruth Burgess), Wild Goose Publications
Pushing the Boat Out: New Poetry, Wild Goose Publications
Starting Where We Are: Liberation Theology in Practice (book and cassette), Wild Goose Publications
Story to Live By, SPCK
Struggles to Love: the Spirituality of the Beatitudes, SPCK
Talking to the Bones: Poems, Prayers and Meditations, SPCK
The Dream of Learning Our True Name, Wild Goose Publications
Walking in Darkness and Light: Sermons and Reflections, St Andrew Press

Tom Gordon:
Need for Living: Signposts on the Journey of Life and Beyond, Wild Goose Publications
New Journeys Now Begin: Learning on the Path of Grief and Loss, Wild Goose Publications

Margaret Legum:
It Doesn't Have To Be Like This: Global Economics: A New Way Forward, Wild Goose Publications

Alastair McIntosh:
Soil and Soul: People Versus Corporate Power, Aurum Press Ltd
Love and Revolution: Poetry, Luath Press

Peter Millar:
An Iona Prayer Book, SCM-Canterbury Press
Finding Hope Again: Journeying Beyond Sorrow, SCM-Canterbury
Iona: Pilgrim Guide, SCM-Canterbury Press
Our Hearts Still Sing: Daily Readings, Wild Goose Publications
Surprise of the Sacred: Finding God in Unexpected Places, SCM-Canterbury Press
Waymarks: Signposts to Discovering God's Presence in the World, SCM-Canterbury Press

J. Philip Newell:
Book of Creation: An Introduction to Celtic Spirituality, SCM-Canterbury Press
Each Day & Each Night: Celtic Prayers from Iona, Wild Goose Publications
Listening to the Heartbeat of God: A Celtic Spirituality, SPCK

Lesley Orr:
In A Unique and Glorious Mission: Women and Presbyterianism in Scotland, 1830–1930, John Donald
In Good Company: Women in the Ministry, Wild Goose Publications

David Osborne:
Owl and the Stereo: An Introduction to Radical Christianity, Wild Goose Publications

Neil Paynter:
Blessed Be Our Table: Graces for Mealtimes and Reflections on Food, Wild Goose Publications
Growing Hope: Daily Readings, Wild Goose Publications
Holy Ground: Liturgies and Worship Resources for an Engaged Spirituality (with Helen

Boothroyd), Wild Goose Publications
Iona Dawn: Through Holy Week with the Iona Community, Wild Goose Publications
Lent & Easter Readings from Iona, Wild Goose Publications
This Is The Day, Volume 1: Readings and Meditations from the Iona Community, Wild Goose Publications

Jan Sutch Pickard:
Dandelions and Thistles: Biblical Meditations from the Iona Community, Wild Goose Publications
Out of Iona: Words from a Crossroads of the World, Wild Goose Publications

Chris Polhill:
Eggs & Ashes: Liturgical & Practical Resources for Lent and Holy Week (with Ruth Burgess), Wild Goose Publications
Pilgrim's Guide to Iona Abbey, Chris Polhill, Wild Goose Publications

David Rhodes:
Faith in Dark Places, SPCK
Sparrow Story: The Gospel for Today, SPCK
See:
www.turbulentbooks.co.uk
www.sparrowstory.com

Eurig Scandrett:
Scotlands of the Future: Towards a sustainable economy, Luath Press Limited

Norman Shanks:
Iona: God's Energy: The Spirituality and Vision of the Iona Community, Hodder & Stoughton

Thom M. Shuman:
Jesse Tree: Daily Readings for Advent, Wild Goose Publications

Helen Steven:
No Extraordinary Power: Prayer, Stillness and Activism, Quaker Books
Roger: an Extraordinary Peace Campaigner, Wild Goose Publications

The Open Door Community:
I Hear Hope Banging at my Back Door: Writings from Hospitality, Ed Loring
A Work of Hospitality: The Open Door Reader, 1982–2002, Peter R. Gathje, Editor, Open Door Community, Atlanta, Georgia

Iain Whyte:
Scotland and the Abolition of Black Slavery, 1756–1838, Iain Whyte, Edinburgh University Press

Some Iona Community classics
A Wee Worship Book, Wild Goose Worship Group, Wild Goose Publications
Bridging the Gap: Has the Church Failed the Poor?, John Harvey, Wild Goose Publications
Chasing the Wild Goose: The Story of the Iona Community, Ron Ferguson, Wild Goose Publications
Daily Readings with George MacLeod, Ron Ferguson, editor, Wild Goose Publications
Every Blessed Thing: An Evening with George MacLeod (Double CD based on the one-man play about the life of George MacLeod) Ron Ferguson and Tom Fleming, Wild Goose Publications
George MacLeod: a Biography, Ron Ferguson, Wild Goose Publications
Iona Abbey Music Book, Wild Goose Publications
Iona Abbey Worship Book, Wild Goose Publications
Iona Community: Today's Challenge, Tomorrow's Hope/Sermon in Stone (DVD and Video, PAL and NTSC formats), Wild Goose Publications
Meditations from the Iona Community, Ian Reid, Wild Goose Publications
Only One Way Left, George MacLeod (Book, e-book), Wild Goose Publications
Reinventing Theology, Ian M. Fraser, (Book, e-book), Wild Goose Publications
The Green Heart of the Snowdrop, Kate McIlhagga, Wild Goose Publications
The Pattern of Our Days, Kathy Galloway, Wild Goose Publications
The Twelve Together, T. Ralph Morton, Wild Goose Publications
The Whole Earth Shall Cry Glory: Iona Prayers, George MacLeod, Wild Goose Publications

Iona can be the home of the New Reformation. But it must recover its genius: keep acting its insights at whatever risk if its insights are to be clarified and the next obedience seen. If, as a community, we write at all it can be no more than passing calculations in the sand, to point to the next Obedience.

George MacLeod